EVALUATING TRAINING PROGRAMS

EVALUATING TRAINING PROGRAMS

THE FOUR LEVELS

SECOND EDITION

DONALD L. KIRKPATRICK

Berrett-Koehler Publishers, Inc.
San Francisco

Berrett-Koehler Publishers, Inc.
450 Sansome Street, Suite 1200
San Francisco, CA 94111-3320
Tel: (415) 288-0260   Fax: (415) 362-2512

ORDERING INFORMATION

Individual sales. Berrett-Koehler publications are available through most bookstores. They can also be ordered direct from Berrett-Koehler at the address above.

Quantity sales. Special discounts are available on quantity purchases by corporations, associations, and others. For details, contact the "Special Sales Department" at the Berrett-Koehler address above.

Orders for college textbook/course adoption use. Please contact Berrett-Koehler Publishers at the address above.

Orders by U.S. trade bookstores and wholesalers. Please contact Publishers Group West, 1700 Fourth Street, Berkeley, CA 94710.
Tel: (510) 528-1444; 1-800-788-3123. Fax: (510) 528-3444.

Printed in the United States of America

Printed on acid-free and recycled paper
that is composed of 50% recovered fiber,
including 10% post-consumer waste.

Library of Congress Cataloging-in-Publication Data

Kirkpatrick, Donald L.
    Evaluating training programs: the four levels / Donald L.
Kirkpatrick — 2nd ed.
        p.   cm.
Includes bibliographical references and index.
ISBN 1-57675-042-6 (hardcover: alk. paper)
1. Employees — Training of — Evaluation.   I. Title.
HF5549.5.T7K569   1998
658.3'12404 — dc21   98-23974
                                            CIP

Second Edition

06   05   04   10   9   8

To my wife Fern,
who has been my inspiration, helper, and encourager
through forty-plus years of happy marriage

Contents

Foreword
to the First Edition

What is quality training? How do you measure it? How do you improve it?

If you ask these questions of training professionals, human resource professionals, and managers of business operations, they inevitably respond with:

"Meets customer needs . . ."

"Students learn what they are supposed to learn . . ."

"Right training, right person, right time, returning to a supportive environment . . ."

"Changes behavior . . ."

Wonderful words and great ideas! If you ask how your training operation is currently measured, the responses typically are:

"Money spent . . ."

"Number of people attending training (known as the "buns in seat" metric) . . ."

"Number of new courses built . . ."

"Number of training hours delivered . . ."

What you typically find in business training operations are the quantitative measures without the qualitative ones. What is needed is a blend between the two, where the training department is held accountable for both! Don Kirkpatrick's four levels of evaluation give you the ability to measure training quality correctly, accurately, and skillfully.

Within any quality system there are two sets of measures that one must respond to when assessing quality: the *internal drivers* that are used to measure your operation and the *external drivers* that your customers use to measure you. These quality measures are the driving forces be-hind quality improvements, as shown in Figure F.1.

Within the framework of the Kirkpatrick model, level 1 and level 2 evaluation results are training departments' internal drivers. They pro-vide the managers who run these departments with information on student satisfaction with the course and whether they have mastered the course content. Levels 3 and 4 then become the external drivers that provide information to business operations on the application of learned skills and on the impact on the business.

Systematically applied from course to course, with quality and im-provement goals documented and measured, these four levels of evalu-ation can be used to assist training departments to become world-class operations.

So what does all this mean to you and your organization? These lev-els of evaluation can help you to make sound training investment deci-sions, they can help the training community to ensure that courses are working, they can help operations departments to identify barriers that are preventing skills from being applied, and they can help your com-pany be confident that the hours your employees spend in training and the dollars that it invests in its people are time and money well spent.

Figure F.1. Quality Assessment Measures

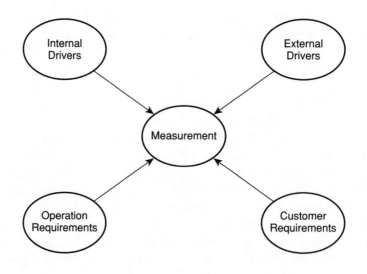

Motorola believes that proper use of the four evaluation levels helps it to achieve its corporate vision of becoming the premier employer in the world by affecting our greatest competitive advantage—our people. It can do the same for you.

Dave Basarab
Manager of Training Operations and Business
Motorola SPS Organization and Human Effectiveness
Austin, Texas

Foreword
to the Second Edition

I am happy to see a second edition of this practical book. It not only contains a revision of Part One, which describes the four levels, but it also contains some new case studies that will be of interest and benefit to readers. For example, the new case study from Intel in Chapter 18 describes how we evaluated a training program at all four levels.

In today's high-tech industries, innovations have life cycles of only a few years. In this type of environment, it is critical that high-quality, cost-effective, just-in-time training be provided to all employees. This training needs to be evaluated and programs need to be improved if the evaluations indicate problems or weaknesses. Kirkpatrick's four levels set the framework for Intel to measure the effectiveness in order to deliver the world-class training required to stay competitive.

No matter how small or large your organization is, you will be able to apply one or more levels in evaluating your programs. Kirkpatrick's guidelines provide a basis for evaluation, and the case studies provide ideas for you to use and modify to implement the guidelines.

Eric Freitag
Manager
Intel University
Chandler, Arizona

Preface

In 1959, I wrote a series of four articles called "Techniques for Evaluating Training Programs," published in *Training and Development,* the journal of the American Society for Training and Development (ASTD). The articles described the four levels of evaluation that I had formulated. I am not sure where I got the idea for this model, but the concept originated with work on my Ph.D. dissertation at the University of Wisconsin, Madison.

The reason I developed this four-level model was to clarify the elusive term *evaluation.* Some training and development professionals believe that *evaluation* means measuring changes in behavior that occur as a result of training programs. Others maintain that the only real evaluation lies in determining what final results occurred because of training programs. Still others think only in terms of the comment sheets that participants complete at the end of a program. Others are concerned with the learning that takes place in the classroom, as measured by increased knowledge, improved skills, and changes in attitude. And they are all right—and yet wrong, in that they fail to recognize that all four approaches are parts of what we mean by *evaluating.*

These four levels are all important, and they should be understood by all professionals in the fields of education, training, and development, whether they plan, coordinate, or teach; whether the content of the program is technical or managerial; whether the participants are or are not managers; and whether the programs are conducted in education, business, or industry. In some cases, especially in academic institutions, there is no attempt to change behavior. The end result is simply to increase knowledge, improve skills, and change attitudes. In these cases, only the first two levels apply. But if the purpose of the training is to get better results by changing behavior, then all four levels apply.

The title of the book, "Evaluating Training Programs: <u>The</u> Four Levels," is bold if not downright presumptuous, since other authors have described different approaches to the evaluation of training. However, in human resource development (HRD) circles, these four levels are recognized widely, often cited, and often used as a basis for research and articles dealing with techniques for applying one or more of the levels. For example, in the June 1993 issue of the ASTD's *Training and Development,* Shelton and Alliger wrote an article entitled "Who's Afraid of Level 4 Evaluation?" in which they quote my 1959 article in these terms: "In 1959, Donald Kirkpatrick proposed a four-level model of criteria for evaluating training: learner reactions, learning, job behavior, and observable results." Many other articles have referred to the four levels as the *Kirkpatrick model.*

I have used the word *training* in the title of this book, and I will use it throughout to include development. Although a distinction is often made between these two terms, for simplicity I have chosen to speak of them both simply as *training* and to emphasize courses and programs designed to increase knowledge, improve skills, and change attitudes, whether for present job improvement or for development in the future. Because of my background, my primary focus will be on supervisory and management training, although the concepts, principles, and techniques can be applied to technical, sales, safety, and even academic courses.

The second edition is divided into two parts. Part One describes concepts, guidelines, principles, and techniques for evaluating at all four levels. Selected references are provided at the end of Chapter 8. Part Two contains case studies from organizations that have evaluated programs at one or more of the levels. Some of the case studies are the same as those in the original edition. Some are revised from the original condition. Eight case studies are new.

I wish to thank Eric Freitag of Intel Corporation for writing the Foreword to this second edition and contributing a new case study (Chapter 18). I am grateful to Sara Jane Hope for reviewing the original manuscript and offering helpful suggestions for improvement. I also wish to thank the American Society for Training and Development (Chapter 9) and *TRAINING* Magazine (Chapter 10) for permission to reprint an article from their magazine. Finally, thanks to those who contributed case studies and provided practical suggestions for evaluation.

Study the case studies to learn what organizations have done to evaluate. Look for forms and procedures you can borrow and adapt to evaluate your own programs.

Best wishes for success in your own evaluation efforts.

Donald L. Kirkpatrick
April 1998
Elm Grove, Wisconsin

PART ONE

CONCEPTS, PRINCIPLES, GUIDELINES, AND TECHNIQUES

Part One contains concepts, principles, guidelines, and techniques for understanding and implementing four levels for evaluating training programs. Most of the content is my own and results from my Ph.D. dissertation on evaluation and my studies and experience since that time. Some modifications were made from the input I received from reviewers that fit in with my objective in writing the book: to provide a simple, practical, four-level approach for evaluating training programs. For those who want information on other principles and techniques, I have provided a selected reading list at the end of Chapter 8.

Chapter 1

Evaluating: Part of a Ten-Step Process

The reason for evaluating is to determine the effectiveness of a training program. When the evaluation is done, we can hope that the results are positive and gratifying, both for those responsible for the program and for upper-level managers who will make decisions based on their evaluation of the program. Therefore, much thought and planning need to be given to the program itself to make sure that it is effective. Later chapters discuss the reasons for evaluating and supply descriptions, guidelines, and techniques for evaluating at the four levels. This chapter is devoted to suggestions for planning and implementing the program to ensure its effectiveness. More details can be found in my book, *How to Train and Develop Supervisors* (New York: AMACOM, 1993).

Each of the following factors should be carefully considered when planning and implementing an effective training program:

1. Determining needs
2. Setting objectives
3. Determining subject content
4. Selecting participants
5. Determining the best schedule
6. Selecting appropriate facilities
7. Selecting appropriate instructors
8. Selecting and preparing audiovisual aids
9. Coordinating the program
10. Evaluating the program

Suggestions for implementing each of these factors follow.

Determining Needs

If programs are going to be effective, they must meet the needs of participants. There are many ways to determine these needs. Here are some of the more common:

1. Ask the participants.
2. Ask the bosses of the participants.
3. Ask others who are familiar with the job and how it is being performed, including subordinates, peers, and customers.
4. Test the participants.
5. Analyze performance appraisal forms.

Participants, bosses, and others can be asked in interviews or by means of a survey. Interviews provide more detailed information, but they require much more time. A simple survey form can provide almost as much information and do it in a much more efficient manner.

A survey form, such as the one shown in Exhibit 1.1, can be readily developed to determine the needs seen both by participants and by their bosses. The topics to be considered can be determined by interviews or simply by answering the question, What are all the possible subjects that will help our people to do their best? The resulting list becomes the survey form.

As Exhibit 1.1 indicates, participants are asked to complete the survey by putting a check in one of three columns for each item. This is a much better process than having them list their needs in order of importance or simply writing down the topics that they feel will help them to do their job better. It is important to have them evaluate each topic so that the responses can be quantified.

After you tabulate their responses, the next step is to weight these sums to get a weighted score for each topic. The first column, *Of great need,* should be given a weight of 2; the second column, *Of some need,* should be given a weight of 1; and the last column, a weight of 0. The weighted score can then be used to arrive at a rank order for individual needs. If two topics are tied for third, the next rank is fifth, not fourth, and if three needs have tied for seventh, the next rank is tenth.

Exhibit 1.1. Survey of Training Needs

In order to determine which subjects will be of the greatest help to you in improving your job performance, we need your input. Please indicate your need for each subject by placing an X in the appropriate column.

Subject	Of great need	Of some need	Of no need
1. Diversity in the workforce—understanding employees			
2. How to motivate employees			
3. Interpersonal communications			
4. Written communication			
5. Oral communication			
6. How to manage time			
7. How to delegate effectively			
8. Planning and organizing			
9. Handling complaints and grievances			
10. How to manage change			
11. Decision making and empowerment			
12. Leadership styles—application			
13. Performance appraisal			
14. Coaching and counseling			
15. How to conduct productive meetings			
16. Building teamwork			
17. How to discipline			
18. Total quality improvement			
19. Safety			
20. Housekeeping			
21. How to build morale—quality of work life (QWL)			
22. How to reward performance			
23. How to train employees			
24. How to reduce absenteeism and tardiness			

25. Other topics of great need
    1.
    2.			

This rank order provides training professionals with data on which to determine priorities. Exhibit 1.2 illustrates the tabulations and the rank order.

The same form can be used to determine the needs seen by the bosses of the supervisors. The only change is in the instructions on the form, which should read: "In order to determine which subjects would be of greatest benefit to supervisors to help improve their performance, we need your input. Please put an X in one of the three columns after each subject to indicate the needs of your subordinates as you see them. Tabulations of this survey will be compared with the needs that they see to decide the priority of the subjects to be offered."

There will be a difference of opinion on some subjects. For example, in a manufacturing organization, the subject of housekeeping might be rated low by supervisors and high by their bosses. Other topics, such as motivation, will probably be given a high rating by both groups. In order to make the final decision on the priority of the subjects to be offered, it is wise to use an advisory committee of managers representing different departments and levels within the organization. The training professional can show the committee members the results of the survey and ask for their input. Their comments and suggestions should be considered advisory, and the training professional should make the final decision.

Participation by an advisory committee accomplishes four purposes:

1. Helps to determine subject content for training programs.
2. Informs committee members of the efforts of the training department to provide practical help.
3. Provides empathy regarding the needs seen by their subordinates.
4. Stimulates support of the programs by involving them in the planning.

The use of tests and inventories is another approach for determining needs. There are two practical ways of doing this. One way is to determine the knowledge, skills, and attitudes that a supervisor should have and develop the subject content accordingly. Then develop a test that measures the knowledge, skills, and attitudes and give it to participants as a pretest. An analysis of the results will provide information regarding subject content.

The other approach is to purchase a standardized instrument that relates closely to the subject matter being taught. The sixty-five-item

Exhibit 1.2. Tabulating Responses to Survey of Training Needs

In order to determine which subjects will be of the greatest help to you in improving your job performance, we need your input. Please indicate your need for each subject by placing an X in the appropriate column.

Rank order	Subject	Weighted score	Of great need	Of some need	Of no need
13	1. Diversity in the workforce—understanding employees	40	15	10	5
4	2. How to motivate employees	51	22	7	1
6	3. Interpersonal communications	48	20	8	2
18	4. Written communication	33	11	11	8
23	5. Oral communication	19	6	7	17
10	6. How to manage time	44	17	10	3
20	7. How to delegate effectively	29	9	11	10
20	8. Planning and organizing	29	6	17	7
14	9. Handling complaints and grievances	39	13	13	4
1	10. How to manage change	56	26	4	0
3	11. Decision making and empowerment	53	24	5	1
6	12. Leadership styles—application	48	19	10	1
16	13. Performance appraisal	36	12	12	6
16	14. Coaching and counseling	36	8	20	2
20	15. How to conduct productive meetings	29	8	13	9
2	16. Building teamwork	55	25	5	0
9	17. How to discipline	47	18	11	1
14	18. Total quality improvement	39	13	13	4
11	19. Safety	43	15	13	2
23	20. Housekeeping	19	6	7	17
5	21. How to build morale—quality of work life (QWL)	50	22	6	2
12	22. How to reward performance	41	17	7	6
6	23. How to train employees	48	19	10	1
19	24. How to reduce absenteeism and tardiness	31	11	9	10

	25. Other topics of great need
	    1.
	    2.				

Note: Tabulated responses from thirty first-level supervisors.

Management Inventory on Managing Change (available from Donald L. Kirkpatrick, 1920 Hawthorne Drive, Elm Grove, WI 53122) is such an instrument. Here are some of the items in it:

1. If subordinates participate in the decision to make a change, they are usually more enthusiastic in carrying it out.
2. Some people are not anxious to be promoted to a job that has more responsibility.
3. Decisions to change should be based on opinions as well as on facts.
4. If a change is going to be unpopular with your subordinates, you should proceed slowly in order to obtain acceptance.
5. It is usually better to communicate with a group concerning a change than to talk to its members individually.
6. Empathy is one of the most important concepts in managing change.
7. It's a good idea to sell a change to the natural leader before trying to sell it to the others.
8. If you are promoted to a management job, you should make the job different than it was under your predecessor.
9. Bosses and subordinates should have an understanding regarding the kinds of changes that the subordinate can implement without getting prior approval from the boss.
10. You should encourage your subordinates to try out any changes that they feel should be made.

Respondents are asked to agree or disagree with each statement. The "correct" answers were determined by the author to cover concepts, principles, and techniques for managing change. It is important to note that the possible answers are "agree" or "disagree" and not "true" or "false."

Five other standardized inventories are available from the source just named: Supervisory Inventory on Communication, Supervisory Inventory on Human Relations, Management Inventory on Time Management, Management Inventory on Performance Appraisal and Coaching, and Management Inventory on Leadership, Motivation, and Decision Making.

Many other approaches are available for determining needs. Two of the most practical—surveying participants and their bosses and giving a pretest to participants before the program is run—have just been described.

Setting Objectives

Once the needs have been determined, it is necessary to set objectives. Objectives should be set for three different aspects of the program and in the following order:

1. What results are we trying to accomplish? These results can be stated in such areas as production, sales, quality, turnover, absenteeism, and morale or quality of work life (QWL). Some organizations set objectives in terms of profits, even on return on investment (ROI). This is usually a mistake, because so many factors determine results like these that evaluation in these terms is often impossible.

2. What behaviors do we want supervisors and managers to have in order to accomplish the results? One such behavior may be management by walking around (MBWA), the concept described by Thomas Peters and Robert Waterman, Jr., in *In Search of Excellence* (New York: Warner Books, 1982). All levels of management at United Airlines and Hewlett–Packard are urged to use this approach to show employees that they care about them. The desired results are better quality of work life, higher morale, and thereby improved productivity.

3. What knowledge, skills, and attitudes do we want participants to learn in the training program? Some programs are aimed at teaching specific knowledge or skills. Others, such as programs on diversity in the workforce, are aimed at increasing knowledge and changing attitudes.

Robert Mager's book *Preparing Instructional Objectives* (Belmont, Calif.: Lake, 1962) describes specific concepts and approaches. (See references at end of Chapter 8.)

Determining Subject Content

Needs and objectives are prime factors when determining subject content. Trainers should ask themselves the question, What topics should be presented to meet the needs and accomplish the objectives? The answers to this question establish the topics to be covered. Some modifications may be necessary depending on the qualifications of the trainers who will present the program and on the training budget. For example, the subject of managing stress may be important, but the instructors available are not qualified, and there is no money to hire a qualified leader or buy videotapes and/or packaged programs on the subject. Other pertinent topics then become higher priorities.

Selecting Participants

When selecting participants for a program, four decisions need to be made:

1. Who can benefit from the training?
2. What programs are required by law or by government edict?
3. Should the training be voluntary or compulsory?
4. Should the participants be segregated by level in the organization, or should two or more levels be included in the same class?

In answer to the first question, all levels of management can benefit from training programs. Obviously, some levels can benefit more than others. The answer to the second question is obvious. Regarding the third question, I recommend that at least some basic programs be compulsory for first-level supervisors if not also for others. If a program is voluntary, many who need the training may not sign up, either because they feel they don't need it or because they don't want to admit that they need it. Those who are already good supervisors and have little need for the program can still benefit from it, and they can also help to train the others. This assumes, of course, that the program includes participatory activities on the part of attendees. To supplement the compulsory programs, other courses can be offered on a voluntary basis.

Some organizations have established a management institute that offers all courses on a voluntary basis. Training professionals may feel that this is the best approach. Or higher-level management may discourage compulsory programs. If possible, the needs of the supervisors, as determined by the procedures described in the preceding section, should become basic courses that should be compulsory. Others can be optional. The answer to the last question depends on the climate and on the rapport that exists among different levels of management within the organization. The basic question is whether subordinates will speak freely in a training class if their bosses are present. If the answer is yes, then it is a good idea to have different levels in the same program. They all get the same training at the same time. But if the answer is no, then bosses should not be included in the program for supervisors. Perhaps you can give the same or a similar program to upper-level managers before offering it to the first-level supervisors.

Determining the Best Schedule

The best schedule takes three things into consideration: the trainees, their bosses, and the best conditions for learning. Many times, training professionals consider only their own preferences and schedules. An important scheduling decision is whether to offer the program on a concentrated basis—for example, as a solid week of training—or to spread it out over weeks or months. My own preference is to spread it out as an ongoing program. One good schedule is to offer a three-hour session once a month. Three hours leave you time for participation as well as for the use of videotapes and other aids. The schedule should be set and communicated well in advance. The day of the program and the specific time should be established to meet the needs and desires of both the trainees and their bosses. Line managers should be consulted regarding the best time and schedule.

I recently conducted a week-long training program for all levels of management at a company in Racine, Wisconsin. Two groups of twenty each attended the program. The first session each day was scheduled from 7:00 to 10:30 A.M. The repeat session for the other group was scheduled from 3:00 to 6:30 P.M. Racine was too far away to go home each day, and what do you do in Racine from 10:30 A.M. to 3:00 P.M. each day for a week? This is the worst schedule I ever had, but it was the best schedule for all three shifts of supervisors who attended. The point is, the training schedule must meet the needs and desires of the participants instead of the convenience of the instructors.

Selecting Appropriate Facilities

The selection of facilities is another important decision. Facilities should be both comfortable and convenient. Negative factors to be avoided include rooms that are too small, uncomfortable furniture, noise or other distractions, inconvenience, long distances to the training room, and uncomfortable temperature, either too hot or too cold. A related consideration has to do with refreshments and breaks. I conducted a training program on managing change for a large Minneapolis company. They provided participants with coffee and sweet rolls in the morning, a nice lunch at noon, and a Coke and cookie break in the afternoon. Participants came from all over the country, including Seattle. In order to save money on transportation and hotel, the company decided to take the program to Seattle, where it had a large operation. In Seattle, no refreshments were offered, and participants were on their own for lunch. Unfortunately, some peers of the participants had attended the same program in Minneapolis. These factors caused negative attitudes on the part of those attending. And these attitudes could have affected their motivation to learn as well as their feeling toward the organization and the training department in particular. Incidentally, more and more companies are offering fruit instead of sweet rolls and cookies at breaks.

Selecting Appropriate Instructors

The selection of instructors is critical to the success of a program. Their qualifications should include a knowledge of the subject being taught, a desire to teach, the ability to communicate, and skill at getting people to participate. They should also be "learner oriented"— have a strong desire to meet learner needs.

Budgets may limit the possibilities. For example, some organizations limit the selection to present employees, including the training director, the Human Resources manager, and line and staff managers. There is no money to hire outside leaders. Therefore, subject content needs to be tailored to the available instructors, or else instructors need to receive special training. If budgets allow, outside instructors can be hired if internal expertise is not available. The selection of these instructors also requires care. Many organizations feel that they have been burned because they selected outside instructors who did a poor job. In order to be sure that a potential instructor will be effective, the best approach is to observe his or her performance in a similar situation. The next best approach is to rely on the recommendations of other training professionals who have already used the individual. A very unreliable method is to interview the person and make a decision based on your impressions.

I recently conducted a workship for eighty supervisors and managers at St. Vincent Hospital in Indianapolis. I had been recommended to Frank Magliery, vice president of Operations, by Dave Neil of ServiceMaster. Dave had been in several of my sessions. In order to be sure that I was the right instructor, Frank attended another session that I did for ServiceMaster. He was able therefore not only to judge my effectiveness but also to offer suggestions about tailoring the training to his organization.

This is the kind of selection process that should be followed when you hire an outside consultant. It not only illustrates a process for selection but also emphasizes the importance of orienting an outside leader to the needs and desires of the specific organization.

Selecting and Preparing Audiovisual Aids

An audiovisual aid has two purposes: to help the leader maintain interest and to communicate. Some aids, hopefully only a few minutes long, are designed to attract interest and entertain. This is fine providing they develop a positive climate for learning. When renting or purchasing videotapes and packaged programs, take care to preview them first to be sure that the benefits for the program outweigh the cost. The extent to which such aids should become the main feature of a program depends on the instructor's knowledge and skills in developing his or her own subject content. Some organizations rely entirely on packaged programs because they have the budget but not the skills needed to develop and teach programs of their own. Other training professionals rely primarily on their own knowledge, skill, and materials and rent or buy videos only as aids. Some organizations have a department that can make effective aids and provide the necessary equipment. Other organizations have to rent or buy them. The important principle is that aids can be an important part of an effective program. Each organization should carefully make or buy the aids that will help it to maintain interest and communicate the message.

Coordinating the Program

Sometimes the instructor coordinates as well as teaches. In other situations a coordinator does not do the teaching. For those who coordinate and do not teach, there are two opposite approaches.

As an instructor, I have experienced two extremes in regard to coordination. At an eastern university offering continuing education, I had to introduce myself, find my way to the lunchroom at noon, tell participants where to go for breaks, conclude the program, and even ask participants to complete the reaction sheets. I couldn't believe that a university that prided itself on professional programming could do such a miserable job of coordinating.

The other extreme occurred in a program that I conducted for State Farm Insurance in Bloomington, Illinois. Steve Whittington and his wife took my wife, Fern, and me out to dinner the evening before the program. He picked me up at the hotel to take me to the training room in plenty of time to set the room up for the meeting. He made sure that I had everything I needed. He introduced me and stayed for the entire program, helping with handouts. He handled the breaks. He took me to lunch and, of course, paid for it. He concluded the meeting by thanking me and asking participants to complete reaction sheets. He took me back to the hotel and thanked me. In other words, he served as an effective coordinator who helped to make the meeting as effective as possible. Of course, the niceties that he included are not necessary for effective coordination, but they do illustrate that it is important to meet the needs of the instructor as well as of the participants.

Evaluating the Program

Details on evaluation are provided in the rest of the book.

As stated at the beginning of this chapter, to ensure the effectiveness of a training program, time and emphasis should be put on the planning and implementation of the program. These are critical if we are to be sure that, when the evaluation is done, the results are positive. Consideration of the concepts, principles, and techniques described in this chapter can help to ensure an effective program.

Chapter 2

Reasons for Evaluating

At a national conference of the National Society for Sales Training Executives (NSSTE), J. P. Huller of Hobart Corporation presented a paper on "evaluation." In the introduction, he says, "All managers, not just those of us in training, are concerned with their own and their department's credibility. I want to be accepted by my company. I want to be trusted by my company. I want to be respected by my company. I want my company and my fellow managers to say, 'We need you.'

"When you are accepted, trusted, respected, and needed, lots and lots of wonderful things happen:

- Your budget requests are granted.
- You keep your job. (You might even be promoted.)
- Your staff keep their jobs.
- The quality of your work improves.
- Senior management listens to your advice.
- You're given more control.

"You sleep better, worry less, enjoy life more. . . . In short, it makes you happy.

"Wonderful! But just how do we become accepted, trusted, respected, and needed? We do so by proving that we deserve to be accepted, trusted, respected, and needed. We do so by evaluating and reporting upon the worth of our training."

This states in general terms why we need to evaluate training. Here are three specific reasons:

1. To justify the existence of the training department by showing how it contributes to the organization's objectives and goals
2. To decide whether to continue or discontinue training programs
3. To gain information on how to improve future training programs

There is an old saying among training directors: When there are cutbacks in an organization, training people are the first to go. Of course, this isn't always true. However, whenever downsizing occurs, top management looks for people and departments that can be eliminated with the fewest negative results. Early in their decision, they look at such overhead departments as Human Resources. Human Resources typically includes people responsible for employment, salary administration, benefits, labor relations (if there is a union), and training. In some organizations, top management feels that all these functions except training are necessary. From this perspective, training is optional, and its value to the organization depends on top executives' view of its effectiveness. Huller is right when he states that training people must earn trust and respect if training is to be an important function that an organization will want to retain even in a downsizing situation. In other words, trainers must justify their existence. If they don't and downsizing occurs, they may be terminated, and the training function will be relegated to the Human Resources manager, who already has many other hats to wear.

The second reason for evaluating is to determine whether you should continue to offer a program. The content of some programs may become obsolete. For example, programs on Work Simplification, Transactional Analysis, and Management by Objectives were "hot" topics in past years. Most organizations have decided to replace these with programs on current hot topics such as Diversity, Empowerment, and Team Building. Also, some programs, such as computer training, are constantly subject to change. Some programs are offered on a pilot basis in hopes that they will bring about the results desired. These programs should be evaluated to determine whether they should be continued. If the cost outweighs the benefits, the program should be discontinued or modified.

The most common reason for evaluation is to determine the effectiveness of a program and ways in which it can be improved. Usually, the decision to continue it has already been made. The question then is, How can it be improved? In looking for the answer to this question, you should consider these eight factors:

1. To what extent does the subject content meet the needs of those attending?
2. Is the leader the one best qualified to teach?
3. Does the leader use the most effective methods for maintaining interest and teaching the desired attitudes, knowledge, and skills?
4. Are the facilities satisfactory?
5. Is the schedule appropriate for the participants?
6. Are the aids effective in improving communication and maintaining interest?
7. Was the coordination of the program satisfactory?
8. What else can be done to improve the program?

A careful analysis of the answers to these questions can identify ways and means of improving future offerings of the program.

When I talked to Matt, a training director of a large bank, and asked him to write a case history on what his organization has done to evaluate its programs, here is what he said: "We haven't really done anything except the 'smile' sheets. We have been thinking a lot about it, and we are anxious to do something. I will be the first one to read your book!"

This is the situation in many companies. They use reaction sheets (or "smile" sheets, as Matt called them) of one kind or another. Most are thinking about doing more. They haven't gone any further for one or more of the following reasons:

- They don't consider it important or urgent.
- They don't know what to do or how to do it.
- There is no pressure from higher management to do more.
- They feel secure in their job and see no need to do more.
- They have too many other things that are more important or that they prefer to do.

In most organizations, both large and small, there is little pressure from top management to prove that the benefits of training outweigh the cost. Many managers at high levels are too busy worrying about profits, return on investment, stock prices, and other matters of concern to the board of directors, stockholders, and customers. They pay little or no attention to training unless they hear bad things about it. As long as trainees are happy and do not complain, trainers feel comfortable, relaxed, and secure.

However, if trainees react negatively to programs, trainers begin to worry, because the word might get to higher-level managers that the program is a waste of time or even worse. And higher-level managers might make decisions based on this information.

In a few organizations, upper-level managers are putting pressure on trainers to justify their existence by proving their worth. Some have even demanded to see tangible results as measured by improvements in sales, productivity, quality, morale, turnover, safety records, and profits. In these situations, training professionals need to have guidelines for evaluating programs at all four levels. And they need to use more than reaction sheets at the end of their programs.

What about trainers who do not feel pressure from above to justify their existence? I suggest that they operate as if there were going to be pressure and be ready for it. Even if the pressure for results never comes, trainers will benefit by becoming accepted, respected, and self-satisfied.

Summary

There are three reasons for evaluating training programs. The most common reason is that evaluation can tell us how to improve future programs. The second reason is to determine whether a program should be continued or dropped. The third reason is to justify the existence of the training department. By demonstrating to top management that training has tangible, positive results, trainers will find that their job is more secure, even if and when downsizing occurs. If top-level managers need to cut back, their impression of the need for a training department will determine whether they say, "That's one department we need to keep" or "That's a department that we can eliminate without hurting us." And their impression can be greatly influenced by trainers who evaluate at all levels and communicate the results to them.

Chapter 3

The Four Levels:
An Overview

The four levels represent a sequence of ways to evaluate programs. Each level is important and has an impact on the next level. As you move from one level to the next, the process becomes more difficult and time-consuming, but it also provides more valuable information. None of the levels should be bypassed simply to get to the level that the trainer considers the most important. These are the four levels:

Level 1—Reaction
Level 2—Learning
Level 3—Behavior
Level 4—Results

Reaction

As the word *reaction* implies, evaluation on this level measures how those who participate in the program react to it. I call it a measure of customer satisfaction. For many years, I conducted seminars, institutes, and conferences at the University of Wisconsin Management Institute. Organizations paid a fee to send their people to these public programs. It is obvious that the reaction of participants was a measure of customer satisfaction. It is also obvious that reaction had to be favorable if we were to stay in business and attract new customers as well as get present customers to return to future programs.

It isn't quite so obvious that reaction to in-house programs is also a measure of customer satisfaction. In many in-house programs, participants are required to attend whether they want to or not. However, they still are customers even if they don't pay, and their reactions can make or break a training program. What they say to their bosses often gets to higher-level managers, who make decisions about the future of training programs. So, positive reactions are just as important for trainers who run in-house programs as they are for those who offer public programs.

It is important not only to get a reaction but to get a positive reaction. As just described, the future of a program depends on positive reaction. In addition, if participants do not react favorably, they probably will not be motivated to learn. Positive reaction may not ensure learning, but negative reaction almost certainly reduces the possibility of its occurring.

Learning

Learning can be defined as the extent to which participants change attitudes, improve knowledge, and/or increase skill as a result of attending the program.

Those are the three things that a training program can accomplish. Programs dealing with topics like diversity in the workforce aim primarily at changing attitudes. Technical programs aim at improving skills. Programs on topics like leadership, motivation, and communication can aim at all three objectives. In order to evaluate learning, the specific objectives must be determined.

Some trainers say that no learning has taken place unless change in behavior occurs. In the four levels described in this book, learning has taken place when one or more of the following occurs: Attitudes are changed. Knowledge is increased. Skill is improved. One or more of these changes must take place if a change in behavior is to occur.

Behavior

Behavior can be defined as the extent to which change in behavior has occurred because the participant attended the training program. Some trainers want to bypass levels 1 and 2—reaction and learning—in order to measure changes in behavior. This is a serious mistake. For example, suppose that no change in behavior is discovered. The obvious conclusion is that the program was ineffective and that it should be discontinued. This conclusion may or may not be accurate. Reaction may have been favorable, and the learning objectives may have been accomplished, but the level 3 or 4 conditions may not have been present.

In order for change to occur, four conditions are necessary:

1. The person must have a desire to change.
2. The person must know what to do and how to do it.
3. The person must work in the right climate.
4. The person must be rewarded for changing.

The training program can accomplish the first two requirements by creating a positive attitude toward the desired change and by teaching the necessary knowledge and skills. The third condition, right climate, refers to the participant's immediate supervisor. Five different kinds of climate can be described:

1. *Preventing:* The boss forbids the participant from doing what he or she has been taught to do in the training program. The boss may be influenced by the organizational culture established by top management. Or the boss's leadership style may conflict with what was taught.

2. *Discouraging:* The boss doesn't say, "You can't do it," but he or she makes it clear that the participant should not change behavior because it would make the boss unhappy. Or the boss doesn't model the behavior taught in the program, and this negative example discourages the subordinate from changing.

3. *Neutral:* The boss ignores the fact that the participant has attended a training program. It is business as usual. If the subordinate wants to change, the boss has no objection as long as the job gets done. If negative results occur because behavior has changed, then the boss may turn into a discouraging or even preventing climate.

4. *Encouraging:* The boss encourages the participant to learn and apply his or her learning on the job. Ideally, the boss discussed the program with the subordinate beforehand and stated that the two would discuss application as soon as the program was over. The boss basically says, "I am interested in knowing what you learned and how I can help you transfer the learning to the job."

5. *Requiring:* The boss knows what the subordinate learns and makes sure that the learning transfers to the job. In some cases, a learning

contract is prepared that states what the subordinate agrees to do. This contract can be prepared at the end of the training session, and a copy can be given to the boss. The boss sees to it that the contract is implemented. Malcolm Knowles's book *Using Learning Contracts* (San Francisco: Jossey-Bass, 1986) describes this process.

The fourth condition, rewards, can be intrinsic (from within), extrinsic (from without), or both. Intrinsic rewards include the feelings of satisfaction, pride, and achievement that can occur when change in behavior has positive results. Extrinsic rewards include praise from the boss, recognition by others, and monetary rewards, such as merit pay increases and bonuses.

It becomes obvious that there is little or no chance that training will transfer to job behavior if the climate is preventing or discouraging. If the climate is neutral, change in behavior will depend on the other three conditions just described. If the climate is encouraging or requiring, then the amount of change that occurs depends on the first and second conditions.

As stated earlier, it is important to evaluate both reaction and learning in case no change in behavior occurs. Then it can be determined whether the fact that there was no change was the result of an ineffective training program or of the wrong job climate and lack of rewards.

It is important for trainers to know the type of climate that participants will face when they return from the training program. It is also important for them to do everything that they can to see to it that the climate is neutral or better. Otherwise there is little or no chance that the program will accomplish the behavior and results objectives, because participants will not even try to use what they have learned. Not only will no change occur, but those who attended the program will be frustrated with the boss, the training program, or both for teaching them things that they can't apply.

One way to create a positive job climate is to involve bosses in the development of the program. Chapter 1 suggested asking bosses to help to determine the needs of subordinates. Such involvement helps to ensure that a program teaches practical concepts, principles, and techniques. Another approach is to present the training program, or at least a condensed version of it, to the bosses before the supervisors are trained.

A number of years ago, I was asked by Dave Harris, personnel manager, to present an eighteen-hour training program to 240 supervisors at A. O. Smith Corporation in Milwaukee. I asked Dave if he could arrange for me to present a condensed, three- to six-hour version to the company's top management. He arranged for the condensed version to be offered at the Milwaukee Athletic Club. After the six-hour program, the eight upper-level managers were asked for their opinions and suggestions. They not only liked the program but told us to present the entire program first to the thirty-five general foremen and superintendents who were the bosses of the 240 supervisors. We did what they suggested. We asked these bosses for their comments and encouraged them to provide an encouraging climate when the supervisors had completed the program. I am not sure to what extent this increased change in behavior over the level that we would have seen if top managers had not attended or even known the content of the program, but I am confident that it made a big difference. We told the supervisors that their bosses had already attended the program. This increased their motivation to learn and their desire to apply their learning on the job.

Much has been written concerning change in behavior, or "transfer of training," as it is often termed. Some of the references at the end of Chapter 8 describe concepts, principles, and techniques.

Results

Results can be defined as the final results that occurred because the participants attended the program. The final results can include increased production, improved quality, decreased costs, reduced frequency and/or severity of accidents, increased sales, reduced turnover, and higher profits. It is important to recognize that results like these are the reason for having some training programs. Therefore, the final objectives of the training program need to be stated in these terms.

Some programs have these in mind on a long-term basis. For example, one major objective of the popular program on diversity in the workforce is to change the attitudes of supervisors and managers toward minorities in their departments. We want supervisors to treat all people fairly, show no discrimination, and so on. These are not tangible results that can be measured in terms of dollars and cents. But it is hoped that tangible results will follow. Likewise, it is difficult if not impossible to measure final results for programs on such topics as leadership, communication, motivation, time management, empowerment, decision making, or managing change. We can state and evaluate desired behaviors, but the final results have to be measured in terms of improved morale or other nonfinancial terms. It is hoped that such things as higher morale or improved quality of work life will result in the tangible results just described.

Summary

Trainers should begin to plan by considering the desired results. These results should be determined in cooperation with managers at various levels. Surveys and/or interviews can be used. A desirable and practical approach is to use an advisory committee consisting of managers from different departments. Their participation will give them a feeling of ownership and will probably increase the chances of their creating a climate that encourages change in behavior. The next step is to determine what behaviors will produce the desired results. Then trainers need to determine what knowledge, skills, and attitudes will produce the desired behavior.

The final challenge is to present the training program in a way that enables the participants not only to learn what they need to know but also to react favorably to the program. This is the sequence in which programs should be planned. The four levels of evaluation are considered in reverse. First, we evaluate reaction. Then, we evaluate learning, behavior, and results—in that order. Each of the four levels is important, and we should not bypass the first two in order to get to levels 3 and 4. Reaction is easy to do, and we should measure it for every program. Trainers should proceed to the other three levels as staff, time, and money are available. The next four chapters provide guidelines, suggested forms, and procedures for each level. The case studies in Part Two of the book describe how the levels were applied in different types of programs and organizations.

Chapter 4

Evaluating Reaction

Evaluating reaction is the same thing as measuring customer satisfaction. If training is going to be effective, it is important that trainees react favorably to it. Otherwise, they will not be motivated to learn. Also, they will tell others of their reactions, and decisions to reduce or eliminate the program may be based on what they say. Some trainers call the forms that are used for the evaluation of reaction *happiness sheets*. Although they say this in a critical or even cynical way, they are correct. These forms really are happiness sheets. But they are not worthless. They help us to determine how effective the program is and learn how it can be improved.

Measuring reaction is important for several reasons. First, it gives us valuable feedback that helps us to evaluate the program as well as comments and suggestions for improving future programs. Second, it tells trainees that the trainers are there to help them do their job better and that they need feedback to determine how effective they are. If we do not ask for reaction, we tell trainees that we know what they want and need and that we can judge the effectiveness of the program without getting feedback from them. Third, reaction sheets can provide quantitative information that you can give to managers and others concerned about the program. Finally, reaction sheets can provide trainers with quantitative information that can be used to establish standards of performance for future programs.

Evaluating reaction is not only important but also easy to do and do effectively. Most trainers use reaction sheets. I have seen dozens of forms and various ways of using them. Some are effective, and some are not. Here are some guidelines that will help trainers to get maximum benefit from reaction sheets:

Guidelines for Evaluating Reaction

1. Determine what you want to find out.
2. Design a form that will quantify reactions.
3. Encourage written comments and suggestions.
4. Get 100 percent immediate response.
5. Get honest responses.
6. Develop acceptable standards.
7. Measure reactions against standards, and take appropriate action.
8. Communicate reactions as appropriate.

The next eight sections contain suggestions for implementing each of these guidelines.

Determine What You Want to Find Out

In every program, it is imperative to get reactions both to the subject and to the leader. And it is important to separate these two ingredients of every program. In addition, trainers may want to get trainees' reactions to one or more of the following: the facilities (location, comfort, convenience, and so forth); the schedule (time, length of program, breaks, convenience, and so forth); meals (amount and quality of food and so forth); case studies, exercises, and so forth; audiovisual aids (how appropriate, effective, and so forth); handouts (how helpful, amount, and so forth); the value that participants place on individual aspects of the program.

Design a Form That Will Quantify Reactions

Trainers have their own philosophy about the forms that should be used. Some like open questions that require a lot of writing. They feel that checking boxes does not provide enough feedback. Some even feel that it amounts to telling trainees what to do. Others keep it as simple as possible and just ask trainees to check a few boxes.

The ideal form provides the maximum amount of information and requires the minimum amount of time. When a program is over, most trainees are anxious to leave, and they don't want to spend a lot of time completing evaluation forms. Some even feel that trainers do not consider their comments anyway.

There are a number of different forms that can provide the maximum information and require a minimum amount of time to complete. Exhibits 4.1, 4.2, 4.3, and 4.4 show forms that can be used

Exhibit 4.1. Reaction Sheet

Please give us your frank reactions and comments. They will help us to evaluate this program and improve future programs.

Leader _____   Subject _____

1. How do you rate the subject? (interest, benefit, etc.)

    _____ Excellent   Comments and suggestions:

    _____ Very good

    _____ Good

    _____ Fair

    _____ Poor

2. How do you rate the conference leader? (knowledge of subject matter, ability to communicate,etc.)

    _____ Excellent   Comments and suggestions:

    _____ Very good

    _____ Good

    _____ Fair

    _____ Poor

3. How do you rate the facilities? (comfort, convenience, etc.)

    _____ Excellent   Comments and suggestions:

    _____ Very good

    _____ Good

    _____ Fair

    _____ Poor

4. How do you rate the schedule?

    _____ Excellent   Comments and suggestions:

    _____ Very good

    _____ Good

    _____ Fair

    _____ Poor

5. What would have improved the program?

Exhibit 4.2. Reaction Sheet

Leader _____ Subject _____

1. How pertinent was the subject to your needs and interests?

    _____ Not at all _____ To some extent _____ Very much

2. How was the ratio of presentation to discussion?

    _____ Too much presentation _____ Okay _____ Too much discussion

3. How do you rate the instructor?

	Excellent	*Very good*	*Good*	*Fair*	*Poor*
a. In stating objectives					
b. In keeping the session alive and interesting					
c. In communicating					
d. In using aids					
e. In maintaining a friendly and helpful attitude					

4. What is your overall rating of the leader?

    _____ Excellent   Comments and suggestions:

    _____ Very good

    _____ Good

    _____ Fair

    _____ Poor

5. What would have made the session more effective?

---

effectively when one leader conducts the entire program. Exhibit 4.5 is unusual because it is truly a "smile" sheet, as many reaction sheets are called. I found it in a hotel in Geneva, Switzerland. The original form was written in French. Exhibits 4.5 and 4.6 show forms that can be used when more than one leader conducts the program and it is not desirable to have trainees complete a separate form for each. All forms

Exhibit 4.3. Reaction Sheet

In order to determine the effectiveness of the program in meeting your needs and interests, we need your input. Please give us your reactions, and make any comments or suggestions that will help us to serve you.

Instructions: Please circle the appropriate response after each statement.

	Strongly disagree	Agree	Strongly agree
1. The material covered in the program was relevant to my job.	1 2 3	4 5	6 7 8
2. The material was presented in an interesting way.	1 2 3	4 5	6 7 8
3. The instructor was an effective communicator.	1 2 3	4 5	6 7 8
4. The instructor was well prepared.	1 2 3	4 5	6 7 8
5. The audiovisual aids were effective.	1 2 3	4 5	6 7 8
6. The handouts will be of help to me.	1 2 3	4 5	6 7 8
7. I will be able to apply much of the material to my job.	1 2 3	4 5	6 7 8
8. The facilities were suitable.	1 2 3	4 5	6 7 8
9. The schedule was suitable.	1 2 3	4 5	6 7 8
10. There was a good balance between presentation and group involvement.	1 2 3	4 5	6 7 8
11. I feel that the workshop will help me do my job better.	1 2 3	4 5	6 7 8

What would have improved the program?

---

can be quantified and used to establish standards for future evaluations. It would be worthwhile to try a form with several groups to see whether trainees understand it and whether it serves the purpose for which it was designed. All the forms illustrated in this chapter need to be tabulated by hand. They can be readily adapted so that they can be tabulated and analyzed by computer if that is easier.

Exhibit 4.4. Reaction Sheet

Please complete this form to let us know your reaction to the program. Your input will help us to evaluate our efforts, and your comments and suggestions will help us to plan future programs that meet your needs and interests.

Instructions: Please circle the appropriate number after each statement and then add your comments.

	High				*Low*
1. How do you rate the subject content? (interesting, helpful, etc.)	5	4	3	2	1

Comments:

2. How do you rate the instructor? (preparation, communication, etc.)	5	4	3	2	1

Comments:

3. How do you rate the facilities? (comfort, convenience, etc.)	5	4	3	2	1

Comments:

4. How do you rate the schedule? (time, length, etc.)	5	4	3	2	1

Comments:

5. How would you rate the program as an educational experience to help you do your job better?	5	4	3	2	1

6. What topics were most beneficial?

7. What would have improved the program?

Exhibit 4.5. Reaction Sheet

Dear Client,

We would like to have your comments and suggestions to enable us to offer you the kind of service you would like.

Would you help us by ticking the face that is most indicative of your feelings:

☐ **breakfast**   ☐ **lunch**   *Very good*   *Good*   *Average*

1. Are you satisfied with the quality of the meals?

2. Are you satisfied with the variety of dishes available?

3. Do you find our prices competitive?

4. What do you think of the service?

5. How do you find the atmosphere in the restaurant?

6. Suggestions:

Name: _____

Address: _____

Exhibit 4.6. Reaction Sheet

Please give your frank and honest reactions. Insert the appropriate number.

Scale: 5 = Excellent   4 = Very good   3 = Good   2 = Fair   1 = Poor

Leader	*Subject*	*Presentation*	*Discussion*	*Audiovisual aids*	*Overall*
Tom Jones					
Gerald Ford					
Luis Aparicio					
Simon Bolivar					
Muhammad Ali					
Chris Columbus					
Bart Starr					

Facilities   Rating _____   Meals   Rating _____

Comments: Comments:

Schedule   Rating _____   Overall program   Rating _____

Comments: Comments:

What would have improved the program?

Encourage Written Comments and Suggestions

The ratings that you tabulate provide only part of the participants' re-actions. They do not provide the reasons for those reactions or suggest what can be done to improve the program. Therefore, it is important to get additional comments. All the forms shown in this chapter give participants opportunities to comment.

Typically, reaction sheets are passed out at the end of a program. Participants are encouraged to complete the forms and leave them on the back table on their way out. If they are anxious to leave, most will not take time to write in their comments. You can prevent this by making the completion of reaction sheets part of the program. For example, five minutes before the program is scheduled to end, the instructor can say, "Please take time to complete the reaction sheet, including your comments. Then I have a final announcement." This simple approach will ensure that you receive comments from all or nearly all the participants.

Another approach is to pass the forms out at the beginning of the program and stress the importance of comments and suggestions.

Get 100 Percent Immediate Response

I have attended many programs at which reaction sheets are distributed to participants with instructions to send them back after they have a chance to complete them. This reduces the value of the reaction sheets for two reasons. First, some, perhaps even most, of the participants will not do it. Second, the forms that are returned may not be a good indication of the reaction of the group as a whole. Therefore, have participants turn in their reaction sheets before they leave the room. If you feel that reactions would be more meaningful if participants took more time to complete them, you can send out a follow-up reaction sheet after the training together with a cover memo that says something like this: "Thanks for the reaction sheet you completed at the end of the training meeting. As you think back on the program, you may have different or additional reactions and comments. Please complete the enclosed form, and return it within the next three days. We want to provide the most practical training possible. Your feedback will help us."

Get Honest Responses

Getting honest responses may seem to be an unnecessary requirement, but it is important. Some trainers like to know who said what. And they use an approach that lets them do just that. For example, they have the participants sign the forms. Or they tell them to complete the form and leave it at their place. In one program, the trainers used a two-sided form. One side was the reaction sheet. The other side sought attendance information: Participants were asked to give their name, department, and so on. I don't know whether the trainers were being clever or stupid.

In some programs, like those at the University of Wisconsin Management Institute, there is space at the bottom of the reaction sheets labeled *signature (optional)*. It is often meaningful to know who made a comment for two reasons: if the comment is positive, so you quote that person in future program brochures, or so that you can contact that person relative to the comment or suggestion.

Where people attend outside programs, they are usually free to give their honest opinion even if it is critical. They see little or no possibility of negative repercussions. The situation can be different in an in-house program. Some participants may be reluctant to make a critical reaction or comment because they fear repercussions. They may be afraid that the instructor or training department staff will feel that the reaction is not justified and there is something wrong with the participant, even that trainers might tell the participant's boss about the negative reaction and that it could affect their future. Therefore, to be sure that reactions are honest, you should not ask participants to sign the forms. Also, you should ask that completed forms be put in a pile on a table so there is no way to identify the person who completed an individual form. In cases where it would be beneficial to identify the individual, the bottom of the form can have a space for a signature that is clearly labeled as *optional*.

Develop Acceptable Standards

A numerical tabulation can be made of all the forms discussed and shown in this chapter. Exhibit 4.7 shows a tabulation of the reactions of twenty supervisors to the form shown in Exhibit 4.1. The following five-point scale can be used to rate the responses on a form.

Excellent = 5   Very good = 4   Good = 3   Fair = 2   Poor = 1

You tally the responses in each category for all items. For each item, you multiply the number of responses by the corresponding weighting and add the products together. Then you divide by the total number of responses received. For example, you calculate the rating for item 1, subject, as follows:

$$(10 \times 5 = 50) + (5 \times 4 = 20) + (3 \times 3 = 9)$$
$$+ (1 \times 2 = 2) + (1 \times 1 = 1) = 82$$

The rating is 82/20 or 4.1

Exhibit 4.7. Tabulating Responses to Reaction Sheets

Please give us your frank reactions and comments. They will help us to evaluate this program and improve future programs.

Leader *Tom Jones*   Subject *Leadership*

1. How do you rate the subject? (interest, benefit, etc.)

    __10__ Excellent   Comments and suggestions:

    __5__ Very good

    __3__ Good   Rating = *4.1*

    __1__ Fair

    __1__ Poor

2. How do you rate the conference leader? (knowledge of subject matter, ability to communicate, etc.)

    __8__ Excellent   Comments and suggestions:

    __4__ Very good

    __5__ Good   Rating = *3.8*

    __2__ Fair

    __1__ Poor

3. How do you rate the facilities? (comfort, convenience, etc.)

    __7__ Excellent   Comments and suggestions:

    __7__ Very good

    __5__ Good   Rating = *4.0*

    __1__ Fair

    __0__ Poor

4. What would have improved the program?

Note: Ratings are on a five-point scale.

You can use these ratings to establish a standard of acceptable performance. This standard can be based on a realistic analysis of what can be expected considering such conditions as budgets, facilities available, skilled instructors available, and so on. For example, at the University of Wisconsin Management Institute, the standard of subjects and leaders was placed at 4.7 on a five-point scale. This standard was based on past ratings. In this situation, budgets were favorable, and most of the instructors were full-time, professional trainers operating in nice facilities. In many organizations, limitations would lower the standard. You can have different standards for different aspects of the program. For example, the standard for instructors could be higher than the standard for facilities. The standards should be based on past experience, considering the ratings that effective instructors have received.

Measure Reactions Against Standards and Take Appropriate Action

Once realistic standards have been established, you should evaluate the various aspects of the program and compare your findings with the standards. Your evaluation should include impressions of the coordinator as well as an analysis of the reaction sheets of participants. Several approaches are possible if the standard is not met.

1. Make a change—in leaders, facilities, subject, or something else.
2. Modify the situation. If the instructor does not meet the standard, help by providing advice, new audiovisual aids, or something else.
3. Live with an unsatisfactory situation.
4. Change the standard if conditions change.

In regard to the evaluation of instructors, I once faced a situation that I'll never forget. At the Management Institute, I selected and hired an instructor from General Electric to conduct a seminar for top management. He had a lot of experience, both of the subject and in conducting seminars both inside and outside the company. His rating was 3.3, far below our standard of 4.7. He saw that we used reaction sheets and asked me to send him a summary. He also said, "Don, I know that you conduct and coordinate a lot of seminars. I would appreciate your personal comments and any suggestions for improvement." I agreed to do it.

I enclosed a thank-you letter with a summary of the comment sheets. My thank-you tactfully offered the following suggestions, which, I indicated, were based on the reaction sheets and on my own observations: "Use more examples to illustrate your points. Give the group more opportunity to ask questions. Ask your audio-visual department to prepare some professional slides and/or transparencies that will help to maintain interest and communicate."

I waited for a thank-you for my constructive suggestions. I am still waiting, and this happened in 1969. I did hear through a mutual friend that the instructor was very unhappy with my letter. He complained that he had taken time from a busy schedule to speak at the University of Wisconsin, he didn't take any fee or expenses, and the only thanks he had gotten was my letter. That was the last time he'd agree to be on our programs.

This example suggests that program coordinators should be very tactful in "helping" instructors by offering suggestions, especially if the instructors are members of top management within their own organization. One practical approach is to let instructors know ahead of time that reaction sheets will be used and that ratings will be compared with a standard. Instructors are usually eager to meet or beat the standard. If they don't, most will either ask for helpful suggestions or decide that someone else should probably do the teaching in the future. This is usually good news for the training staff, who may want to make a change anyway.

Obviously, all reactions that can be tabulated should be tabulated and the ratings calculated. In regard to comments, trainers can either record all comments on a summary sheet or summarize the comments that are pertinent. Tabulations can even be made of similar comments.

Communicate Reactions as Appropriate

Trainers are always faced with decisions regarding the communication of reactions to programs. Obviously, if instructors want to see their reaction sheets, they should be shown them or at least a summary of the responses. Other members of the training department should certainly have access to them. The person to whom the training department reports, usually the manager of Human Resources, should be able to see them. Communicating the reactions to others depends on two factors: who wants to see them and with whom training staff want to communicate.

Regarding who wants to see them, training staff must decide whether it is appropriate. Is it only out of curiosity, or does the requester have legitimate reasons?

Regarding the desire of training staff to communicate the reactions, the question is how often the information should be communicated and in what detail. Those who make decisions about staffing, budgets, salary increases, promotions, layoffs, and so on should be informed. Also, as I suggested in Chapter 1, if there is an advisory committee, its members should be informed. If the concepts and principles described in Chapter 1 have been implemented, the reactions will be favorable, and top management will respect the training department and realize how much the organization needs it in good and bad times.

Summary

Measuring reaction is important and easy to do. It is important because the decisions of top management may be based on what they have heard about the training program. It is important to have tangible data that reactions are favorable. It is important also because the interest, attention, and motivation of participants has much to do with the learning that occurs. Still another reason why it is important is that trainees are customers, and customer satisfaction has a lot to do with repeat business.

This chapter has provided guidelines, forms, procedures, and techniques for measuring reaction effectively. Reaction is the first level in the evaluation process. It should be evaluated for all training programs. The responses to reaction sheets should be tabulated, and the results should be analyzed. The comments received from participants should be considered carefully, and programs should be modified accordingly. This measure of customer satisfaction can make or break a training department. It is only the first step, but it is an important one.

P.S. If you refer to reaction sheets as "smile" sheets, smile when you do so and hope that participants are smiling when they leave the program!

Chapter 5

Evaluating Learning

There are three things that instructors in a training program can teach: knowledge, skills, and attitudes. Measuring learning, therefore, means determining one or more of the following:

What knowledge was learned?
What skills were developed or improved?
What attitudes were changed?

It is important to measure learning because no change in behavior can be expected unless one or more of these learning objectives have been accomplished. Moreover, if we were to measure behavior change (level 3) and not learning and if we found no change in behavior, the likely conclusion is that no learning took place. This conclusion may be very erroneous. The reason why no change in behavior was observed may be that the climate was preventing or discouraging, as described in Chapter 3. In these situations, learning may have taken place, and the learner may even have been anxious to change his or her behavior. But because his or her boss either prevented or discouraged the

Note: In the guidelines for levels 2, 3, and 4 no information has been given on how to use statistics. This subject is too complex to be included here. I encourage readers to consider statistical analysis. Consult people within your organization who are knowledgeable, and ask them to help you apply statistics to level 2 as well as to levels 3 and 4. Chapters 13, 14, 16, 18, 19, and 21 use statistics to determine the effectiveness of training.

trainee from applying his or her learning on the job, no change in behavior took place.

The measurement of learning is more difficult and time-consuming than the measurement of reaction. These guidelines will be helpful:

Guidelines for Evaluating Learning

1. Use a control group if practical.
2. Evaluate knowledge, skills, and/or attitudes both before and after the program.
3. Use a paper-and-pencil test to measure knowledge and attitudes.
4. Use a performance test to measure skills.
5. Get a 100 percent response.
6. Use the results of the evaluation to take appropriate action.

The remainder of this chapter suggests ways of implementing these guidelines.

Use a Control Group If Practical

The term *control group* will be used in levels 3 and 4 as well as here in level 2. It refers to a group that does not receive the training. The group that receives the training is called the *experimental group.* The purpose of using a control group is to provide better evidence that change has taken place. Any difference between the control group and the experimental group can be explained by the learning that took place because of the training program.

The phrase *whenever practical* is important for several reasons. For example, in smaller organizations, there will be a single training program in which all the supervisors are trained. In larger organizations, there are enough supervisors that you can have a control group as well as an experimental group. In this case, you must take care to be sure that the groups are equal in all significant characteristics. Otherwise, comparisons are not valid. It could be done by giving the training program only to the experimental group and comparing scores before training with scores after training for both the experimental and control groups. The control group would receive the training at a later time. The example of test scores later in this chapter will illustrate this.

Evaluate Knowledge, Skills, and/or Attitudes

The second guideline is to measure attitudes, knowledge, and/or attitudes before and after the program. The difference indicates what learning has taken place.

Evaluating Increase in Knowledge and Changes in Attitudes

If increased knowledge and/or changed attitudes is being measured, a paper-and-pencil test can be used. (This term must have been coined before ballpoint pens were invented.) I'll use the Management Inventory on Managing Change (MIMC) described in Chapter 1 to illustrate.

Example 1 in Table 5.1 shows that the average score of the experimental group on the pretest (that is, on the test given before the program started) was 45.5 on a possible score of 65. The average score of the experimental group on the posttest (the same test given at the conclusion of the program) was 55.4—a net gain of 9.9.

Example 1 also shows that the average score of the control group on the pretest was 46.7 and that the score of the control group on the posttest was 48.2. This means that factors other than the training

Table 5.1. Pretest and Posttest Scores
on the Management Inventory on Managing Change

		Experimental group	*Control group*
Example 1	Pretest	45.5	46.7
	Posttest	55.4	48.2
	Gain	+9.9	+1.5
	Net Gain 9.9 − 1.5 = 8.4		
		Experimental group	*Control group*
Example 2	Pretest	45.5	46.7
	Posttest	55.4	54.4
	Gain	+9.9	+7.7
	Net Gain 9.9 − 7.7 = 2.2		

program caused the change. Therefore, the gain of 1.5 must be deducted from the 9.9 gain of the experimental group to show the gain resulting from the training program. The result is 8.4.

Example 2 in Table 5.1 shows a different story. The net gain for the control group between the pretest score of 46.7 and the posttest score of 54.4 is 7.7. When this difference is deducted from the 9.9 registered for the experimental group, the gain that can be attributed to the training program is only 2.2.

This comparison of total scores on the pretest and posttest is one method of measuring increased knowledge and/or changes in attitude. Another important measure involves the comparison of pretest and posttest answers to each item on the inventory or test. For example, this is item 4 of the MIMC described in Chapter 1: "If a change is going to be unpopular with your subordinates, you should proceed slowly in order to obtain acceptance."

Table 5.2 shows that seven of the twenty-five supervisors in the experimental group agreed with item 4 on the pretest, and eighteen disagreed. It also shows that twenty agreed with it on the posttest, and five disagreed. The correct answer is *Agree,* so the positive gain was 11. Table 5.2 also shows the pretest and posttest responses from the control group. For it, the gain was 1. Therefore, the net gain due to the training program was 10.

Item 8 in Table 5.2 shows a different story. Item 8 states: "If you are promoted to a management job, you should make the job different than it was under your predecessor."

Five of those in the experimental group agreed on the pretest, and twenty disagreed. On the posttest, six agreed, and nineteen disagreed. The correct answer is *Agree.* The net gain was 1. The figures for the control group were the same. So there was no change in attitude and/or knowledge on this item.

This evaluation of learning is important for two reasons. First, it measures the effectiveness of the instructor in increasing knowledge and/or changing attitudes. It shows how effective he or she is. If little or no learning has taken place, little or no change in behavior can be expected.

Just as important is the specific information that evaluation of learning provides. By analyzing the change in answers to individual items, the instructor can see where he or she has succeeded and where he or she has failed. If the program is going to be repeated, the in-

Table 5.2. Responses to Two Items
on the Management Inventory on Managing Change

Item 4. "If a change is going to be unpopular with your subordinates, you should proceed slowly in order to obtain acceptance." (The correct answer is *Agree*.)

	Experimental group		Control group	
	Agree	Disagree	Agree	Disagree
Pretest	7	18	6	19
Posttest	20	5	7	18
Gain	+13		+1	

Net Gain 13 − 1 = 12

Item 8. "If you are promoted to a management job, you should make the job different than it was under your predecessor." (The correct answer is *Agree*.)

	Experimental group		Control group	
	Agree	Disagree	Agree	Disagree
Pretest	5	20	5	20
Posttest	6	19	6	19
Gain	+1		+1	

Net Gain 1 − 1 = 0

structor can plan other techniques and/or aids to increase the chances that learning will take place. Moreover, if follow-up sessions can be held with the same group, the things that have not been learned can become the objectives of these sessions.

These examples have illustrated how a control group can be used. In most organizations, it is not practical to have a control group, and the evaluation will include only figures for those who attended the training program.

It almost goes without saying that a standardized test can be used only to the extent that it covers the subject matter taught in the training program. When I teach, I use the various inventories that I have developed as teaching tools. Each inventory includes much of the content of the corresponding program. The same principles and techniques can and should be used with a test developed specifically for the organization. For example, MGIC, a mortgage insurer in Milwaukee, has developed an extensive test covering information that its supervisors need to know.

Much of this information is related to the specific policies, procedures, and facts of the business and organization. Some of the items are true or false, while others are multiple choice, as Exhibit 5.1 shows.

The training people have determined what the supervisors need to know. Then they have written a test covering that information. They

Exhibit 5.1. Sample Items from a MGIC Test to Evaluate Supervisor Knowledge

---

1. T or F   When preparing a truth-in-lending disclosure with a financed single premium, mortgage insurance should always be disclosed for the life of the loan.

2. T or F   GE and MGIC have the same refund policy for refundable single premiums.

3. T or F   MGIC, GE, and PMI are the only mortgage insurers offering a non-refundable single premium.

4. _____   Which of the following is not a category in the loan progress reports?

   a. Loans approved

   b. Loans-in-suspense

   c. Loans denied

   d. Loans received

5. _____   Which of the following do not affect the MGIC Plus buying decision?

   a. Consumer

   b. Realtor

   c. MGIC underwriter

   d. Secondary market manager

   e. Servicing manager

   f. All the above

   g. None of the above

   h. Both b and c

   i. Both c and e

6. _____   The new risk-based capital regulations for savings and loans have caused many of them to

   a. Convert whole loans into securities

   b. Begin originating home equity loans

   c. Put MI on their uninsured 90s

   d. All the above

   e. Both e and c

   f. Both b and c

---

have combined true-or-false statements with multiple-choice items to make the test interesting. A tabulation of the pretest responses to each item will tell the instructors what the supervisors do and do not know before they participate in the program. It will help them to determine the need for training. If everyone knows the answer to an item before the program takes place, there is no need to cover the item in the program. A tabulation of posttest responses will tell the instructor where he or she has succeeded and where he or she has failed in getting the participants to learn the information that the test covers. It will help instructors to know what they need to emphasize and whether they need to use more aids in future programs. It will also tell them what follow-up programs are needed.

This type of test is different from the inventories described earlier. Participants must know the answers to the questions in Exhibit 5.1. Therefore, those who take the posttest put their name on it, and they are graded. Those who do not pass must take further training until they pass the test.

In regard to the inventories, there is no need to identify the responses and scores of individual persons. The scoring sheet shown in Exhibit 5.2 is given to supervisors. They score their own inventory and circle the number of each item that they answered incorrectly. They keep their inventory and turn in the scoring sheet. These can be tabulated to determine both the total score and the responses to individual items. You can then use the resulting numbers as shown in Tables 5.1 and 5.2.

Both the MIMC and the MGIC examples are typical of efforts to measure increase in knowledge and/or changes in attitudes.

Exhibit 5.2. Scoring Sheet for the Management Inventory on Managing Change

---

Management Inventory on Managing Change   Date _____

Please circle by number those items you answered incorrectly according to the scoring key. Then determine your score by subtracting the number wrong from 65.

1	2	3	4	5	6	7	8	9	10	11	12	13	14	15	16	17	18
19	20	21	22	23	24	25	26	27	28	29	30	31	32	33	34
35	36	37	38	39	40	41	42	43	44	45	46	47	48	49	50
51	52	53	54	55	56	57	58	59	60	61	62	63	64	65

Score   65 −   =

Evaluating Increase in Skills

If the objective of a program is to increase the skills of participants, then a performance test is needed. For example, some programs aim at improving oral communication skills. A trained instructor can evaluate the level of proficiency. Other participants may also be qualified if they have been given standards of performance. For the pretest, you can have each person give a short talk before any training has been given. The instructor can measure these talks and assign them a grade. During the program, the instructor provides principles and techniques for making an effective talk. The increase in skills can be measured for each succeeding talk that participants give. The same approach can be used to measure such skills as speaking, writing, conducting meetings, and conducting performance appraisal interviews. Chapter 13 describes such a program.

The same principles and techniques apply when technical skills, such as using a computer, making out forms, and selling, are taught. Of course, the before-and-after approach is not necessary where the learner has no previous skill. An evaluation of the skill after instruction measures the learning that has taken place.

Get a 100 Percent Response

Anything less than a 100 percent response requires a carefully designed approach to select a sample group and analyze the results statistically. It is not difficult to get everyone in the group to participate, and tabulations become simple. Tables 5.1 and 5.2 show how this can be done. It is desirable to analyze the tabulations shown in Tables 5.1 and 5.2 statistically, but in most organizations it is not necessary.

Take Appropriate Action

There is an old saying that, if the learner hasn't learned, the teacher hasn't taught. This is a good philosophy for each instructor to have. It is only too easy to blame a learner for not learning. How many times have we trainers said (or perhaps only thought) to someone whom we are teaching, "How many times do I have to tell you before you catch on?" And usually the tone makes it clear that we are criticizing the learner, not simply asking a question. Another old saying applies pretty well to the same situation: When you point a finger at another person, you are pointing three fingers at yourself! This saying, too, can be applied in many teaching situations.

The important point is that we are measuring our own effectiveness as instructors when we evaluate participants' learning. If we haven't succeeded, let's look at ourselves and ask where we have failed, not what is the matter with the learners. And if we discover that we have not been successful instructors, let's figure how we can be more effective in the future. Sometimes the answer is simply better preparation. Sometimes it's the use of aids that help us to maintain interest and communicate more effectively. And sometimes the answer is to replace the instructor.

Summary

Evaluating learning is important. Without learning, no change in behavior will occur. Sometimes, the learning objective is to increase knowledge. Increased knowledge is relatively easy to measure by means of a test related to the content of the program that we administer before and after the training. If the knowledge is new, there is no need for a pretest. But if we are teaching concepts, principles, and techniques that trainees may already know, a pretest that we can compare with a posttest is necessary.

We can measure attitudes with a paper-and-pencil test. For example, programs on diversity in the workforce aim primarily at changing attitudes. We can design an attitude survey that covers the attitudes we want participants to have after taking part in the program. A comparison of the results from before and after training can indicate what changes have taken place. In such cases, it is important not to identify learners so we can be sure that they will give honest answers, not the answers that we want them to give.

The third thing that can be learned is skills. In these situations, a performance test is necessary. A pretest will be necessary if it is possible that they already possess some of the skills taught. If you are teaching something entirely new, then the posttest alone will measure the extent to which they have learned the skill.

Chapter 6

Evaluating Behavior

W hat happens when trainees leave the classroom and return to their jobs? How much transfer of knowledge, skills, and attitudes occurs? That is what level 3 attempts to evaluate. In other words, what change in job behavior occurred because people attended a training program?

It is obvious that this question is more complicated and difficult to answer than evaluating at the first two levels. First, trainees cannot change their behavior until they have an opportunity to do so. For example, if you, the reader of this book, decide to use some of the principles and techniques that I have described, you must wait until you have a training program to evaluate. Likewise, if the training program is designed to teach a person how to conduct an effective performance appraisal interview, the trainee cannot apply the learning until an interview is held.

Second, it is impossible to predict when a change in behavior will occur. Even if a trainee has an opportunity to apply the learning, he or she may not do it immediately. In fact, change in behavior may occur at any time after the first opportunity, or it may never occur.

Third, the trainee may apply the learning to the job and come to one of the following conclusions: "I like what happened, and I plan to continue to use the new behavior." "I don't like what happened, and I will go back to my old behavior." "I like what happened, but the boss and/or time restraints prevent me from continuing it." We all hope that the rewards for changing behavior will cause the trainee to come to the first of these conclusions. It is important, therefore, to provide help, encouragement, and rewards when the trainee returns to the job from the training class. One type of reward is intrinsic. This term refers to the inward feelings of satisfaction, pride, achievement, and happiness that can occur when the new behavior is used. Extrinsic rewards are also important. These are the rewards that come from the outside. They include praise, increased freedom and empowerment, merit pay increases, and other forms of recognition that come as the result of the change in behavior.

In regard to reaction and learning, the evaluation can and should take place immediately. When you evaluate change in behavior, you have to make some important decisions: when to evaluate, how often to evaluate, and how to evaluate. This makes it more time-consuming and difficult to do than levels 1 and 2. Here are some guidelines to follow when evaluating at level 3.

Guidelines for Evaluating Behavior

1. Use a control group if practical.
2. Allow time for behavior change to take place.
3. Evaluate both before and after the program if practical.
4. Survey and/or interview one or more of the following: trainees, their immediate supervisor, their subordinates, and others who often observe their behavior.
5. Get 100 percent response or a sampling.
6. Repeat the evaluation at appropriate times.
7. Consider cost versus benefits.

The remainder of this chapter suggests ways of implementing these guidelines.

Use a Control Group If Practical

Chapter 5 described the use of control groups in detail. A comparison of the change in behavior of a control group with the change experienced by the experimental group can add evidence that the change in behavior occurred because of the training program and not for other reasons. However, caution must be taken to be sure the two groups are equal in all factors that could have an effect on behavior. This may be difficult if not impossible to do.

Allow Time for Behavior Change to Take Place

As already indicated, no evaluation should be attempted until trainees have had an opportunity to use the new behavior. Sometimes, there is an immediate opportunity for applying it on the job. For example, if the training program is trying to change attitudes toward certain subordinates by teaching about diversity in the workforce, participants have an immediate opportunity to change attitudes and behavior as soon as they return to the job. Or if the program teaches management by walking around (MBWA), as encouraged by United Airlines and Hewlett-Packard, participants have an opportunity to use the technique right away. However, if the purpose of the training is to teach a foreman how to handle a grievance, no change in behavior is possible until a grievance has been filed.

Even if a participant has an immediate opportunity to transfer the training to the job, you should still allow some time for this transfer to occur. For some programs, two or three months after training is a good rule of thumb. For others, six months is more realistic. Be sure to give trainees time to get back to the job, consider the new suggested behavior, and try it out.

Evaluate Both Before and After the Program If Practical

Sometimes evaluation before and after a program is practical, and sometimes it is not even possible. For example, supervisors who attend the University of Wisconsin Management Institute training programs sometimes do not enroll until a day or two before the program starts. It would not be possible for the instructors or designated research students to measure their behavior before the program. In an in-house program, it would be possible, but it might not be practical because of time and budget constraints.

It is important when planning a supervisory training program to determine the kind of behavior that supervisors should have in order to be most effective. Before the training program, you measure the behavior of the supervisors. After the program, at a time to be determined as just outlined, you measure the behavior of the supervisors again to see whether any change has taken place in relation to the knowledge, skills, and/or attitudes that the training program taught. By comparing the behaviors observed before and after the program, you can determine any change that has taken place.

An alternative approach can also be effective. Under this approach, you measure behavior after the program only. Those whom you interview or survey are asked to identify any behavior that was different than it had been before the program. This was the approach that we used at the Management Institute to evaluate the three-day supervisory training program called Developing Supervisory Skills. Chapter 15 describes this evaluation.

In some cases, the training professionals and/or persons whom they select can observe the behavior personally.

Survey and/or Interview Persons Who Know the Behavior

As the guideline suggests, evaluators should survey and/or interview one or more of the following: trainees, their immediate supervisor, their subordinates, and others who are knowledgeable about their behavior.

Four questions need to be answered: Who is best qualified? Who is most reliable? Who is most available? Are there any reasons why one or more of the possible candidates should not be used?

If we try to determine who is best qualified, the answer is probably the subordinates who see the behavior of the trainee on a regular basis. In some cases, others who are neither boss nor subordinate have regular contact with the trainee. And, of course, the trainee knows (or should know) his or her own behavior. Therefore, of the four candidates just named, the immediate supervisor may be the person least qualified to evaluate the trainee unless he or she spends a great deal of time with the trainee.

Who is the most reliable? The trainee may not admit that behavior has not changed. Subordinates can be biased in favor of or against the trainee and therefore give a distorted picture. In fact, anyone can give a distorted picture, depending on his or her attitude toward the trainee or the program. This is why more than one source should be used.

Who is the most available? The answer depends on the particular situation. If interviews are to be conducted, then availability is critical. If a survey questionnaire is used, it is not important. In this case, the answer depends on who is willing to spend the time needed to complete the survey.

Are there any reasons why one or more of the possible candidates should not be used? The answer is yes. For example, asking subordinates for information on the behavior of their supervisor may not set well with the supervisor. However, if the trainee willing to have subordinates questioned, this may be the best approach of all.

A significant decision is whether to use a questionnaire or an interview. Both have their advantages and disadvantages. The interview gives you an opportunity to get more information. The best approach is to use a patterned interview in which all interviewees are asked the same questions. Then you can tabulate the responses and gather quantitative data on behavior change.

But interviews are very time-consuming, and only a few can be conducted if the availability of the person doing the interviewing is limited. Therefore, a small sample of those trained can be interviewed. However, the sample may not be representative of the behavior change that took place in trainees. And you cannot draw conclusions about the overall change in behavior. Exhibit 6.1 shows a patterned interview that can be used as is or adapted to your particular situation.

A survey questionnaire is usually more practical. If it is designed properly, it can provide the data that you need to evaluate change in behavior. The usual problem of getting people to take the time to complete it is always present. However, you can overcome this problem by motivating the people whom you ask to complete the survey. Perhaps there can be some reward, either intrinsic or extrinsic, for doing it. Or a person can be motivated to do it as a favor to the person doing the research. Producing information for top management as the reason for doing it may convince some. If the instructor, the person doing the evaluation, or both have built a rapport with those who are asked to complete the survey, they usually will cooperate. Exhibit 6.2 shows a survey questionnaire that you can use as is or adapt to your organization.

Exhibit 6.1. Patterned Interview

The interviewer reviews the program with the interviewee and highlights the behaviors that the program encouraged. The interviewer then clarifies the purpose of the interview, which is to evaluate the effectiveness of the course so that improvements can be made in the future. Specifically, the interview will determine the extent to which the suggested behaviors have been applied on the job. If they have not been applied, the interview will seek to learn why not. The interviewer makes it clear that all information will be held confidential so that the answers given can be frank and honest.

1. What specific behaviors were you taught and encouraged to use?

2. When you left the program, how eager were you to change your behavior on the job?

   _____ Very eager _____ Quite eager _____ Not eager

   Comments:

3. How well equipped were you to do what was suggested?

   _____ Very _____ Quite _____ Little _____ None

4. If you are <u>not doing</u> some of the things that you were encouraged and taught to do, why not?

	How Significant?		
	Very	*To some extent*	*Not*
a. It wasn't practical for my situation.			
b. My boss discourages me from changing.			
c. I haven't found the time.			
d. I tried it, and it didn't work.			
e. Other reasons.			

5. To what extent do you plan to do things differently in the future?

   _____ Large extent _____ Some extent _____ No extent

6. What suggestions do you have for making the program more helpful?

Exhibit 6.2. Survey Questionnaire

Instructions: The purpose of this questionnaire is to determine the extent to which those who attended the recent program on leadership methods have applied the principles and techniques that they learned there to the job. The results of the survey will help us to assess the effectiveness of the program and identify ways in which it can be made more practical for those who attend. Please be frank and honest in your answers. Your name is strictly optional. The only reason we ask is that we might want to follow up on your answers to get more comments and suggestions from you.

Please circle the appropriate response after each question.

5 = Much more   4 = Some more   3 = The same   2 = Some less   1 = Much less

Understanding and Motivating	*Time and energy spent after the program compared to time and energy spent before the program*				
1. Getting to know my employees	5	4	3	2	1
2. Listening to my subordinates	5	4	3	2	1
3. Praising good work	5	4	3	2	1
4. Talking with employees about their families and other personal interests	5	4	3	2	1
5. Asking subordinates for their ideas	5	4	3	2	1
6. Managing by walking around	5	4	3	2	1
Orienting and Training					
7. Asking new employees about their families, past experience, etc.	5	4	3	2	1
8. Taking new employees on a tour of the department and other facilities	5	4	3	2	1
9. Introducing new employees to their coworkers	5	4	3	2	1
10. Using the four-step method when training new and present employees	5	4	3	2	1
11. Being patient when employees don't learn as fast as I think they should	5	4	3	2	1
12. Tactfully correcting mistakes and making suggestions	5	4	3	2	1
13. Using the training inventory and timetable concept	5	4	3	2	1

What would have made the program more practical and helpful to you?

Name (optional) _____

Get 100 Percent Response or a Sampling

The dictum that something beats nothing can apply when you evaluate change in behavior. The person doing the evaluation can pick out a few "typical" trainees at random and interview or survey them. Or you can interview or survey the persons most likely not to change. The conclusion might be that, if Joe and Charlie have changed their behavior, then everyone has. This conclusion may or may not be true, but the approach can be practical. Obviously, the best approach is to measure the behavior change in all trainees. In most cases, this is not practical. Each organization must determine the amount of time and money that it can spend on level 3 evaluation and proceed accordingly.

Repeat the Evaluation at Appropriate Times

Some trainees may change their behavior as soon as they return to their job. Others may wait six months or a year or never change. And those who change immediately may revert to the old behavior after trying out the new behavior for a period of time. Therefore, it is important to repeat the evaluation at an appropriate time.

I wish I could describe what an appropriate time is. Each organization has to make the decision on its own, the kind of behavior, the job climate, and other significant factors unique to the situation. I would suggest waiting two or three months before conducting the first evaluation, the exact number depending on the opportunity that trainees have to use the new behavior. Perhaps another six months should elapse before the evaluation is repeated. And, depending on circumstances and the time available, a third evaluation could be made three to six months later.

Consider Cost Versus Benefits

Just as with other investments, you should compare the cost of evaluating change in behavior with the benefits that could result from the evaluation. In many organizations, much of the cost of evaluation at level 3 is in the staff time that it takes to do. And time is money. Other costs of evaluation can include the hiring of an outside expert to guide or even conduct the evaluation. For example, I have recently been hired by Kemper Insurance, Ford, GE, Blockbuster, and Northern States Power to present and discuss the four levels of evaluation with their training staff. At Kemper, I was asked to offer specific suggestions and return three months later to comment on the evaluations that they had done. (Chapter 12 describes one of their evaluations.) In these instances, I was called in not to evaluate a specific program but to provide guidelines and specific suggestions on how programs could be evaluated at all four levels. Other consultants can be called in to evaluate the changes in behavior that result from a specific program. You should consider such costs as these when you decide whether to evaluate changes in behavior.

The other factor to consider is the benefits that can be derived from evaluation including changes in behavior and final results. The greater the potential benefits, the more time and money can be spent on the evaluation not only of behavior change but in level 4 also. Another important consideration is the number of times the program will be offered. If it is run only once and it will not be repeated, there is little justification for spending time and money to evaluate possible changes in behavior. However, if a program is going to be repeated, the time and money spent evaluating it can be justified by the possible improvements in future programs.

It is important to understand that change in behavior is not an end in itself. Rather, it is a means to an end: the final results that can be achieved if change in behavior occurs. If no change in behavior occurs, then no improved results can occur. At the same time, even if change in behavior does occur, positive results may not be achieved. A good example is the principle and technique of managing by walking around (MBWA). Some organizations, including United Airlines and Hewlett-Packard, have found that higher morale and increased productivity can result. These organizations therefore encourage managers at all levels to walk among the lowest-level employees to show that they care. Picture a manager who has never shown concern for people. He attends a seminar at which he is told to change his behavior by walking around among lower-level employees to show that he cares. So the manager—for the first time—changes his behavior. He asks one employee about the kids. He comments to another employee regarding a vacation trip that the employee's family is planning. And he asks another employee about Sam, the pet dog. (The manager has learned about these things before talking to the three employees.) What are the chances that the three employees are now going to be motivated to increase their productivity because the manager really cares? Or will they look with suspicion on the new behavior and wonder what the boss is up to? The manager's change in behavior could even have negative results. This possibility underlines the fact that some behavior encouraged in the classroom is not appropriate for all participants. Encouraging supervisors to empower employees is a behavior that would not be appropriate in departments that had a lot of new employees, employees with negative attitudes, or employees with limited knowledge.

Summary

Level 3 evaluation determines the extent to which change in behavior occurs because of the training program. No final results can be expected unless a positive change in behavior occurs. Therefore, it is important to see whether the knowledge, skills, and/or attitudes learned in the program transfer to the job. The process of evaluating is complicated and often difficult to do. You have to decide whether to use interviews, survey questionnaires, or both. You must also decide whom to contact for the evaluation.

Two other difficult decisions are when and how often to conduct the evaluation. Whether to use a control group is still another important consideration. The sum of these factors discourages most trainers from even making an attempt to evaluate at level 3. But something beats nothing, and I encourage trainers to do some evaluating of behavior even if it isn't elaborate or scientific. Simply ask a few people, Are you doing anything different on the job because you attended the training program?

If the answer is yes, ask, Can you briefly describe what you are doing and how it is working out? If you are not doing anything different, can you tell me why? Is it because you didn't learn anything that you can use on the job? Does your boss encourage you to try out new things, or does your boss discourage any change in your behavior? Do you plan to change some of your behavior in the future? If the answer is yes, ask, What do you plan to do differently?

Questions like these can be asked on a questionnaire or in an interview. A tabulation of the responses can provide a good indication of changes in behavior.

If the program is going to be offered a number of times in the future and the potential results of behavior changes are significant, then a more systematic and extensive approach should be used. The guidelines in this chapter will prove helpful.

Chapter 7

Evaluating Results

Now comes the most important and perhaps the most difficult of all—determining what final results occurred because of attendance and participation in a training program. Trainers consider questions like these:

How much did quality improve because of the training program on total quality improvement that we have presented to all supervisors and managers? How much has it contributed to profits?

How much did productivity increase because we conducted a program on diversity in the workforce for all supervisors and managers?

What reduction did we get in turnover and scrap rate because we taught our foremen and supervisors to orient and train new employees?

How much has "management by walking around" improved the quality of work life?

What has been the result of all our programs on interpersonal communications and human relations?

How much has productivity increased and how much have costs been reduced because we have trained our employees to work in self-directed work teams?

What tangible benefits have we received for all the money we have spent on programs on leadership, time management, and decision making?

How much have sales increased as the result of teaching our sales-people such things as market research, overcoming objections, and closing a sale?

What is the return on investment for all the money we spend on training?

All these and many more questions usually remain unanswered for two reasons: First, trainers don't know how to measure the results and compare them with the cost of the program. Second, even if they do know how, the findings probably provide evidence at best and not clear proof that the positive results come from the training program. There are exceptions, of course. Increases in sales may be found to be directly related to a sales training program, and a program aimed specifically at reducing accidents or improving quality can be evaluated to show direct results from the training program.

A number of years ago, Jack Jenness, a friend of mine at Consolidated Edison in New York, was asked by his boss to show results in terms of dollars and cents from an expensive program on leadership that they were giving to middle- and upper-level managers. The company had hired consultants from St. Louis at a very high fee to conduct the program. I told Jack, "There is no way it can be done!" He said, "That's what I told my boss." Jack then asked me to come out to his organization to do two things: Conduct a workshop with their trainers on the four levels of evaluation, and tell his boss that it couldn't be done. I did the first. I didn't get a chance to do the second because the boss had either been convinced and didn't see the need, or he didn't have the time or desire to hear what I had to say.

This example is unusual at this point in history, but it might not be too unusual in the future. Whenever I get together with trainers, I ask, "How much pressure are you getting from top management to prove the value of your training programs in results, such as dollars and cents?" Only a few times have they said they were feeling such pressure. But many trainers have told me that the day isn't too far off when they expect to be asked to provide such proof.

When we look at the objectives of training programs, we find that almost all aim at accomplishing some worthy result. Often, it is improved quality, productivity, or safety. In other programs, the objective is improved morale or better teamwork, which, it is hoped, will lead to better quality, productivity, safety, and profits. Therefore, trainers look at the desired end result and say to themselves and others, "What behavior on the part of supervisors and managers will achieve these results?" Then they decide what knowledge, skills, and attitudes supervisors need in order to behave in that way. Finally, they determine the training needs and proceed to do the things described in Chapter 1. In so doing, they hope (and sometimes pray) that the trainees will like the program; learn the knowledge, skills, and attitudes taught; and transfer them to the job. The first three levels of evaluation attempt to determine the degree to which these three things have been accomplished.

So now we have arrived at the final level, What final results were accomplished because of the training program? Here are some guidelines that will be helpful:

Guidelines for Evaluating Results

1. Use a control group if practical.
2. Allow time for results to be achieved.
3. Measure both before and after the program if practical.
4. Repeat the measurement at appropriate times.
5. Consider cost versus benefits.
6. Be satisfied with evidence if proof is not possible.

Do these guidelines look familiar? They are almost the same ones that were listed in Chapter 6 for evaluating change in behavior. Some have the same principles and difficulty. At least one (number 3) is much easier.

Use a Control Group If Practical

Enough has been said about control groups in Chapters 5 and 6 that I do not need to dwell on it here. The reason for control groups is always the same: to eliminate the factors other than training that could have caused the changes observed to take place. In a sales training program, for example, it might be quite easy to use control groups. If salespeople in different parts of the country are selling the same products, then a new sales training program can be conducted in some areas and not in others. By measuring the sales figures at various times after the program and comparing them with sales before the program, you can readily see differences. The increase (or decrease) in sales in the regions where the new sales program has been presented can easily be compared to the increase (or decrease) in areas where the program has not been presented. This does not prove that the difference resulted from the training program, even if the control and experimental groups were equal. Other factors may have influenced the sales. These factors can include such things as these: a new competitor has entered the marketplace, a good customer has gone out of business, the economy in a region has gone bad, a competitor has gone out of business, a new customer has moved into the region, or a present customer got a new order that requires your product. These and other factors force us to use the term *evidence* in place of *proof.*

Allow Time for Results to Be Achieved

In the sales example just cited, time has to elapse before the evaluation can be done. How long does it take for a customer to increase orders? There is no sure answer to the question because each situation is different. Likewise, if a program aims to teach such subjects as leadership, communication, motivation, and team building, the time between training and application on the job may be different for each individual. And improved results, if they occur, will lag behind the changes in behavior. In deciding on the time lapse before evaluating, a trainer must consider all the factors that are involved.

Measure Both Before and
After the Program If Practical

This is easier to do when you are evaluating results than when you are evaluating changes in behavior. Records are usually available to determine the situation before the program. If a program aims at reducing the frequency and severity of accidents, figures are readily available. Figures are also available for the sales example just used. The same is true for quality, production, turnover, number of grievances, and absenteeism. For morale and attitudes, preprogram figures may also be available from attitude surveys and performance appraisal forms.

Repeat the Measurement at Appropriate Times

Each organization must decide how often and when to evaluate. Results can change at any time in either a positive or negative direction. It is up to the training professional to determine the influence of training on these results. For example, sales may have increased because of a big push and close supervision to use a new technique. When the push is over and the boss has other things to do, the salesperson may go back to the old way, and negative results may occur.

Consider Cost Versus Benefits

How much does it cost to evaluate at this level? Generally, it isn't nearly as costly as it is to evaluate change in behavior. The figures you need are usually available. The difficulty is to determine just what figures are meaningful and to what extent they are related, directly or otherwise, to the training. I almost laugh when I hear people say that training professionals should be able to show benefits in terms of return on investment (ROI) from a company standpoint. The same thought occurs to me when they expect trainers to relate training programs directly to profits. Just think of all the factors that affect profits. And you can add to the list when you consider all the things that affect ROI.

The amount of money that should be spent on level 4 evaluation should be determined by the amount of money that the training program costs, the potential results that can accrue because of the program, and the number of times that the program will be offered. The higher the value of potential results and the more times the program will be offered, the more time and money should be spent. The value of the actual results (if it can be determined accurately) should then be compared to the cost of the program. The results of this evaluation should determine whether the program should be continued.

How Much Evidence Is Needed?

How much evidence does your top management expect from you? The two O. J. Simpson trials illustrate the difference that exists in different organizations. In the first trial (for murder), the jury had to be unanimous in finding Simpson guilty "beyond a reasonable doubt." They arrived at a "not guilty" verdict. In the second trial (for money), only nine members of the jury had to agree that the "preponderance of evidence" proved him guilty. They agreed unanimously that over 50 percent of the evidence pointed to his guilt, so they reached a verdict of "guilty."

The top management of some organizations requires "evidence beyond a reasonable doubt," whereas others only require "preponderance of evidence," which can be just what they have heard about the program from those who have attended and/or their bosses. Human resource professionals need to know what their top management expects and/or demands and evaluate accordingly. Following is an example that would probably be sufficient evidence for most top executives.

Turnover in a certain company was far too high. The main reason for the turnover, as determined by the training department, was that supervisors and foremen were doing a poor job of orienting and training new employees. Therefore, a training program on how to orient and train employees was conducted in April for all supervisors and foremen. Here are the turnover figures before and after the April training.

Oct.	Nov.	Dec.	Jan.	Feb.	Mar.	Apr.	May	June	July	Aug.	Sept.
6%	7%	5%	7%	6%	7%	6%	4%	2%	2%	2%	3%

It seems obvious that the training program caused the positive results. After all, the objective of the training program was to reduce turnover, and turnover certainly dropped. But some wise guy asks, "Are you sure that some other factor didn't cause the reduction?" And the trainer says, "Like what?" And the wise guy says, "The unemployment figure in your city went way up, and new employees got a nice raise, and the figures for last year were about the same, and I understand that your employment department is hiring more mature people instead of kids right out of high school." I would consider this to be a "preponderance of evidence" but not "evidence beyond a reasonable doubt." But this is an objective way to measure results and show that the objective of reducing turnover was reached.

Summary

Evaluating results, level 4, provides the greatest challenge to training professionals. After all, that is why we train, and we ought to be able to show tangible results that more than pay for the cost of the training. In some cases, such evaluation can be done and quite easily. Programs that aim at increasing sales, reducing accidents, reducing turnover, and reducing scrap rates can often be evaluated in terms of results. And the cost of the program isn't too difficult to determine. A comparison can readily show that training pays off.

Most of the programs that I teach have results in mind. When I conduct a management workshop on how to manage change, I certainly hope that those who attend will make better changes in the future and that the changes will be accepted and implemented enthusiastically. The results will be such things as better quality of work, more productivity, more job satisfaction, and fewer mistakes. When I teach how to improve communication effectiveness, I expect participating supervisors to communicate better on the job afterward and the result to be fewer misunderstandings, fewer mistakes, improved rapport between supervisor and subordinate, and other positive results. When I teach leadership, motivation, and decision making, I expect participants to understand what I teach, accept my ideas, and use them on the job. This will, of course, end up with tangible results. But how can I tell? Can I prove or even find evidence beyond a reasonable doubt that the final results occur? The answer is a resounding no. There are too many other factors that affect results.

So what should a trainer do when top management asks for tangible evidence that training programs are paying off? Sometimes, you can find evidence that positive results have occurred. In other situations, you will have to go back a level or two and evaluate changes in behavior, learning, or both. In many cases, positive reaction sheets from supervisors and managers will convince top management. After all, if top management has any confidence in the management team, isn't it enough to know that the supervisors and managers feel the training is worthwhile?

If your programs aim at tangible results rather than teach management concepts, theories, and principles, then it is desirable to evaluate in terms of results. Consider the guidelines given in this chapter. And most important, be satisfied with evidence, because proof is usually impossible to get.

P.S. The most frequent question I am asked is, How do you evaluate level 4? Be prepared for my answer if you ask this question. I will probably describe at length all four levels, beginning with level 1.

Chapter 8

Implementing the Four Levels

Everybody talks about it, but nobody does anything about it. When Mark Twain said this, he was talking about the weather. It also applies to evaluation—well, almost. My contacts with training professionals indicate that most use some form of reaction, "smile," or "happiness" sheets. Some of these sheets are, in my opinion, very good and provide helpful information that measures customer satisfaction. Others do not meet the guidelines that I listed in Chapter 4. And many trainers ignore critical comments by saying, "Well, you can't please everybody" or "I know who said that, and I am not surprised."

Where do I start? What do I do first? These are typical questions from trainers who are convinced that evaluation is important but have done little about it.

My suggestion is to start at level 1 and proceed through the other levels as time and opportunity allow. Some trainers are anxious to get to level 3 or 4 right away because they think the first two aren't as important. Don't do it. Suppose, for example, that you evaluate at level 3 and discover that little or no change in behavior has occurred. What conclusions can you draw? The first conclusion is probably that the training program was no good, and we had better discontinue it or at least modify it. This conclusion may be entirely wrong. As I described in Chapter 3, the reason for no change in job behavior may be that the climate prevents it. Supervisors may have gone back to the job with the necessary knowledge, skills, and attitudes, but the boss wouldn't allow change to take place. Therefore, it is important to evaluate at level 2 so you can determine whether the reason for no change in behavior was lack of learning or negative job climate.

The first step for you to take in implementing the evaluation concepts, theories, and techniques described in the preceding chapters is to understand the guidelines of level 1 and apply them in every program. Use a philosophy that states, "If my customers are unhappy, it is my fault, and my challenge is to please them." If you don't, your entire training program is in trouble. It is probably true that you seldom please everyone. For example, it is a rare occasion when everyone in my training classes grades me excellent. Nearly always some participants are critical of my sense of humor, some content that I presented, or the quality of the audiovisual aids. I often find myself justifying what I did and ignoring their comments, but I shouldn't do that. My style of humor, for example, is to embarrass participants, I hope in a pleasant way so that they don't resent it. That happens to be my style, and most people enjoy and appreciate it. If I get only one critical comment from a group of twenty-five, I will ignore it and continue as I did in the past. However, if the reaction is fairly common because I have overdone it, then I will take the comment seriously and change my approach.

I used to tell a funny story in class. It was neither dirty nor ethnic. Nearly everyone else thought it was funny, too, and I had heard no objections to it. One day, I conducted a training class with social workers. I told the story at the beginning of the class and proceeded to do the training. After forty minutes, I asked whether anyone had a comment or question. One lady raised her hand and said, "I was offended by the joke you told at the beginning of the session, and I didn't listen to anything you said after that!"

I couldn't believe it. I was sure she was the only one who felt that way, so I asked the question, "Did any others feel the same way?" Seven other women raised their hands. There were about forty-five people in the class, so the percentage was very much in my favor. But I decided that that particular joke had no place in future meetings. If she had been the only one, I probably would still be telling it.

The point is this: Look over all the reaction sheets, and read the comments. Consider each one. Is there a suggestion that will improve future programs? If yes, use it. If it is an isolated comment that will not improve future programs, appreciate it, but ignore it.

Evaluating at level 2 isn't that difficult. All you need to do is to decide what knowledge, skills, and attitudes you want participants to have at the end of the program. If there is a possibility that one or more of these three things already exist, then a pretest is necessary. If you are presenting something entirely new, then no pretest is necessary. You can use a standardized test if you can find one that covers the things you are teaching. Several examples were given in Chapter 5. Or you can develop your own test to cover the knowledge and attitudes that you are teaching. An example from MGIC was also given in Chapter 5. Study the guidelines and suggestions from Chapter 5, and then do it!

Levels 3 and 4 are not easy. A lot of time will be required to decide on an evaluation design. A knowledge of statistics to determine the level of significance may be desirable. Check with the research people in your organization for help in the design. If necessary, you may have to call in an outside consultant to help you or even do the evaluation for you. Remember the principle that the possible benefits from an evaluation should exceed the cost of doing the evaluation, and be satisfied with evidence if proof is not possible.

There is an important principle that applies to all four levels: You can borrow evaluation forms, designs, and procedures from others, but you cannot borrow evaluation results. If another organization offers the same program as you do and they evaluate it, you can borrow their evaluation methods and procedures, but you can't say, "They evaluated it and found these results. Therefore, we don't have to do it, because we know the results we would get."

Learn all you can about evaluation. Find out what others have done. Look for forms, methods, techniques, and designs that you can copy or adapt. Ignore the results of these other evaluations, except out of curiosity.

And now for some specific suggestions.

1. Study the case studies in Part Two of this book. They illustrate all four levels.
2. Read one or more of the following books:

Basarab, David J., and Root, Darrel K. *The Training Evaluation Process.* Norwell, Mass.: Kluwer, 1992.

Brown, Stephen M., and Seidner, Constance J. *Evaluating Corporate Training Models and Issues.* Boston: Kluwer Academic, 1997.

Holcomb, Jane. *Making Training Worth Every Penny.* Playa del Rey, Calif.: On-Target Training, 1993.

Mager, Robert F. *Preparing Instructional Objectives.* (3rd ed.)
   Atlanta: Center for Effective Performance, 1997.
Parry, Scott, B. *Evaluating the Impact of Training.* Alexandria, Va.:
   American Society for Training and Development, 1997.
Phillips, Jack. *Training Evaluation and Measurement Methods.* (2nd
   ed.) Houston: Gulf, 1991.
Robinson, Dana, and Robinson, James. *Training for Impact.* San
   Francisco: Jossey-Bass, 1989.

3. Contact the American Society for Training and Development
   for further information on evaluation (phone: 703/683-8100).
   They have booklets and other materials for sale.
4. If advisable and cost-effective, hire a qualified consultant to
   help you with your evaluation.

In teaching management courses, I usually start by telling the group
about a study made by the Society for Advancement of Management, a
branch of the American Management Association. A special task force
was assigned the job of deciding on a definition of management. The
task force decided that management is a science and an art. It defined
these two words as follows: "As a science, it is organized knowledge—
concepts, theory, principles, and techniques. As an art, it is the application of the organized knowledge to realities in a situation, usually with
blend or compromise, to obtain desired practical results."

I would like to use the same definition for *evaluation*. It is a science
and an art. This book provides the organized knowledge—concepts,
theory, principles, and techniques. It is up to you to do the application. May you be successful in doing it.

PART TWO

CASE STUDIES OF IMPLEMENTATION

In order to make this book as practical and helpful as possible, I invited a number of training professionals to describe an evaluation that they had done in implementing one or more of the four levels. I looked for variety in terms of the type of program as well as the type of organization in which the evaluation had been done. I also wanted case studies of evaluations that ranged from the simple to the complex. The case studies from Motorola, Arthur Andersen, and Intel were written by evaluation specialists. All three organizations have a separate department to evaluate programs.

All the case studies were written especially for this book with the exception of Chapters 9 and 10. These chapters reprint articles that appeared in *Training and Development,* a publication of the American Society for Training and Development, and *TRAINING* magazine.

When you study these cases, it is important to understand that you can borrow forms, designs, and techniques and adapt them to your own organization. This may save you a lot of time and frustration when making decisions on what to evaluate and how to do it. If you want more details on the evaluations, I am sure that the authors will be happy to oblige.

Chapter 9

Making a Play
for Training Evaluation

This article appeared in the April 1994 issue of *Training and Development,* which is published by the American Society for Training and Development. It describes the four levels and how each can be applied. The company, Montac, is hypothetical and provides the setting for a practical discussion on evaluation between a training specialist and the head of the training department. The article, which is well written, describes the benefits and the importance of each level.

Montac, A Fictitious Company

Theodore Krein and Katherine Weldon
Instructional Design Department
Ernst & Young, Vienna, Virginia

The setting is the corporate headquarters of Montac, a hypothetical diversified company with many divisions. Mary Hoskins is Montac's training director. She is based at corporate headquarters, but her staff provides support to all divisions.

In addition to developing and administering some programs that are available to employees throughout the corporation, Mary's staff provides internal consulting on improving performance. Often the consulting leads to the development of training programs specific to the needs of a division. The consulting may also result in recommendations for non-training solutions to performance problems.

Pete Elston is a training specialist on Mary's staff. He joined the company six months ago, after graduating with a liberal arts degree from the local university. Mary hired Pete because she saw real potential in him. His education did not include courses in learning design, but Mary was convinced that she could develop Pete into a competent training professional—sort of a Pygmalion story. In addition to encouraging Pete to take courses in instructional technology at night, Mary has made it her personal mission to coach Pete.

Under Mary's guidance, Pete has been working on a performance-improvement project for the Granville Division of Montac. He has completed the front-end analysis and has prepared a set of potential performance objectives to be achieved by a training program, which has yet to be developed. We enter the scene as Pete enters Mary's office.

Pete Elston Reporting

Pete   Mary, you asked me to check back with you after the design meeting with the client, once we had the objectives pretty well developed. As you know, we determined that the problems at Granville are caused by a lack of knowledge and skill. So training seems to be an appropriate way to overcome the performance gap.

Mary   You've done a great job of expressing most of your objectives in performance terms. That will be important as we move ahead with this project. When we state objectives in performance language, it's easier to know for sure whether we've achieved them. The reason I wanted to meet with you today is to begin discussing the evaluation plan for your program.

Pete   Isn't it premature to talk about evaluation so early? I haven't even begun developing the program.

Mary   I know what you mean. We usually think of evaluation happening *after* we hold a training program, so it must seem as if we're jumping the gun by talking about evaluation now. But here's why we're not.

The jargon of our profession includes two general terms—summative evaluation and formative evaluation. In today's meeting we'll concentrate on summative evaluation. This is evaluation of a program after it's been offered, to learn whether the training achieved what we wanted it to achieve. But I also want you to be aware of formative evaluation.

Formative evaluation involves checks we make during the program-development process to make sure that the program will meet our criteria of excellence. One formative evaluation technique is to have another experienced training professional go over the initial draft of a training design. That reviewer can consider a lot of different criteria, including the design's appropriateness for achieving the program's objectives.

We can take several other steps during development that increase the likelihood that participants will learn what we want them to learn. For example, we might test a case study on some experienced staff to see if it makes sense to them. Is it relevant to their jobs? Is it consistent with the company's culture? Do the instructions make sense?

When we get into program development, we will talk about the kinds of formative evaluation that might be appropriate for our program. For now, let's get back to the topic at hand—evaluation after the fact.

Program Objectives Versus the Ultimate Objectives

Pete   You said we needed to develop an evaluation plan. What did you have in mind?

Mary   What outcomes do you want from your program?

Pete   I want the program to achieve the objectives we have on my list. For example, here's one of them: "At the end of the program, the new market-research analyst will be able to conduct an interview to determine what the client wants to learn from the market study."

Mary   At what point do you want participants to show they can do these things? I mean, is this an objective you can check on at the end of the course, or does it apply to what these analysts will do when they return to their jobs?

Pete   I guess I want it to be both. I'd like to know at the end of the course that they have met the objectives and can perform the skills. If they can, I can assume they'll be able to do them on the job.

Mary   I know that seems logical. But there's a catch. It's true that your ultimate objective is to influence job performance. That's always our intent—usually assumed, but seldom stated—when we create a training program. At the moment the program is finished, we can't know whether it really will be successful in improving job performance. The best we can tell at the end of the program is whether the participants learned what they were supposed to learn.

We use our best judgment and experience to design training that will have an on-the-job impact. We want transfer of learning to the job. But at times, even our best judgment fails us, and we don't get the ultimate outcomes we want.

Pete   So you're telling me that I can't know whether my training really has an impact?

Four Levels of Evaluation

Mary   What I'm saying is you can't know at the end of the program whether it will have the desired on-the-job effects. Let me give you a scheme for evaluating programs. Donald Kirkpatrick developed it at the University of Wisconsin. He described four levels of evaluating training:

- Level 1—how participants reacted to the program
- Level 2—what participants learned from the program
- Level 3—whether what was learned is being applied on the job
- Level 4—whether that application is achieving results

Pete   I didn't know there could be so much to evaluation. To be honest, I didn't know there was so much involved in putting together training programs. It wasn't all that long ago that I assumed someone would just sit down and figure out all the topics a program should cover, develop a bunch of lectures to cover the topics, and then go ahead and put on the course. It was a new experience for me when you spent all that time showing me how to arrive at performance objectives. And we still haven't begun developing the program.

Mary   Billions of dollars are spent each year in the United States on training. Much of that money is wasted because many trainers don't know the appropriate steps to take to ensure that their training addresses a real business need. And they don't know how to check to see whether that business need has been satisfied. In between those two are many other steps that are required if we are to do a truly professional job in training.

Pete   You mentioned the four levels. I recently spoke with somebody who said that level 1 evaluation really isn't worth much. Now that you've described the other levels, I can see why he might feel that way.

Mary   Each of the four levels has value. The mistake many people make about level 1 is to assume that if they get favorable participant reactions to their program, then that's all they need to conclude it's effective. It's not that level 1 evaluation does not have value. It's a matter of recognizing what the value is—and what the limitations are.

Level 1: Reacting to Training

Mary   First, let's see what level 1 evaluation can do for us. We'll look at five possible advantages:

- Level 1 can tell us how relevant participants thought the training was.
- It can tell us whether they were confused by any of the training.
- It can point out any areas in which trainees thought information was missing.
- It can give us an idea of how engaged the trainees felt by the training.
- It can tell us how favorable overall participant reactions were.

By the way, Pete, I don't mean to imply that this is all we can get from level 1 evaluation. But these five information items should make my point.

First, relevance. We know that adults learn better when they can relate a presentation to their previous experience and when they can see the relevance of the program to their jobs. Most adults are serious enough about their jobs that they do not welcome attending a program they perceive to be a waste of time. If the program will not help them to do their jobs better, then they probably won't be pleased with it. We shouldn't be pleased with it, either.

Second is potential participant confusion. Are participants having trouble understanding the concepts we're trying to teach them? If there are places in the program where that's a problem, then we need to know about it. If, in their evaluation comments, several participants report similar points of confusion, then we have gained valuable information to help us make corrections—either in the program design, or in its delivery.

Summative evaluations—those that come at the end of a program —can be used to make improvements in the program. But when we use summative evaluation to improve a program, the evaluation also is formative. Some people argue that all evaluation is formative evaluation, since it's hard to imagine not making changes to a program when we discover deficiencies in midstream.

The third benefit of level 1 evaluation is its potential for pointing out missing content areas. Participants are usually painfully aware of problems they have when they try to perform their jobs. Many expect the training to provide solutions to those problems. It is useful for us to know whether the training has failed to provide those solutions.

Don't let me mislead you. I'm not necessarily talking about missing instructional content in a program. Problems in this area might simply mean that we failed to clearly communicate what participants should expect from the program. It might also tell us that there are participant needs that can be addressed in some other way.

Fourth, did participants feel engaged? We know that adults learn better when they are involved in the learning process than when they feel like passive targets of information dumping. If they did not feel involved in the training program, then their learning probably wasn't what we'd like it to be. We'd want to take a look at why. Is it a fault of the design, a fault of the presentation, or a combination of the two?

The fifth factor is how favorable participants felt toward the program as a whole. Often we can infer this from their answers to other questions. Merely learning that participants did not like the program isn't very helpful to us. It doesn't tell us what we might do about it. So we need participants to give us some specifics.

Participants' favorable feelings don't ensure learning. But they can influence the chances that there will be a market for the program in the future. Bad press can scuttle a program, even one that teaches valuable knowledge and skills.

So you see, it is useful to gather level 1 evaluation information.

Level 2: Learning from Training

Pete What happens in level 2 evaluation?

Mary This is where we check to see whether participants can perform according to the course objectives. And an important key to measuring the performance after training is stating the desired performance properly, during training.

Let's look at the objective you chose earlier: "The new market-research analyst will be able to conduct an interview to determine what the client wants to learn from the market study."

How might we be able to tell—during the training program—whether the new market-research analyst can conduct that interview?

Pete It seems to me we could create a simulation role play—in which we ask the participant to conduct a simulated interview. We could watch the participant and judge whether she or he performed well.

Mary Good. But I want to make sure there's no confusion here between on-the-job performance—ultimate performance—and performance at the end of the training program. So let's add some information on measurement to the description of that objective. We might restate the objective to incorporate measurement like this:

"Given a role play that simulates an interview with a client, the new market-research analyst will be able to conduct the interview to determine what the client wants to learn from the market study."

Now we have spelled out the conditions under which we can check to see whether the participant can satisfy the objective.

Pete We might even create a checklist to use in evaluating the role-play performance.

Mary   That would be a great idea. We could include in that checklist all the specific interviewing principles we want the participant to demonstrate in the interview. Then we could add to our performance objective a criterion of satisfactory performance in the role play. Then the objective might look like this:

"Given a role play that simulates an interview with a client, the new market-research analyst will be able to conduct the interview to determine what the client wants to learn from the market study, demonstrating at least eight of the ten interviewing principles presented in the training program."

Pete   As I recall, that would be a test to learn whether the participant could apply what he or she learned in class. And I guess the checklist would help guarantee that the same evaluation standard would be used to evaluate the interview performance of each program participant.

Mary   You're grasping this stuff very quickly, Pete. Now, you have some other objectives for your program that refer to the participant's knowledge of the subject. Let's look at a couple of them:

- "The participant will be able to explain the difference between a product-centered approach to selling and a client-centered approach to selling."
- "The participant will be able to recognize the five indicators of client resistance and the principal response to each."

Remember, we want to be able to tell, either during the training program or at the very end of the program, whether we have achieved these objectives. Look carefully at each and tell me what you would do to determine whether we have achieved them.

Pete   For the first one, we could ask the participant to explain to the program leader the difference between a product-centered approach and a client-centered approach.

Mary   Good. We see objectives like this for many classroom courses. Many program leaders never conduct that actual test. Instead, a leader judges the class's performance from his or her impressions of participants' understanding in class discussion.

That may be OK if the objective isn't crucial. But if we've spent the time analyzing what participants need in order to do their jobs, and we've included this objective in our program because it is important, then it's worth the effort to find out whether individual participants achieved the objective.

A key point to remember is that the verb we choose for a performance objective usually makes clear how we can test the performance. In this case, the verb is *explain*. So the participant must explain. It's clear that a true/false or multiple-choice question would not be adequate for measuring that performance. Instead, the participant would need to explain the differences between the two approaches—verbally, or in a short written paragraph.

Pete   The second objective we listed is about being able to recognize the five indicators of resistance and the responses to them. That one looks trickier, because it involves two different performances.

Mary   That's right. It is best to state each objective so that it contains only a single performance. So we probably should break this objective in two. But just for fun, let's see whether we could create a test item that would satisfy both parts of this objective. Start with the verb—*to recognize*. Now, what would—or wouldn't—we have participants do if we want them to recognize something?

Pete   Well, the objective suggests that they should know it when they see it. It doesn't require them to write a sentence or even to drag something out of their memories with any clues other than the key words in the objective.

So what would a test item look like that asks for recognition? The question would contain the items we want trainees to recognize. So if it's a paper-and-pencil test, the five indicators would appear on the printed page. I suppose we could present the five indicators and ask, "Are these the five indicators?" But that makes the question require only a simple yes-no response. And half the participants could get it right by guessing. That wouldn't give us much comfort that participants had learned what we want them to learn about the indicators.

What if we listed ten items, including the five indicators, and asked the participants to pick out the five? I think that would be a better question.

Mary   I agree. And if that were all we wanted to know, that question would do the job. But we also said we'd test for recognition of the appropriate responses to the five types of resistance. How might you modify the question to test for both dimensions of the objective?

Pete   It looks to me as though we could do it with a matching test item. On the left we'd have the ten items, only five of which would be indicators. On the right we'd have descriptions of responses to resistance.

You said something the other day about one question giving away the answer to another question—something to avoid. It seems that if we only put five response descriptions on the right, they might provide clues to the five indicators on the left. So I think I'd put more than five response descriptions on the right—add some distracters. Then the likelihood of participants getting the question right by chance is reduced a lot.

Mary   I think that would do it. You analyzed that very well. And I'm pleased that you remembered our discussion about the challenge of developing effective test questions. That's a task you'll soon need to undertake for your program. Because you need to develop the test for level 2 evaluation after you develop your objectives—but before you develop the training program.

There's another important point. We want to know that it is the training program that's responsible for participants achieving the objectives. So we need a before-program measure. If we don't administer a pretest, we will miss the possibility that participants could have achieved the objectives before training.

Pete   Now I understand why you were saying that we need to plan for program evaluation while we are planning for program development.

Mary   That's right. Now, to help you get ready for developing the test for learning, I'm going to give you this book, *Criterion-Referenced Test Development,* by Sharon A. Shrock and William C. C. Coscarelli. It's one of the better ones I know of. It's scholarly without being complicated, and it will give you the right foundation.

Level 3: Applying Learning

Pete   So what about level 3 evaluation—applying learning to the job?

Mary   Now we're getting to your ultimate objectives—ensuring that the training has had a positive influence on job performance. Unfortunately, many trainers completely ignore this evaluation level. They seem to assume that the logic that led to their training design is good enough to ensure that the desired results are happening on the job.

But that's a shaky assumption. And it's even worse than it sounds, because many trainers never bother with level 2 measurement, either. The only data they have are from their level 1 evaluations. So the trainers can't even tell whether participants actually learned what they were supposed to—let alone whether they are applying what they learned on the job.

So what would you do? How would you evaluate your training program at Kirkpatrick's third level?

Pete I guess I'd ask the training participants whether they're using what they learned. I'd ask them to describe to me what they do differently now, compared to what they did before they went through the training. I'd ask for specific examples of how they are applying the knowledge and skills they learned in the training program.

Mary Do you see any limitations in asking the participants themselves how they are using what they learned?

Pete I suppose they might be biased. They might even want to look good or make me or the interviewer feel good. That could bias the data.

To overcome that bias, I could talk to their managers. I suppose I could also watch the training participants doing their jobs. But that might be harder to pull off.

Mary One thing to remember is that you're trying to get a handle on changes in performance that might be attributable to the training. Unless you have a "before" performance measure, sometimes referred to as a baseline measure, it would be difficult to find out whether the "after" performance you observe is different.

Pete So if we want to do the level 3 evaluation properly, we should gather baseline measures before people attend the training program—just like giving those pretests in order to make level 2 evaluation meaningful.

Mary Right. And that brings us back to the importance of planning the evaluation of a program during the program-development process.

Your idea of talking to those who have participated in the training and to their managers is a good one. One-on-one interviews—face-to-face—probably give us the most useful information. But sometimes they aren't practical. The people we want to talk to may be spread out geographically. Or individual interviews may take too much time. One reason level 3 evaluation is performed so seldom is that it can be costly to gather the information.

Questionnaires can help us reduce the cost of level 3 evaluation. They require careful design. If you choose the questionnaire approach, you'll have to get someone involved who is experienced in questionnaire design. You may have to make some follow-up telephone calls to participants, as well. Telephone interviews aren't as effective as face-to-face interviews, but they can be more cost-effective.

Focus groups are also useful for gathering information. They can provide information more efficiently than individual interviews. We won't explore at this time all the factors to consider in using focus groups. Let me just say that this technique also requires specialized experience.

Some people think that level 3 evaluation is unnecessary. They say we need only to focus on whether we are getting on-the-job results—level 4. But that idea overlooks a crucial fact: If we didn't have a level 3 measure, we wouldn't know the reason behind a lack of results on the job. It could result from trainees' failure to learn what was intended. But it could also result from something going on in the work environment.

When you plan your information-gathering activities for level 3 evaluation, you'll need to take into account possible factors in the job environment that could prevent the application of newly learned knowledge and skill. All too frequently, we hear comments like this from the supervisors of newly trained employees: "I know that's what they taught you. Now I'm going to show you how we really do it."

If trainees don't receive proper, on-the-job reinforcement of what they learned in the formal training program, then we've wasted most or all of our investment in training.

Level 4: Measuring Results from Training

Mary   A lot of specialized knowledge and skill goes into developing evaluation strategies. And the greatest challenge of all is figuring out how to perform level 4 evaluation. In level 4 evaluation, we're interested in business results. What effect does the program have on measures that are important to the business? For example:

- Reduced employee turnover
- Reduced costs
- Improved quality
- Increases in favorable comments from customers
- Increased sales
- Fewer grievances filed; for example, harassment complaints
- Increased profitability

Pete   It seems like a pretty big leap from learning in the classroom to results in the real world. Can we really tell whether it was training that succeeded—or failed—when a change in results occurs?

Mary   That's the big question. In many cases, we can't tell without a great deal of research. That may involve a considerable investment of time and money. So many training directors judge that the benefits of level 4 evaluation are not great enough to justify the investment required.

Pete   So level 4 evaluation isn't practical?

Mary   It can be. In some settings, the business results may be simple to measure. For example, say that we observe a significant increase in sales and profitability after sales training. If other factors have been held constant, then we have strong evidence that the training was responsible for the gains.

Or say that we provide advanced training to some machine operators in how to minimize scrap. If we then observe a reduction in the amount and cost of scrap from those operators, then we have good evidence that the training was at least a major contributor to the result.

Pete   Why the hedge? Isn't it obvious that training was the factor that caused the result?

Mary   Unless we conduct a carefully designed study, using experimental and control groups, we have to recognize the possibility that other variables could have contributed to the result. We need to think in terms of evidence, not proof. We have evidence that training influenced the result. But we cannot state positively that training was the sole cause.

The examples I've given are simple ones. Measuring the effects of, say, supervisory or management training becomes much more difficult. Frequently, the skills participants learn in supervisory training programs are not reinforced in the workplace. After training, a supervisor may return to a job in which she or he works for a manager who does not have the skills.

In such instances we could say there's a lack of congruence between formal training and the workplace. It is somewhat like taking golf lessons when the game to be played is baseball. In general, organizations need to do a better job of connecting formal training to the work environment.

Pete   Mary, I appreciate the short course in evaluation. I know I have a lot to learn. But I think I have a better understanding now—at least of evaluation fundamentals. I'm looking forward to talking with you about how we can apply formative evaluation to the program as we develop it.

Chapter 10

Balancing Your Evaluation Act

This challenging article from *TRAINING* magazine describes an approach for measuring results, level 4, and cautions that *results* and *return on investment* (ROI) should not be considered synonyms. It emphasizes that trying to measure effectiveness in terms of ROI is not necessarily desirable. Instead, the writer describes a performance measurement index for measuring performance improvement.

Karie A. Willyerd, Manager, Training and Development
Lockheed Martin Tactical Aircraft Systems, Fort Worth, Texas

Last year I attended a workshop at a training conference in which the presenter spent most of the session verbally beating up the people in the room for not measuring the financial return on investment (ROI) of training. "ROI is where it's at in business today," he kept saying.

At the same time, others contend that ROI is a flawed financial yardstick—a dead science and a throwback to the days when bean counters determined business value.

What's a trainer to do?

Some different performance measurement tools that have been proposed for general business use may provide a more balanced approach to evaluation. These tools ensure that a training or performance solution is strategically aligned, objectively evaluated, and quantitatively measured for results.

The question is, What kind of results should we really be looking for?

ROI or Results?

In 1959, University of Wisconsin management professor Donald Kirkpatrick proposed that training programs can be evaluated for success at four different "levels." His model is still widely accepted in the training field.

Level 1 measures *reaction*. The most obvious artifact associated with it is what trainers call "smile sheets." The primary purpose of level 1 evaluation is to measure customer satisfaction. Usually it is conducted immediately following the training event.

Level 2 is *learning*. Kirkpatrick says learning happens when attitudes are changed, knowledge is increased, or skill is improved. The primary artifact associated with level 2 is a test administered at the completion of the training event.

Level 3 is *behavior*. This is the extent to which a person's behavior changes due to attending the training. Usually such change is measured after the person has been back on the job some period of time, perhaps three months. For better or worse, the primary artifact associated with level 3 is a survey.

Finally, level 4 is *results*. All the final results that occurred because of the training are measured at this level. The artifact most often associated with level 4 evaluation is a financial analysis, usually an ROI or cost-benefit analysis. The idea generally is to "prove the training was worth it."

Many in the training profession mistakenly call Kirkpatrick's level 4 "ROI," but Kirkpatrick specifically labeled it "results." This is an important distinction. As the friendly number crunchers in your organization probably could tell you, ROI and other traditional financial measures have three major shortfalls. First, they usually do not capture all of a company's strategic objectives. Second, ROI is a snapshot in time that tells you where you've been; it has no ability to predict where you'll go. Finally, since ROI is a lagging indicator, it is not a good diagnostic tool.

In short, even if we are concerned only with hard-nosed business indicators as opposed to mushy, humanistic measures of "success," ROI does not necessarily live up to its reputation as the ultimate measure of "results" from a training program or any other intervention.

The Balanced Scorecard

The financial and strategic planning world is starting to look seriously at a performance measurement called the balanced scorecard. "The traditional financial measures worked well for the industrial era, but they are out of step with the skills and competencies companies are trying to measure today," wrote Robert S. Kaplan and David P. Norton in a 1992 *Harvard Business Review* article.

Kaplan, the Arthur Lowes Dickinson professor of accounting at Harvard Business School, and Norton, president of Renaissance Solutions, Inc., a management consulting and systems integration firm in Lincoln, Massachusetts, developed the balanced scorecard to counteract this weakness in traditional financial measures. The balanced scorecard tracks the key elements of a company's strategy using both financial and operational measures. The operational measures are the drivers of *future financial performance.*

Much of the training in which our organizations invest is geared toward future financial performance; after all, training is often an investment in the long-term performance of people. So measuring results with financial tools that look backward is misleading at best. We need to use performance indicators that look to the future.

Before we discuss how to use the balanced scorecard in level 4 evaluation, we need to understand a little more about how the balanced scorecard works at the organizational level. Like Kirkpatrick's model, the balanced scorecard looks at four key areas of performance by providing answers to four basic questions:

- How do we look to our shareholders? (financial perspective)
- How do customers see us? (customer perspective)
- What must we excel at? (internal perspective)
- Can we continue to improve and create value? (innovation and learning perspective)

How many times as trainers and performance technologists have we complained that hard-nosed financial measures are too short-sighted? The balanced scorecard helps ensure that all the critical performance measures are evaluated. It provides a check and balance so that one area isn't overemphasized at the expense of another.

Short-Sighted Solutions

For example, let's assume the shipping department has asked you to help it streamline processes and develop training and performance aids so employees can become more efficient (an internal measure closely linked to a financial measure). You create a stellar set of solutions that indeed drives the shipping department to increased internal efficiency at a substantial return on investment. Your customer is happy, and the ROI analysis looks great, so you're happy.

But let's suppose that one of your solutions was a recommendation that the department pack full trucks for designated geographic regions. This required some agile scheduling, which was one of the more difficult performance challenges you addressed; you had to install an electronic performance support system to meet the challenge. It was well worth the investment, however, since substantial savings have resulted from reducing the number of trips made by half-empty delivery trucks. The shipping department employees all get bonuses at the end of the year.

Shortly thereafter, you get a call from the sales department. Sales are down; you need to come up with a new sales class to motivate the salespeople. Being faithfully committed to good front-end analysis, you discover that lagging sales to existing customers are the real problem. So you interview a few key people, take a look at the customer complaint log, and find out that the number 1 complaint is the time it now takes to get products shipped. Seems your company just adopted a new shipping process that increased product ship time by three days. Sorry, your customers are saying, they just can't wait that long to receive orders. They're taking their business elsewhere.

This example demonstrates a couple of important points. First, this situation could have been avoided had the shipping department—with your help—ensured that it solicited a balanced approach to performance improvement. In this case, the customer perspective was completely neglected. Shipping full trucks is not a virtue if your customers will desert you while you're waiting for the trucks to fill.

Second, it's possible to accept less-than-optimal results in one measurement area, as long as the overall picture indicates strategic alignment. Perhaps the shipping department should be allowed to be "inefficient" in order to achieve a greater goal of getting products to the customer when the customer wants them. Likewise, perhaps achieving desired results from the customer, internal, and innovation perspectives is exactly what the organization needs your performance solutions to do in order to manage its strategy.

Here's the heresy to some: lower financial results in the targeted area (the shipping department) may represent success because the investment in training or performance solutions pays off in the future.

For another example of neglecting one area of organizational performance, we turn to the Apocryphal Buggy Whip Company. Apocryphal was scoring extremely well on internal processes, customer satisfaction, and financial results. All other buggy whip companies benchmarked against it. But since Apocryphal didn't have the ability to innovate and learn, it eventually had to close its doors.

Since the performance measures are derived from strategy, the balanced scorecard ensures that the measures used will help strategically manage the organization. The more you can align your results to organizational strategy, the more your performance solutions will contribute value.

Balancing Act

In a 1993 article in the *Harvard Business Review,* Kaplan and Norton provided some step-by-step instructions for building a balanced scorecard. Figure 10.1 provides a quick overview of those steps.

The first step, defining the vision, must be inclusive enough to provide guidance for each of the four levels. John Kotter's latest book, *Leading Change,* sums up some of the characteristics of an effective vision. It must be desirable for the long-term interests of the stakeholders, feasible, focused enough to guide decision making, flexible, and easy to communicate.

The next step is to define the critical success factors, the areas that will drive performance to the vision. For example, part of the vision

Figure 10.1. Building a Balanced Scorecard

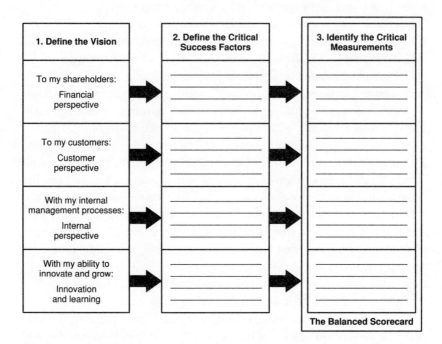

for a reengineering project might be to increase responsiveness to customers while reducing costs and maintaining employee satisfaction. Some related critical success factors might be reduced customer wait time, total budget costs below $100,000, no layoffs due to reengineering, and so on.

The final step is to identify the specific critical measurements. As trainers, we have long obsessed about performance measurements at the financial level. Critical measurements in that area might be net income, return on net assets, cash flow, and so on. Performance measurements tied to the customer perspective might be percent of repeat customers, percent of customer complaints, number of new accounts, and so on. Internal business perspective measures might be product development time, engineering change notifications, scrap and rework, or customer response time. Innovation and learning measures might be total process cycle time, number of new products developed, and employee satisfaction.

Some of these measures can be converted into immediate financial results. Scrap and rework, for instance, are readily translated into cost data. On the other hand, customer response time is neither easily nor accurately translated into cost data. Still, it is a legitimate measure of organizational performance.

Later, we'll combine the balanced scorecard with an index that quantitatively tracks progress toward goals. But first let's look at an example of how the balanced scorecard might be applied to a training course or performance solution.

The process is the same as the one described in Figure 10.1 for the organizational level. To ensure the course is strategically aligned with your customer's business objectives, collect the department's vision and mission statements. If the customer doesn't have one, offer to assist in developing one, explaining that it will help you ensure that your product fully aligns with the department's business objectives. Ask for any information on strategic initiatives that are in place.

When you ask for performance standards during your front-end analysis, ask for critical success factors and measures in all four areas. Table 10.1 identifies some questions that will elicit these measures.

Since you have collected potential measures early in the analysis stage, agree on a set of measures with the customer. It may take some negotiation. Even when top management supports the idea of establishing a workable set of measures, it can be a challenge.

It's not essential to include measures from all four perspectives, but do so if you can. Remember, ideally these measures flow down from company strategy. If the training program or performance solution you are developing is helping the department with a specific perspective, say innovation and growth, you may be able to negotiate suboptimal results in another measure. Ultimately, it's your customer's decision.

The measures you finally select will work best when:

- You have control over what is measured.
- They are easily quantified.
- Everyone in the customer organization can be involved in the measurement.
- They are measured as close to the front line—the people who do the work—as possible.
- They are viewed as an improvement tool, not as punishment.

Table 10.1. Questions to Solicit Measurement Data

Balanced Scorecard Dimension	*Potential Analysis Questions*
Financial perspective	• What is the backlog? • What is the inventory? • What do you bid as a cost per task? • What current financial measures do you track?
Internal perspective	• How many hours does it take to complete the job now? • What is the total cycle time of the task? • How many rework hours are there per job? • What is the absenteeism rate?
Customer perspective	• What's the number of transactions per day? • How is customer satisfaction measured? • What is the number of referrals?
Innovation and learning	• What are the number of new employee suggestions? • How do you track employee satisfaction? • What is the number of new products introduced per year?

Charting Performance

If we do not eventually convert all of these measures into dollars, how will we know that our solution has made an impact? One tool is the performance measurement index, also called an objectives matrix. It enables us to create a sort of Dow Jones industrial average for measuring performance. Furthermore, it is a performance tracking tool for customers that they maintain themselves.

Figure 10.2 is a blank performance measure chart, with the selected metrics across the top of each column. These are the metrics for a group's overall performance and include measurements from all four scorecard perspectives. The columns correspond to the measurements that you select with your customer. Everything else on the chart is standardized. Since it is so standardized, we at Lockheed Martin developed a customized spreadsheet that we give to our internal customers to help them track their measures.

Figure 10.2. Performance Measurement Chart

Design Group

Percent of reworked drawings	Hours expended per drawing	Percent overtime	Department expense per drawing	Percent of drawings overdue	Percent of training time	Dept. 42
						Month Jan
						Performance
						10
						9
						8
						7
						6
						5 Score
						4
						3
						2
						1
						0
						Score
						Weight
						Value =

Jan	Feb	Mar	Apr	May	Jun	Jul	Aug	Sep	Oct	Nov	Dec

Here are the steps for completing the chart:

1. *Finalize the measurements with the customer.* Those become the column headings.
2. *Establish the current performance level for each metric.* Enter this at performance level 3 on the chart.
3. *Establish an improvement goal for each metric.* These should be set at realistic levels and pegged to a date one year hence. Enter this goal at level 10 on the chart.
4. *Establish intermediate goals.* These are progress goals between the current state (3) and the desired state (10). Enter these goals at levels 4 to 9.
5. *Establish lower performance goals.* Performance may actually get worse, perhaps due to slack periods or other variables that

are unpredictable. The index allows you to track these as well. Enter these at levels 0 to 2.

6. *Assign weights to each metric.* This is somewhat subjective, but try to retain a balance among the four perspectives. The weights should total 100. Enter these on the row marked "Weight." You may develop the chart to this point very early in the analysis stages to allow the customer group time to refine measures and goals before you begin training.

7. *Calculate the index.* To calculate the monthly index, determine the measurement that has been achieved for each metric, and record the corresponding score at the bottom of the column. For example, in Figure 10.3, if the number of drawings overdue was 26, the score would be 4, since a 5 was not yet achieved. Multiply the score times the weight

Figure 10.3. Performance Measurement Chart

Design Group

Percent of reworked drawings	Hours expended per drawing	Percent overtime	Department expense per drawing	Percent of drawings overdue	Percent of training time	Dept. 42 Month Feb
19%	12.5	6.1%	314	27%	5%	Performance
0–5	5.3	0.0	143	15	10	10 ⌐
6–8	6.5	0.5	164	17	9	9
9–11	7.7	1.0	185	19	8	8
12–14	8.9	1.5	206	21	7	7
15–17	10.1	2.0	227	23	6	6
18–20	11.3	2.5	248	25	5	5 Score
21–23	12.5	3.0	269	27	4	4
24–26	13.7	3.5	290	29	3	3
27–28	14.9	4.0	311	31	2	2
29–30	16.1	4.5	332	33	1	1
Over 30	17.3	5.0	353	35	0	0 ⌐
5	4	0	1	4	5	Score
10	30	10	20	20	10	Weight
50	120	0	20	80	50	Value = 320

Jan	Feb	Mar	Apr	May	Jun	Jul	Aug	Sep	Oct	Nov	Dec
300	320										

to get the value for the metric. The sum of the values is the performance index for the month.

If all the metrics were achieving goal, the score would be 1,000. If performance stayed the same as when the project began, the score would be 300. Any score above 300 demonstrates improvement. The tool also allows you to identify problem areas so you can refine any training or performance solutions that affect the metric. Tracking monthly performance is important to gain timely insight into performance.

Now you have assembled a tool for selecting strategically aligned measures—a balanced scorecard—and a tool for tracking performance improvement results—the performance measurement index. Combining these tools will help you track strategically aligned results in a quantifiable fashion.

That's what level 4 evaluation is all about.

For Further Reading

Felix, Glenn H., and James L. Riggs. "Productivity Measurement by Objectives." *National Productivity Review,* Autumn 1983.

Jackson, Terence. *Evaluation: Relating Training to Business Performance.* San Diego: University Associates, 1989.

Kaplan, Robert S., and David P. Norton. "The Balanced Scorecard—Measures that Drive Performance." *Harvard Business Review,* January-February 1992, 71–79.

Kaplan, Robert S., and David P. Norton. "Putting the Balanced Scorecard to Work." *Harvard Business Review,* September-October 1993, 134–147.

Kaplan, Robert S., and David P. Norton. "Using the Balanced Scorecard as a Strategic Management System." *Harvard Business Review,* January-February 1996, 75–85.

Kirkpatrick, Donald L. *Evaluating Training Programs: The Four Levels.* San Francisco: Berrett-Koehler, 1994.

McWilliams, Brian. " The Measure of Success." *Across the Board,* 1996. (Available—http://www.mediapool.com/offtherecord/atbpsc.html)

McWilliams, Brian. "ROI Revisited." *Client/Server Journal,* 1995. (Available—http://www.mediapool.com/offtherecord/csjroi.html)

Robinson, Dana G., and James C. Robinson. *Training for Impact: How to Link Training to Business Needs and Measure the Results.* San Francisco: Jossey-Bass, 1989.

Terhoeve, Anne D. "Performance Measurement Index: A Powerful Tool for Monitoring Metrics." Paper presented at the International Society for Performance and Instruction Conference, 1996.

Wilson, David. "Exploring New Values and Measurements for the Knowledge Area." Paper, 1996. (Available—http://www.cica.ca/new/pa/explore.html)

Worthen, Blaine R., and James R. Sanders. *Educational Evaluation: Alternative Approaches and Practical Guidelines.* White Plains, N.Y.: Longman, 1987.

Chapter 11

Evaluating a Training Program
for Nonexempt Employees

This case study is an example of a relatively simple approach for evaluating at all four levels. It includes a reaction sheet and a survey form that can be tabulated on a computer. The evaluation of results compared turnover figures for those trained with figures on those who were not trained. These figures were then converted into dollar savings. The design of the evaluation is readily adaptable to other organizations.

First Union National Bank

Patrick O'Hara, Assistant Vice President
Human Resources Division, Training and Development,
First Union National Bank, Charlotte, North Carolina

CARE

A major goal of First Union is to let employees know how much they and their contribution to the success and growth of First Union are valued. Personal development is one strategy.

CARE I is a program that was developed to provide a developmental opportunity for the nonexempt employees who historically have not been the focus of personal development training. As the corporation has expanded over the last several years, there has been tremendous change and upheaval. During mergers and consolidations, employees have the pressures that all this change has brought to bear. CARE is a one-day program devoted to the bank's largest population, the nonexempt employees who have shouldered major responsibilities throughout this growth cycle at First Union.

CARE is an acronym for Communication, Awareness, Renewal, and Empowerment. The learning objectives are:

- Increase self-awareness by use of self-assessment tools and group feedback.
- Increase understanding of communication styles and develop flexibility in one's own communication style.
- Increase communication effectiveness by exposure to and practice in assertiveness concepts and skills.
- Understand and implement the steps of goal setting as a tool in career renewal.

Input from employee focus groups was instrumental in developing the course design.

The program is offered on an ongoing basis for new employees. The majority of CARE I training occurred in 1991. More than 10,000 employees have attended CARE I.

Here is a brief description of the CARE program, with an indication of the activities and materials used:

Morning:
- Johari Window
- Self-awareness: DESA instrument explained and processed
- Assertiveness in communication, lecturette, role playing, discussion on using a journal to help increase assertive behavior
Lunch: As a group
Afternoon:
- Assertiveness continued
- Creating your future: goal-setting process as a tool for personal renewal (process explained and exercises processed)
- Personal empowerment: where and how it begins (discussion to tie the day's activities to the overriding theme of empowerment)

Closing Ceremony: three gifts
- Gift from corporation: a mustard seed in a lucite cube with the CARE logo
- Gift from each other: positive quotes for other participants sealed in an envelope to be opened in one month
- Gift to self: have participants write down what they want to give themselves in the coming year (could be a healthier body, etc.), put in sealed envelope, and open in two months

Evaluation Plan

Because this was such a massive effort on the part of the corporation, it was decided that the results should be evaluated. It was decided to start with the four-level Kirkpatrick evaluation model and create several measurement instruments.

1. Participant reactions

Our standard end-of-course evaluation form was modified to fit the CARE program. Because it was a personal development course, the intent was to ask participants how it related to their personal development. The questionnaires were administered at the end of the day by the trainer and collected and returned to the Corporate Training and Development Department for processing. Exhibit 11.1 shows the evaluation form.

2. and 3. Learning gains and behavior changes

Again, because CARE was a personal development course, it was felt that both the learning and any resulting changes in behavior were of a very subjective and personal nature. To evaluate on the second and third levels (learning gain and behavior change), the company sent a questionnaire to a random sample of the participants asking them about their learning and changes in their behavior. This instrument was mailed to participants at the end of each quarter, so that the longest period of time between the class and the questionnaire was about ninety days. The completed forms were returned to the Corporate Training and Development Department for processing. Exhibit 11.2 shows the questionnaire.

4. Organizational impact

It was determined that the best way to evaluate the impact on the organization was to look at turnover. The rationale was that, if employees

Exhibit 11.1. CARE Evaluation Form, National Computer Systems

---

Name of Instructor _____

Location _____

Date _____

National Computer Systems

Instructions: When marking each answer:

- Use a No. 2 pencil only.
- Circle appropriate number.
- Cleanly erase any marks you wish to change.

Please use the following scale to record your thoughts about the course content:

1 = *Disagree strongly*
2 = *Disagree*
3 = *Neither agree nor disagree*
4 = *Agree*
5 = *Agree strongly*

Content

1. The skills taught in this class are relevant to my personal development. 1 2 3 4 5

2. This class helped me develop those skills. 1 2 3 4 5

3. The material was clearly organized. 1 2 3 4 5

4. The course content met my needs. 1 2 3 4 5

5. Comments:

Instruction

The course instructor

6. Facilitated class discussions effectively. 1 2 3 4 5

7. Listened carefully to participants. 1 2 3 4 5

8. Assisted in linking concepts to actual interpersonal situations. 1 2 3 4 5

9. Had excellent presentation skills. 1 2 3 4 5

10. Comments:

Overall

11. Rank your overall satisfaction with the program. 1 2 3 4 5

Thank you for taking the time to give constructive feedback on this course. Your responses will be used to improve future courses.

Exhibit 11.2. Insti-Survey, National Computer Systems

Directions: Thank you for taking the time to complete this short survey.

Please use a No. 2 pencil. Cleanly erase any responses you want to change.

Please use the following scale:

A = *Agree strongly*
B = *Agree somewhat*
C = *Neutral*
D = *Disagree somewhat*
E = *Disagree strongly*

Because of my CARE Class, I

1. Am more self-aware.	A	B	C	D	E
2. Am better able to communicate with others.	A	B	C	D	E
3. Am seeking more feedback on strengths and areas to improve.	A	B	C	D	E
4. Feel more personally empowered.	A	B	C	D	E
5. Can better respond to aggressive behavior.	A	B	C	D	E
6. Can better respond to nonassertive behavior.	A	B	C	D	E
7. Am more likely to assert myself now.	A	B	C	D	E
8. Am better able to set goals for myself now.	A	B	C	D	E
9. See how goal setting helps me make some positive changes.	A	B	C	D	E
10. Feel more valued as a First Union Employee now.	A	B	C	D	E

---

did indeed feel valued by the company, they would be less likely to leave. Turnover is also one of the most reliable bits of information tracked at First Union.

Numbers on turnover were kept not only for employees who had participated in the program but also for those who had not. The employees selected to participate in the CARE program were determined in a fairly random manner, since the intent of the program was that eventually all nonexempt employees would participate. An extra step was taken, and statistics were run on other information kept in our Human Resource database to determine whether we had other information about participants that might be related to turnover. Last, some simple calculations were made to determine what a reduction in turnover might have saved the corporation in real dollars.

Evaluation Results

The results of the evaluations were surprising, to say the least.

1. Participants' reactions

Our course evaluation was separated into three categories: content, instruction, and an overall evaluation of the program. We used a five-point scale to scale responses, with 5 being the highest response possible and 1 the lowest. For the CARE program, we consistently received the following scores:

Content	4.45
Instruction	4.76
Overall	4.69

While it is felt that these scores can always be improved, they are high.

2. and 3. Learning gains and behavior changes

The responses to the various questions are combined to determine a score for the achievement of the course objectives overall. Once again, a five-point scale was used in which 5 was the best and 1 signaled cause for concern. On this measure, an average of 3.9 was received. Given the fact that time had passed and that learning and behavior changes normally drop off over time, this, too, is a very good score.

4. Organizational impact

The results of the level 4 evaluation were probably the most exciting from an organizational perspective. We found that the difference in turnover was 14 percent. Turnover rates for the CARE group were running at about 4.2 percent for the year, while for the non-CARE group they were 18.2 percent. This finding was extremely exciting.

In addition, we pulled several pieces of data from the corporate Human Resources database on all participants. We checked things like gender, age, and time with the company to see whether some other variable might affect the results. We brought in a consultant to help determine what information might be looked at, and the consultant ran a discriminant analysis on the resulting data for us. Nothing else could be found that seemed to be contributing to the reduction in turnover among the CARE group. This was pretty good evidence that the program was influencing the reduction in turnover.

As the last step in the process, we calculated real dollar savings for the program. To do this, we determined our cost for hiring and training tellers. First Union has a lot of tellers, and we know a lot about their hiring and training costs. Tellers also made up about 33 percent of the CARE participants.

It costs $2,700 to hire and train a teller. It costs $110 to put a teller through CARE. If CARE training saves the company from having to hire and train a teller, we save $2,590. Given the number of tellers put through the CARE program, the estimated savings to the company were over $1,000,000 in 1991, and that was for only one-third of the CARE group. It is expected that the costs of hiring and training for the other two-thirds are the same or higher on average. This means that the corporation saved a lot of money by offering the program to employees. This saving would have more than funded the entire CARE program.

After conducting what is felt to be a fairly rigorous evaluation of the CARE program in a business environment, we know that

- Participants reacted very favorably to the program.
- Participants feel that they learned and are using new skills.
- More participants than nonparticipants are staying at First Union.
- First Union not only helped employees grow and develop personally but also benefited in a real, quantifiable way.

Chapter 12

Evaluating a Training Course on Performance Appraisal and Coaching

T his study is one of the most complete that I have seen. The evaluation covered all four levels. The program evaluated was a pilot program conducted at the Charlotte, North Carolina, branch of the Kemper National Insurance Companies. The evaluation was planned and implemented by the Corporate Education Department in the home office. Of special interest is the summary of results communicated to executives concerned with the program.

Kemper National Insurance Companies

Judith P. Clarke, Training Manager
Corporate Education Department, Long Grove, Illinois

Need and Purpose

Our training program is a success if it accomplishes four objectives: participants like the program, participants gain needed knowledge and skills, participants apply what they learned to their jobs, and participants assist the company in achieving its mission and objectives. The purpose of the program is to improve performance. The purpose of evaluation is to verify and improve the effectiveness of training. The evaluation design includes ways and means of measuring the effectiveness of the program in achieving each of the four objectives just defined.

The Training Course

The program was conducted at the Charlotte branch of Kemper. All supervisors and managers attended the course during a three-month period between December 1989 and March 1990. The program and its evaluation received the complete support of the branch manager. Exhibit 12.1 (grouped with the other exhibits at the end of the chapter) describes the program content and objectives.

Evaluation Design

Both quantitative and qualitative data were collected. Data collection techniques included existing tools as well as measurements designed for this evaluation. This section describes the data collection tools that we used for the four levels on which we evaluated the training program.

1. *Reaction:* How well did the participants like the training? Each participant completed the reaction sheet shown in Exhibit 12.2 at the end of the course. The results were tabulated and summarized.

2. *Learning:* What knowledge and skills did participants gain from the program? We collected data by administering the Performance Appraisal Skills Inventory (King of Prussia, Pa.: Organization Design and Development, 1987) before and after training. The inventory contains eighteen performance appraisal situations. For each situation, the participant selects the best answer from four possible choices.

3. *Behavior:* To what extent have participants transferred knowledge and skills learned in the program to their jobs in these four areas: preparing for the performance appraisal, establishing two-way communication with subordinates, gaining agreement on the appraisal, and documenting the report form.

To collect data, we used results from the Performance Appraisal Report Form Checklist shown in Exhibit 12.3, administered before and after training, the Performance Appraisal Questionnaire for Managers shown in Exhibit 12.4, the Performance Appraisal Questionnaire for Employees shown in Exhibit 12.5, and unobtrusive data, which included informal observations obtained from many sources, including the Human Resources manager, the immediate supervisor of those completing forms and conducting interviews, and those who completed forms and conducted interviews.

4. ***Results:*** To assess the results, we asked this question: What gain has there been in the achievement of the following two Human Resources objectives? Ninety-five percent of all performance appraisals are completed on schedule, and the quality and accuracy of the appraisals improve in five areas: candidness, completeness, developmental plans, ratings, and feedback.

Data were collected through an analysis by the branch Human Resources manager of completed performance appraisals.

Evaluation Results

The evaluations were conducted as planned, and the results were communicated to executives and other interested and concerned persons as follows:

The performance appraisal and coaching course was designed to improve the skills of managers and supervisors in coaching effectively during the performance appraisal discussion and in writing the performance appraisal report.

The Charlotte branch was selected as the site for piloting the course and for evaluating its effectiveness. The training received the enthusiastic support of the branch manager, Jim Murphy, and of the branch Human Resources manager, Peggy Jones, and it was positively received by the Charlotte supervisors and managers. Forty-one branch supervisors and managers completed the course between December and March, a fact that made it possible to study the effectiveness of training with an entire management staff.

Procedure and Findings

Evaluation that verifies and improves the effectiveness of training is conducted at four levels: reaction, learning, behavior, and results. Evidence to determine the effectiveness of training must be gathered at each level. Table 12.1 lists the questions that need to be answered at each level of evaluation and the data collection tools that were used in answering each question.

The findings at each level of evaluation indicate that the performance appraisal and coaching course makes a difference in increasing

Table 12.1. Evaluation Questions and Data Collection Tools

	Evaluation question	*Data collection tool*
Reaction	How did the participants react to the training?	Course reaction sheets
Learning	What information and skills were gained?	Performance appraisal checklist administered before and after training
Behavior	How have participants transferred knowledge and skills to their jobs?	Performance appraisal checklist administered before and after training Manager and employee questionnaires Anecdotal data
Results	What effect has training had on the organization and achievement of its objectives? (Timeliness and quality in performance appraisals are a corporate goal.)	Performance appraisal checklist

both the quality of the coaching that takes place during the discussion and the quality of the performance appraisal report.

Reaction

Level 1 findings indicate that course participants were satisfied customers. The course evaluations received confirmed that participants reacted positively to the course. Positive reactions increase participants' receptivity to the knowledge and skills presented in the course. The majority of participants felt that the course objectives had been met and that the course was highly relevant to their jobs. The average overall rating on a five-point scale was 4.37.

Learning

Level 2 findings indicate that course participants made gains in the knowledge and skills needed to conduct and document quality performance appraisals. Data gathered from administration of the quality checklist before and after training indicate that 94 percent of the performance appraisals written by participants after the course were of higher quality than the appraisals that they had written before training. It was also significant that, while appraisal quality was as low as 54 percent before training, the lowest quality observed after training was 78 percent.

Behavior

Level 3 findings provide evidence that course participants applied the knowledge and skills acquired in the course when they conducted subsequent performance appraisals. Data gathered with the quality checklist before and after training highlighted three areas of particular improvement: two-way discussion, documentation of attributes, and objectives. The course provides practice sessions to enhance skills needed to involve employees in the performance appraisal discussion and to show evidence of discussion and employee input in the performance appraisal report. Appraisals conducted after participation in the course showed nearly four times more two-way discussion after the course than before it.

Performance appraisals are audited by branch Human Resources staff to identify errors and potential problems. When errors are found, a performance appraisal is returned to the appraising supervisor for improvement. Strong evidence that participants applied knowledge and skills learned in the course on the job was provided by an immediate decline in the number of returns. Before the training program, eight appraisals were returned for improvement in one month. After the program, no more than two appraisals per month were returned.

The Charlotte branch Human Resources manager reported that, from the conclusion of the study through the fourth quarter, the number of appraisals returned through the audit had remained low in comparison to previous years. Her report shows the percentage of audited appraisals that were of acceptable quality each quarter after the program.

Q3	90%
Q4	96
Q1	95
Q2	80
Q3	95
Q4	96

The lower quality of appraisals during the second quarter of the second year reflects the fact that five appraisals were returned for clarification of objectives and documentation of the achievement of prior objectives and that one appraisal lacked proper documentation of attendance. The Charlotte branch Human Resources manager is continuing to coach the management staff in these areas, but she states that the narratives now indicate much more two-way discussion than she saw before the training took place.

Another indication that participants applied new knowledge and skills was the results of two questionnaires. One questionnaire was designed for management staff who were trained and the other for the employees who reported to them.

The manager questionnaire showed that 77 percent of the management staff considered handling performance problems within the performance appraisal to be easier after taking the course. Because the skills needed to coach employees with performance improvement needs effectively are practiced during the course, supervisors and managers are likely to find handling performance problems easier because they are more skilled at doing so.

The employee questionnaire was designed to determine how the employees who had been appraised by the trained supervisors felt about how they had been coached. Evidence provided by employees indicated that supervisors were effective in three important areas: employees felt that supervisors listened (83 percent), that supervisors valued their input highly (75 percent), and that agreement was reached on main issues of the performance appraisal (77 percent).

Anecdotal data provided by the Human Resources manager and the participants themselves confirmed that the course had made a difference in the quality of the performance appraisals being written. By the end of the first quarter after the program, the Human Resources manager stated that she was seeing a marked difference in the overall quality of performance appraisals. Participants commented that it was much easier to do the appraisal after they had completed the course.

Results

Level 4 findings were drawn from data collected with the quality checklist before and after training. The course increased the quality of performance appraisals in several important areas: objectives, performance feedback, and completeness. Specific objectives that met the quality criteria presented in the course increased by 36 percent after training.

Performance feedback, both in recognizing employee strengths and in coaching for performance improvement, was of higher quality after the course. The number of appraisals containing attributes supported by behavioral examples of how the employee exhibited the attribute on the job increased by 49 percent.

Additional evidence of effective feedback on performance improvement needs was provided by the 36 percent increase found in specific objectives, which clearly state what the employee will do to maintain or improve performance and how measurement will take place. The language used to document objectives indicates that employees are becoming more involved in discussing and finding solutions to performance issues. Data from the checklist after training showed a 35 percent increase in evidence of discussion.

Conclusions and Recommendations

The evidence presented in this report supports the assumption that the performance appraisal and coaching course results in supervisors and managers who are more confident and competent in conducting quality performance appraisals. The evidence also shows an increase in the number of performance appraisal reports documented correctly.

Skills and knowledge gained during training need to be reinforced on the job. Reinforcement is achieved when all staff are trained with support from top management. Managers who have themselves been trained can coach the supervisors who report to them. Human resources staff can also provide ongoing coaching.

Training all supervisors and managers in one location creates a great opportunity for affecting the culture in terms of the overall desired outcome of the course. The evaluation clearly shows that supervisors now use a joint problem-solving approach to encourage employees to assume responsibility for their own performance. It also shows that supervisors provide candid feedback on all aspects of performance. Managers and supervisors who are more comfortable with the authoritarian management style may find this approach uncomfortable, but when it is modeled and reinforced by their own manager and peers, change is likely to occur.

Exhibit 12.1. Performance Appraisal and Coaching Seminar

Objectives

During this course, participants will

1. Self-assess individual strengths and weaknesses in the skill areas necessary to establish two-way communication and gain agreement in the six steps of the performance appraisal discussion:

- Building trust
- Opening
- Accomplishments and concerns
- Planning
- Evaluating and rating
- Closing

2. Identify individual improvement goals for strengthening skills needed for conducting effective performance appraisal discussions.

3. Practice applying the following coaching process to the six steps of the performance appraisal discussion:

- Identify the situation.
- Clarify information.
- Explore options.
- Agree on actions.
- Follow up.

4. Learn to recognize when specific coaching techniques can be used to establish two-way communication and reduce defensiveness during the performance appraisal discussion.

5. Analyze various ways in which both the employee and the supervisor can prepare for the performance appraisal discussion:

- Reviewing objectives, standards, and reports
- Employee self-appraisal
- Input from next-level manager

6. Define each section of the performance appraisal report form and explain how to use it as a tool in the performance appraisal discussion.

7. Explain how the wording of the performance appraisal report form can enhance the clarity of the completed form and reinforce the interactive tone of the overall process.

8. Demonstrate ability in writing

- Performance improvement needs
- Performance improvement objectives
- Achievement of prior objectives

9. Identify the criteria for a timely, high-quality performance appraisal report form through the use of a checklist.

Exhibit 12.2. Reaction Sheet

Course Title: _____

Instructor(s): _____   Date: _____

Your evaluation of this course will assist in making future courses more effective.

A. *Instructions:* Please indicate a rating for each
   statement below by circling a number on
   the scale to the right:

	Strongly agree				Strongly disagree

1. Course objectives were clearly stated and easily   5   4   3   2   1
   understood.
   Comments:

2. Course objectives were met.   5   4   3   2   1
   Comments:

3. Course met my personal expectations.   5   4   3   2   1
   Comments:

4. Time allotted for various segments was appropriate. 5   4   3   2   1
   Comments:

	High				Low

5. To what degree was the course relevant   5   4   3   2   1
   to your job?
   Comments:

6. How would you rate your personal interest   5   4   3   2   1
   in this course?
   Comments:

B. To what degree did the following contribute
   to your achieving the course objectives?

7. Printed participant materials (participant guide, 5   4   3   2   1
   handouts, etc.).
   Comments:

8. Audiovisual materials (tapes, videos, overheads, etc.). 5   4   3   2   1
   Comments:

9. Discussion(s) with other participants.   5   4   3   2   1
   Comments:

Exhibit 12.3. Performance Appraisal Report Form Checklist

On the basis of the completed appraisals that you have brought to the course, how would you answer these questions?

	Yes	No
Performance Standards		
• Do standards reflect the current job?	☐	☐
• Are standards attached and evaluated?	☐	☐
Attendance		
• Are attendance problems documented according to policy?	☐	☐
• Have you refrained from describing the personal reasons for absences?	☐	☐
Achievement of Prior Objectives		
• Are prior objectives restated and evaluated?	☐	☐
• If prior objectives are not met, are clear circumstances or reasons stated?	☐	☐
• If prior objectives are not met, will an outside reader know how this will affect the performance rating?	☐	☐
Attributes		
• Are attributes coded properly and supported by job-specific behavioral examples?	☐	☐
• Are attributes used to recognize and reinforce past performance?	☐	☐
Performance Improvement Needs: Immediate Needs		
• Do the needs relate to failure to meet standards or achieve objectives?	☐	☐
• Do supporting comments indicate a sense of urgency about the need?	☐	☐
• Are supporting comments job related and specific?	☐	☐
• Do supporting comments reflect input that the employee provided about the need?	☐	☐
Performance Improvement Needs: Other		
• Are the needs specific, and do they involve job-related areas that require improvement?	☐	☐
• Are they related to the current position?	☐	☐
• Do supporting comments reflect input that the employee provided about the need?	☐	☐
Objectives		
• Are performance improvement objectives listed first and linked to the need in Section F?	☐	☐
• Do they state specifically how well the employee should do or achieve?	☐	☐
• Do they state specifically what the employee should do or achieve to be acceptable?	☐	☐
• Do they state specifically under what conditions (time frame, resources, training) the employee should perform?	☐	☐
• Do supporting comments reflect input that the employee provided about the objectives?	☐	☐

Exhibit 12.3. Performance Appraisal Report Form Checklist *(continued)*

Performance Rating	*Yes*	*No*
• Is the rating consistent with the results and narrative of the entire performance analysis?	☐	☐
• Is the rating based on the principle of zero-based appraisal?	☐	☐

Development Objectives (if applicable)

	Yes	*No*
• Is it clear that development objectives are not used in determining the performance indicator?	☐	☐
• Is it clear that they are not requirements or standards of the current job?	☐	☐
• Are these objectives specific in terms of what the employee should do, how well, and under what conditions?	☐	☐
• Do supporting comments reflect input that the employee provided about the objective?	☐	☐

Promotability

	Yes	*No*
• Do identified position(s) fit the employee's experience and skills?	☐	☐
• Are listed position(s) properly titled and coded?	☐	☐
• If the employee is immediately promotable to another functional area, has the performance appraisal been signed by another department manager?	☐	☐

Relocation

	Yes	*No*
• Did you discuss current relocation preferences with the employee at the time of the appraisal?	☐	☐

Supervisor's Comments

	Yes	*No*
• Are the comments job related and consistent with the rest of the appraisal?	☐	☐
• Does the Comments section effectively summarize the appraisal?	☐	☐

Other

	Yes	*No*
• Have you completed each section with all the required documentation?	☐	☐
• If the employee is participating in the career development program, is the career development plan properly completed and attached?	☐	☐
• Does the appraisal reflect evidence of two-way communication?	☐	☐
• Does the appraisal language reflect employee input?	☐	☐
• If a third party reviewed the completed appraisal, would the documentation be clear and consistent throughout each section?	☐	☐
• Is the appraisal free of references to personal issues and circumstances of employee's life?	☐	☐
• Has the appraisal been completed by the due date?	☐	☐

Exhibit 12.4. Performance Appraisal Questionnaire for Managers

---

Instructions: This survey is designed to describe your experiences in conducting performance appraisals since completing the performance appraisal and coaching course.

Please answer the questions below by circling the number that corresponds to your response.

1. Characterize your preparation for conducting performance appraisals since completing the course.

	Much easier		*Same*		*More difficult*
Preparation is 5	5	4	3	2	1

Comments:

2. Characterize the actual performance appraisal discussions that you have conducted since completing the course.

	Much easier		*Same*		*More difficult*
• Discussing employee strengths 5	5	4	3	2	1
• Discussing performance problems 5	5	4	3	2	1
• Overcoming defensiveness 5	5	4	3	2	1
• Developing an improvement plan 5	5	4	3	2	1

3. Characterize your documentation of the performance appraisal report form since completing the course.

	Much easier		*Same*		*More difficult*
• Documenting performance improvement needs 5	5	4	3	2	1
• Writing objectives 5	5	4	3	2	1
• Documenting achievement of prior objectives 5	5	4	3	2	1

4. To what degree have you been successful in reaching agreement with your employees on the main issues of the performance appraisal discussion since completing the course?

	High		*Medum*		*Low*
	5	4	3	2	1

Comments:

Exhibit 12.4. Performance Appraisal Questionnaire for Managers *(continued)*

---

5. Which aspects of the performance appraisal process are still the most difficult for you? Check your response(s):

_____ Preparing for the performance appraisal

_____ Discussing employee strengths

_____ Discussing performance problems

_____ Developing an improvement plan

_____ Overcoming defensiveness

_____ Conducting the performance appraisal discussion

_____ Reaching agreement on main issues

_____ Documenting performance improvement needs

_____ Writing objectives

_____ Documenting achievement of prior objectives

Please comment on the items that you have checked.

What other comments would you like to make on conducting performance appraisals? (Use the back of this sheet if necessary.)

Please use the enclosed envelope to return the completed questionnaire. Thank you for your cooperation.

Exhibit 12.5. Performance Appraisal Questionnaire for Employees

---

Instructions: Your manager recently completed a course on performance appraisal. In order to better understand the effectiveness of this course, we are interested in your reactions to your most recent performance appraisal.

Since this questionnaire is anonymous, do *not* sign your name.

Please answer the questions below by circling your response or the number that corresponds to your response.

1. Has your most recent performance appraisal   Yes   No
   occurred within the last six months?

2. Were you asked to prepare for the performance   Yes   No
   appraisal discussion?

   If yes, please explain what you did to prepare.

3. During the performance appraisal discussion,
   what percentage of time did you spend talking?   _____ %

   Comments:

4. Overall, how would you rate your degree
   of involvement in your most recent performance   *High*   *Medium*   *Low*
   appraisal discussion?   5   4   3   2   1

   Comments:

5. To what degree did your manager listen to your   *High*   *Medium*   *Low*
   input during the performance appraisal discussion?   5   4   3   2   1

   Comments:

6. To what degree did your manager consider your
   ideas to be important during the performance   *High*   *Medium*   *Low*
   appraisal discussion?   5   4   3   2   1

   Comments:

7. To what degree were you and your manager
   successful in reaching agreement on the main   *High*   *Medium*   *Low*
   issues of the performance appraisal discussion?   5   4   3   2   1

   Comments:

Please use the enclosed envelope to return the completed questionnaire. Thank you for your cooperation.

Chapter 13

Evaluating a Training Program on Presentation Skills

A t Arthur Andersen & Co., presentation skills are considered to be very important. To meet the need, a training program was developed and offered to those who could benefit from it. Evaluation was done at levels 2 and 3 to measure the effectiveness of the program. Pretests and posttests were used to determine whether the course resulted in persistent changes in knowledge, skills, and attitudes and the extent to which changes in behavior occurred. The evaluation services group developed a sophisticated design for the Management Development Department to use in evaluating the program.

———

Arthur Andersen & Company

Steven Bond, Manager, Center for Professional Education
Arthur Andersen & Co., St. Charles, Illinois

The Context

The Centers for Professional Education

Arthur Andersen and Andersen Consulting are professional services providers that make up the Arthur Andersen Worldwide Organization. Arthur Andersen provides auditing, business advisory services, and tax consultation, and Andersen Consulting offers business integration and information systems to clients around the world. At its centers for professional education in St. Charles, Illinois, and Veldhoven, The Netherlands, more than 260 education professionals comprising the Professional Education Division design and develop training programs offered to Andersen's 60,000 employees at training sites and offices around the world. The 6,000,000 hours of training delivered annually cover technical areas, business strategy, and management and leadership development.

Management Development

Traditionally, the Arthur Andersen Worldwide Organization has promoted people from within the organization to management levels. Therefore, it has a tradition of management development programming that includes training, job assignment, and other personal development experiences. The management development training group provides a wide variety of personal, professional, and interpersonal programs as part of this overall development process. These programs are based on needs assessment findings and are evaluated formatively throughout the development process. Occasional summative evaluations are also completed.

Evaluation Services

Beginning in 1979, the centers for professional development have used an independent evaluation function separate from the training development groups. This function provides a variety of services ranging from survey research and needs assessment to follow-up studies for program evaluation. The specialists in this evaluation group work cooperatively with the training development teams to ensure quality in the training programs and to provide decision makers with accurate, timely information.

This report summarizes a follow-up evaluation of an Effective Presentations course conducted by the evaluation services group for Management Development.

The Course

In a professional services relationship, where confidence in an individual is often the determining factor in obtaining and retaining a client, it is important for the service provider not only to exhibit deep technical competence but also to inspire interpersonal confidence. An ability to make oral presentations in a self-assured, professional manner is a part of projecting an image of poise and self-control to the client.

The two-day Effective Presentations course, which has a maximum class size of sixteen participants, is offered approximately 120 times per year. Instructor-led periods are followed by sessions in which participants have opportunities to practice the skills presented in lecture. Participants give six presentations. Each is videotaped and critiqued by fellow participants and instructors. The objectives of the course are to help to improve the participants' eye contact; vocal projection; stance, gestures, and animation; and use of visuals, silence, and pauses and to help them organize effectively what they say.

The Evaluation

Purpose and Overall Design

The purpose of the summative evaluation of the Effective Presentations course was to determine whether the course resulted in persistent changes in participants' knowledge, behaviors, or attitudes related to the making of presentations. The focus of the evaluation was to assess participants' behavior while actually making presentations, to determine whether participants' self-assessment changed during the course, and to assess whether participants retained changes in knowledge, attitudes, and behaviors over time. A pre-post follow-up within-subjects design was used. This design had the following structure:

Measure——Train——Measure——Wait——Measure

Information was obtained from participants on three occasions: at the beginning of the course, at the end of the course, and after the course. On each occasion, participants completed a questionnaire and were videotaped while making a presentation.

Data Collection Process

Information was collected at four different sessions of the course. These sessions were selected not at random but because they were scheduled within the time frame of the study. During each session, an evaluator observed the instruction, administered questionnaires before and after the training to each participant, ensured that the videotap-ings were completed correctly and retained, conducted informal in-terviews with participants, and provided information to participants about the follow-up phase of the evaluation. Beginning six months after the first session, follow-up questionnaires were distributed, and arrangements were made to complete follow-up videotapings with participants from five U.S. and four European offices. The time that elapsed between completion of the course and follow-up taping ranged from about one to eight months.

Questionnaires

The three questionnaires included items that obtained participants' self-assessments in the following areas: demographics; training and ex-perience related to the making of presentations; self-ratings on general presentation skills; self-reported confidence in making presentations; and performance in specific areas, such as eye contact, gestures, voice projection, stance and posture, use of visuals, question-and-answer ses-sions, and organization of content. To avoid introducing participants to specific course content before the course began, some questions were not asked on the questionnaire administered before training.

Videotaping

Each participant included in the final behavioral analysis was video-taped before and after training and at the follow-up session.

Before Training. The first presentation made by participants in the course served as the premeasure. Participants had been presented with no course content at the time when they made this presentation. In the event that this first presentation was too short to obtain an adequate sample of be-havior, the first portion of the second presentation was used to assess the skills for which a participant had not yet received instruction.

After Training. The last (sixth) presentation in the course served as the postmeasure. At that point, participants had received all course con-tent. However, they did receive feedback on the presentation subse-quent to taping.

Follow-up Session. Arrangements were made with participants to pre-pare and deliver a five-to-ten minute presentation in their office. These presentations were either presentations to other office employees, or they were practice for upcoming client presentations. Most of these presentations were attended by either a Management Development or an evaluation services staff person, who videotaped the session.

Behavioral Rating System

A coding structure and observation checklist were created for analysis of the videotaped presentations. The structure was based on two considerations: course content and ability to measure differences in performance in a videotaped presentation. The rating system had six general categories: head movement and eye contact, gestures and upper body movement, lower body movement and stance, voice quality, organization of content, and overall presentation. Each category represents the translation of a major area of course content into a set of specific behavioral measures.

The frequency of behaviors in the first four categories were recorded during four fifteen-second periods for a total of one minute for each. The presentation was then replayed, and raters recorded information and assigned ratings for voice projection and speed (subcategories of the voice quality category), organization of content, and overall presentation.

Four raters were trained to use the behavioral rating system. Two raters simultaneously viewed and coded each videotaped presentation. Raters were rotated so that three of the four individuals rated tapes with at least two other raters. Tapes were rated in random order. Interrater reliabilities were computed across each pair of raters and across the behavioral categories. The lowest reliabilities were in the more subjective areas, such as voice quality, but overall the intercorrelations were modest to strong, with about half being above .80 and more than two-thirds above .60.

Use of visuals and question-and-answer sessions were excluded from the behavioral rating system because participants did not have an opportunity to demonstrate these skills on all presentations. The next six sections describe the categories rated.

Head Movement and Eye Contact. It was not possible to discern the duration of participants' eye contact accurately while observing the taped presentations. Therefore, shifts in head movement were used instead. (Individuals often break eye contact without shifting their head, but they are not likely to shift their head while retaining eye contact with a specific individual. If an individual made three head shifts in a fifteen-second period, it was assumed that eye contact was being held for an average of five seconds. If fifteen shifts occurred, the average duration of eye contact was calculated to have been one second.) This is a conservative measure that gives participants credit for more effective eye contact than was likely to have occurred.

Two types of behavior were recorded. The first was the number of head shifts, and the second was the number of glances directed at something other than the audience, such as the ceiling, floor, or walls (ineffective behavior).

Gestures and Upper Body Movement. Three subcategories were established that subsumed the majority of possible behaviors likely to be seen. Participants were rated as gesturing effectively (moving one or both hands above elbow height), assuming a "parade rest" stance (with arms and hands relaxed at sides), or doing something ineffective (for example, holding their hands in fig leaf or praying positions, holding onto a flipchart or podium, or making small, low gestures).

Lower Body Movement and Stance. Three subcategories were used. Participants were assessed as standing appropriately (feet stationary and shoulder-width apart, weight evenly distributed), moving with purpose, or doing something ineffective (weight unevenly distributed, pacing, rocking, or standing turned toward the flipchart or overhead screen).

Voice. Three subcategories were used. Nonwords (*umh*'s, *ahh*'s, fillers, words or sentences restarted) were counted. Voice projection (strong/loud, acceptable, or too soft) and speed (too fast, appropriate, or too slow) were rated at the end of the taped presentation.

Organization of Content. The introduction, body, and conclusion of each presentation were rated as present/effective, acceptable, or weak/absent.

Overall Presentation. Ratings were assigned to the overall presentation on a scale ranging from 1 (very poor) to 5 (very good). Pluses and minuses could also be assigned. This resulted in a fourteen-point scale ranging from 1 to 5+.

Participant Sample

Data on performance before and after training were obtained from forty-six participants in the four sessions. Follow-up questionnaires were distributed to all participants with the exception of four individuals who had left the firm or who had taken the course in preparation to be certified to teach it. The follow-up questionnaire was completed by thirty participants (71 percent). Follow-up videotapes were obtained from nineteen participants. These nineteen individuals were from nine offices; six of them were from European offices. Follow-up questionnaires were received from eighteen of the nineteen individuals for whom there were follow-up tapes. The data analyses were based on the data available from this group of nineteen participants. Key characteristics of this group (years with the firm, experience and training related to the making of presentations, and self-assessment of overall presentation ability) were compared with the characteristics of participants for whom the data were incomplete. No significant differences were found. Therefore, conclusions based on the sample of nineteen individuals appeared to be generalizable.

Data Analysis Approach for Questionnaires and Tape Ratings

Participants' performances during videotaped presentations and their responses on questionnaires were analyzed to determine the changes that had occurred. To assess whether any changes in participants' behavior or questionnaire responses were statistically significant, the evaluators used t-tests (paired comparison). Comparisons were completed for each of the categories identified in the preceding section.

Performing numerous t-tests increases the probability that chance differences due to sampling error rather than to the effect of the training will occur. To control for this, the criterion for concluding that differences were statistically significant was made more strict than it would have been if fewer comparisons had been made. Use of a strict criterion (.01) for individual comparisons increased the confidence with which conclusions about the effects of the course in numerous specific areas could be made.

The Findings

General Findings

Results of the analysis on each of the categories for which questionnaire and behavioral data were collected were summarized. Mean responses on the pre, post, and follow-up questionnaires and results of the related significance tests were calculated, and information about the frequency and effectiveness of specific behaviors during the video-taped pre, post, and follow-up presentations was provided.

Overall, participants' self-assessments significantly improved in all areas included on the questionnaires. Participants' actual behaviors while making presentations improved in several areas, including overall effectiveness, gestures and upper body movement, stationary feet, voice projection, avoiding nonwords, and providing an effective conclusion. Improved performance levels were retained from the post to follow-up presentations in each of these areas with the exception of effectiveness in delivering conclusions (a part of organization of content).

A Word About Self-Reported Reaction Data on Overall Effectiveness

Participants' self-assessments of their overall presentation ability improved significantly. Self-assessment of their overall presentation ability did not change between the time immediately after training and follow-up.

Raters' assessments of participants' overall effectiveness while making the videotaped presentations concurred with participants' self-assessments. There was a significant improvement in the overall ratings of the presentations at the end of the course over ratings at the beginning of the course. There was no significant change in participants' overall effectiveness between the end of training and the follow-up presentations, which suggests that the improvements made during the course were retained over time. These quantitative results parallel participants' verbal comments offered during and after the course.

Concluding Comments

The study just described was designed to be a rigorous look at retention of learned behaviors and application of those behaviors in a non-training setting. While the follow-up sessions were not training per se, they were not fully real-world applications either. This reflects a constraint in practice. It is sometimes simply not feasible to follow the trainee into his or her workplace in order to measure the trainee's performance. Significant impact questions are left unanswered by this type of research. Do changed presentation skills make a difference in a person's professional relationship-building capability? Do superior presentation skills translate into reduced cost and/or increased revenue and therefore greater long-run profits? Before these questions of impact can be addressed realistically, two fundamental questions must be answered: Did the training result in a behavioral change? And did the change persist? This evaluation is an example of one step in the overall evaluation process that should accompany training designed to affect organizational performance.

Chapter 14

Evaluating the Creative Manager Training Program

The evaluating of training is so important at Motorola that Motorola University has a separate department that is specifically for that purpose on a worldwide basis. The department was managed by Dave Basarab, who contributed the foreword to this book. This case study describes the process and results for evaluating at levels 1, 2, and 3. The sophisticated design that it outlines will interest any organization that takes evaluation seriously.

Motorola Corporation

Dave Basarab, Manager of Training Operations and Business
Motorola SPS Organization and Human Effectiveness,
Austin, Texas

Introduction

Every year, Motorola invests more than 4.4 million hours of employee time and more than 200 million dollars in training. With this kind of investment, the business portions of Motorola asked Motorola University (a corporate entity) for help in determining whether the money invested in training results in the performance expected on the job. To address their concern, Motorola University formed the Evaluation Department.

This department functions as a central source for the processing of training evaluation data from around the world. More than sixty-five Motorola training departments are currently served, with locations including China, Korea, Malaysia, Japan, the United Kingdom, Phoenix, Chicago, Austin, and greater Boston. The Evaluation Department is composed of a full-time staff dedicated to consultation on evaluation procedures and to the processing and reporting of evaluation information.

Motorola University has adopted the Kirkpatrick model for training evaluation, but it has added its own unique focus to the effort. We define evaluation as a systematic process to collect data and convert those data into usable information. Training evaluation information is used to improve training programs, measure the effects of training, help in decision making, determine and track the quality of training, and act on the results. Motorola's use of the four Kirkpatrick evaluation levels is shown in Table 14.1.

We use a systematic process to evaluate training at all levels. The process consists of specific steps and criteria to follow when conducting an evaluation study. It is much more than a map. It is a guide complete with process specifications and examples that help users to plan, develop, collect, analyze, and report various types of evaluation data at all levels. It is flexible enough to walk you through a simple descriptive analysis and detailed enough to guide you through advanced causal comparative and correlational studies. The process used at Motorola is shown in Figure 14.1.

Table 14.1. Motorola's Evaluation Levels

Evaluation level	Kirkpatrick definition	Motorola's use
Level 1	Reaction	Customer satisfaction index from participants
Level 2	Learning	Mastery of knowledge and skills
Level 3	Behavior	Application of knowledge and skills on the job
Level 4	Results	Organizational impact

Figure 14.1. Motorola's Evaluation Process

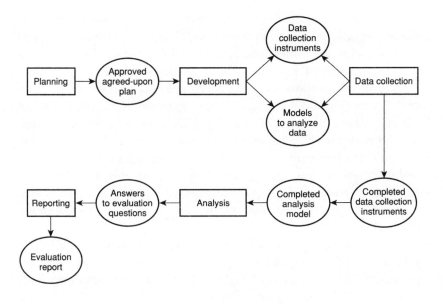

The Creative Manager

The evaluation of a program called the Creative Manager illustrates Motorola's evaluation process. The three-day program was designed, developed, and delivered by Motorola University throughout the world. It focuses on a manager's ability to recognize and develop the creative potential in himself or herself and in others by applying the creative process to generate, develop, and champion unique ideas.

Participants in this skill-based course not only develop new definitions of creativity but also assess their own innate creative potential, apply an eight-step creative process to various topics, and develop their ability to use creative techniques to generate ideas. The target audience for this course is all Motorola managers and team leaders.

The program has three goals: to develop creative behaviors, to apply the creative process to various topics, and to learn and use tools that can develop creativity in oneself and in others.

Planning the Evaluation

The evaluation process calls for the identification and interviewing of evaluation stakeholders—individuals who have a vested interest in the training and its outcomes. The primary stakeholder for this evaluation was the manager of the Motorola University competency center for management education. She was interviewed to determine the purpose of the evaluation and the intended use of its results, her commitment to the evaluation, any constraints on data collection and observation, on-the-job performance goals and expectations, organizational issues that may inhibit performance, any significant issues affecting performance, evaluation study time frames, report format, whether the study was aimed at the discovery of possible causes for behavior transfer, and whether we needed to explore the magnitude of the relationship between two variables.

After the interviews, an evaluation plan was written and signed by the stakeholder. The plan stated that the purpose of the evaluation was to determine what the participants liked and disliked about the training (level 1 evaluation), the learning that occurred because of the training (level 2 evaluation), and the degree to which participants have successfully transferred skills learned in the course to their jobs (level 3 evaluation).

The information collected was used in two ways: to identify and correct problems associated with the training and thereby improve the program (formative evaluation) and to verify the worth and merit of the training itself (summative evaluation).

Developing the Data Collection
Instruments and Analysis Models

This phase of the evaluation process develops the data collection instruments and analysis models (tools used to summarize the data) specified in the evaluation plan. According to the plan, we built instruments for three levels.

Level 1

Level 1 evaluation at Motorola studies the satisfaction of participants with the training event. The Participant Assessment (PA) form was used to capture level 1 evaluation data on participants' overall satisfaction with course relevancy, design, perceived learning, instructor performance, materials, and learning environment. Data collected from the Participant Assessment form are completely anonymous.

The individual items on the Participant Assessment form assess the following: relevancy (items 1–4), perceived learning (item 5), course design (items 6–13), instructor (items 14–20), training facility (item 21), printed materials (item 22), and overall satisfaction (item 23). Each response on the Participant Assessment form is considered as falling into one of the following three categories: satisfied, dissatisfied, or null (neither satisfied nor dissatisfied).

From these responses, we calculate a customer satisfaction percentage for each item, each category of items, and the entire assessment. This is the formula:

$$\text{Customer satisfaction} = \left(\frac{\text{Satisfied responses}}{\text{Total responses} - \text{Null responses}} \right) \times 100$$

A training session has met the quality goal if customer satisfaction meets or exceeds 90 percent for each category of responses (relevancy, course design, instructor, and so on). If the training session is considered a pilot, the course is released if it meets or exceeds 80 percent customer satisfaction in the categories of relevancy and course design.

The Motorola University Evaluation Department uses a customer system called AdEPT (*Ad*vanced *E*valuation *P*articipant *T*echnology) as its analysis model in support of its training evaluation activities. AdEPT is an automated system that allows Motorola University to gather level 1 and level 2 evaluation data and provide reports to its clients. The gathering and reporting of level 1 and level 2 evaluation data can be used to improve a course during its design, development, and initial implementation or to pinpoint opportunities for improvement after the course has been implemented. The primary benefit to Motorola University and its clients is timely access to data that provide a starting point for improving the quality of training.

Level 2

Level 2 evaluation is known at Motorola University as the *mastery assessment process*. The mastery assessment process determines the effectiveness of a course in providing participants with the knowledge and skills prescribed by the objectives. Level 2 data are used to evaluate courses, not personnel. In other words, data collected by giving tests are used to look for patterns within the results so that action plans to improve learning can be implemented. The data collected are not used to grade participants, imply passing or failing a course, or provide input for participants' performance reviews.

Quality goals are documented during development, and evaluation data are collected on training sessions that are reported to evaluation clients. The heart of the mastery assessment process is called the *mastery matrix of learning.* Table 14.2 shows the mastery matrix of learning for the Creative Manager program.

The matrix concept allows the designer to select the objectives that are to be evaluated, the tests used to collect data on learning, and the minimum test score that a participant needs to obtain in order to indicate mastery of an objective. To take into account that people learn differently and take tests differently and that instructors teach differently (together, these differences are known as *process variation*), we calculate a lower control limit for each test. This value estimates three standard deviations below the mastery score for a population of a given size. This value then accounts for any process variation in the instructional event. This is the formula used for calculating the lower control limit:

$$LCL = P - 3\sqrt{\frac{P(1-P)}{n}}$$

where LCL = lower control limit, P = defined mastery score, and n = the number of people to be trained. A training session meets the quality criterion if 80 percent of the participants score at or above the lower control limit on all tests. The quality goal must be achieved at pilot test for the course to be released.

Table 14.2. Mastery Matrix of Learning for the Creative Manager Program

Objective being evaluated	Test number	Mastery score	Lower control limit
1	1	80%	77%
2	2	80	77
3	3	80	77
4	4	80	77
5	5	80	77

Note: Quality goal: 80 percent of the participants score at or above the lower control limit for each objective; N = 2,000

Level 2 evaluation data are captured by administering the Motorola University mastery assessment to all students as specified in the course's instructor guide.

Level 3

Level 3 evaluation at Motorola is a process that collects data to determine whether the skills learned in training are being applied on the job or, if they are not, why and to identify the training, cultural, and organizational issues that may inhibit application of the skills learned.

For the Creative Manager course, participants provided the names of three associates who would be able to comment on their effective use of the creative process. A follow-up survey regarding behavioral transfer was mailed to the participants and the associates whom they named. The first fifty participants who attended the Creative Manager program were surveyed in an attempt to answer the following evaluation questions:

1. Has the participant exhibited the behaviors learned in the course on the job? If the answer is yes, how often were the behaviors exhibited?
2. Did the participant perceive the results of his or her behaviors to be positive or negative?
3. Does the participant feel that the behaviors that he or she exhibited should be continued?
4. If the skills were exhibited more than once, did the participant feel that improvement occurred as a result of training (if applicable)?
5. Did environmental influences help or hinder the use of the skills on the job?
6. Does the participant consider the Creative Manager program to be valuable for teaching and promoting the components of creativity, traits, idea-finding techniques, and the creative problem-solving process?

A second survey was administered to the 150 coworkers whom they had identified as people who would have an opportunity to observe their use of creative skills and behaviors within ninety days of training. Responses from this survey were used to answer the following evaluation questions:

1. Have associates observed the participant exhibiting the behaviors learned in the course on the job? If behaviors were observed,

how often were they observed? If behaviors were not observed, is it the associate's perception that the participant had the opportunity to exhibit the behaviors taught in the course?

2. Did associates perceive the results of the participant's behaviors to be positive or negative?
3. Do associates feel that the participant's behaviors should be continued?
4. If the skills were exhibited more than once, did associates feel that improvement occurred as a result of training (if applicable)?

Collecting Evaluation Data

The data collection phase of the Motorola University training evaluation process involves the gathering of data to address the evaluation questions posed in the evaluation plan. Data sources include people, documents, and performance data. The data collection effort for the Creative Manager program followed the timetable shown in Figure 14.2.

Level 1 and level 2 evaluation data were collected for all classes. One level 3 data collection was conducted.

Figure 14.2. Evaluation Data Collection Timetable

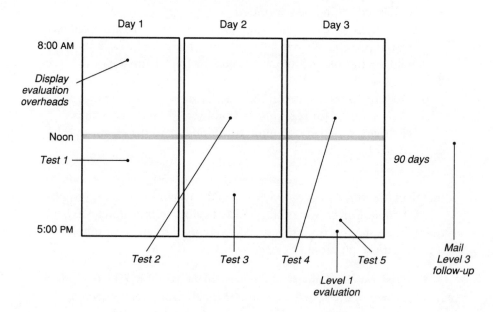

Analyzing the Data

In the analysis phase, the data collected are interpreted. This phase answers the evaluation questions posed in the evaluation plan. Figures 14.3 through 14.5 show the results for the Creative Manager program by evaluation level.

Figure 14.3. Level 1: Customer Satisfaction

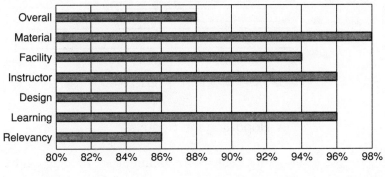

Note: N = 211

Figure 14.4. Level 2: Mastery of Objectives

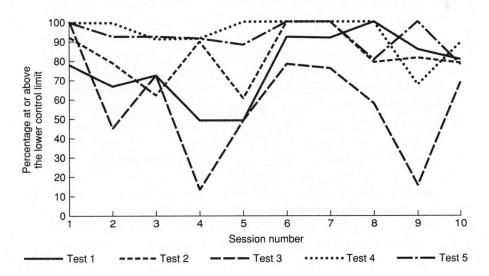

Figure 14.5. Level 3: Application of Skills on the Job

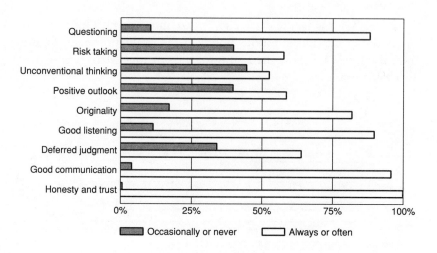

Reporting the Results

The purpose of reporting results is to communicate training evaluation information to stakeholders and interested audiences so they can use the information for decision making. Table 14.3 shows the reporting structure for level 1 and level 2 data from the Creative Manager program. Reports were distributed through electronic mail.

Twenty-eight of the fifty participants who attended the Creative Manager training completed and returned the survey designed to collect level 3 data. Of the 149 associates identified by participants, 102 people completed and returned the survey.

Overall, the majority of the training participants and their associates felt that the skills and traits of creativity were being used on the job. However, agreement between training participants and their associates was not reached when they were asked about the job circumstances under which the skills and traits of creativity were being applied. Significantly more participants than associates reported that the participants were using the skills and traits in each circumstance.

Both groups surveyed agreed that the results of displaying the skills and traits were generally positive.

Regarding organizational influences on the use of the skills and traits of creativity, more than half of the participants agreed that em-

Table 14.3. Reporting Structure, Level 1 and Level 2 Data

Report	Frequency	Purpose
Level 1		
Weekly report	Every Thursday	Provides a summary report of customer satisfaction for all training sessions in the preceding week
Monthly report	First two business days of the month	Summarizes the distribution of responses to the target audience question, by course, for the preceding month
Quarterly report (management summary)	First two business days of the quarter	Summarizes the results of responses to items dealing with instructor performance, by instructor, for the preceding quarter
Level 2		
Weekly report	Every Thursday	Provides a summary report on achievement of the learning quality goal for all sessions
Learning history	Every Thursday for each session where learning quality is below goal and on demand	Documents all learning throughout the life of the course, helps to determine root cause when quality has not been achieved

ployee recognition programs (71 percent), availability of resources (54 percent), and personal attitudes and values (75 percent) helped them back on the job. Hindrances to using the skills and traits included organizational, social, and political attitudes (56 percent).

Overall, 96 percent of the participants found the training program to be of value to them on the job.

Chapter 15

Evaluating a Training Program on Developing Supervisory Skills

This case study is based on a research project that was designed to measure changes in behavior and results. The program covered six topics and lasted for three days. Patterned interviews were conducted three months after the program with the participants and their immediate supervisors.

Management Institute, University of Wisconsin

Donald L. Kirkpatrick,
Professor Emeritus
University of Wisconsin, Milwaukee

Developing Supervisory Skills, a three-day institute conducted by the University of Wisconsin Management Institute, included six three-hour sessions on the following topics: giving orders, training, appraising employee performance, preventing and handling grievances, making decisions, and initiating change. All the leaders were staff members of the University of Wisconsin Management Institute. Teaching methods included lecture, guided discussion, "buzz" groups, role playing, case studies, supervisory inventories, and films and other visual aids.

Research Design

Each participant completed a questionnaire at the start of the program. Interviews of each participant were conducted at his or her workplace between two and three months after the conclusion of the program. On the same visit, the participant's immediate supervisor was also interviewed. Out of a total enrollment of fifty-seven participants, data were obtained from forty-three and from their bosses, and those data are included in this study. Exhibit 15.1 shows the findings on demographics and general issues.

Exhibit 15.1. Questionnaire Responses: Demographics

1. Describe your organization:
   a. Size
      - (4) Less than 100 employees
      - (10) 100–500 employees
      - (3) 500–1,000 employees
      - (26) More than 1,000 employees
   b. Products
      - (15) Consumer
      - (11) Industrial
      - (12) Both
      - (5) Other

2. Describe yourself:
   a. Title
      - (33) Foreman or supervisor
      - (10) General foreman or superintendent
   b. How many people do you supervise?
      - (1) 0–5
      - (9) 6–10
      - (6) 11–15
      - (8) 6–20
      - (19) More than 20
   c. Whom do you supervise?
      - (26) All men
      - (11) Mostly men
      - (6) Mostly women
   d. What kind of workers do you supervise?
      - (14) Production, unskilled
      - (23) Production, semiskilled
      - (12) Production, skilled
      - (2) Maintenance
      - (9) Office

Exhibit 15.1. Questionnaire Responses: Demographics *(continued)*

---

   e. Before attending the program, how much were you told about it?
   - (3)   Complete information
   - (8)   Quite a lot
   - (20) A little
   - (12) Practically nothing
   f. To what extent do you feel that you will be able to improve your supervisory performance by attending this program?
   - (21) To a large extent
   - (22) To some extent
   - (0)   Very little

3. How would you describe your top management?
   - (31) Liberal (encourages change and suggestions)
   - (9)   Middle-of-the-road
   - (3)   Conservative (discourages change and suggestions)

4. How would you describe your immediate supervisor?
   - (35) Liberal
   - (8)   Middle-of-the-road
   - (0)   Conservative

5. How often does your supervisor ask you for ideas to solve departmental problems?
   - (19) Frequently
   - (19) Sometimes
   - (5)   Hardly ever

6. To what extent will your supervisor encourage you to apply the ideas and techniques you learned in this program?
   - (14) To a large extent
   - (14) To some extent
   - (1)   Very little
   - (14) Not sure

Research Results

In this situation, it was not possible to measure on a before-and-after basis. Instead, interviews were used to determine how behavior and results after the program compared with behavior before the program. Both the participant and his or her immediate supervisor were interviewed, and their responses were compared.

The first part of each interview determined overall changes in behavior and results. Exhibit 15.2 shows the responses. The second part

Exhibit 15.2. Questionnaire Responses: Behavior Changes

---

1. To what extent has the program improved the working relationship between the participant and his or her immediate supervisor?
   - (23, 12) To a large extent
   - (51, 32) To some extent
   - (26, 56) No change
   - (0, 0) Made it worse

2. Since the program, how much two-way communication has taken place between the participant and his or her immediate supervisor?
   - (12, 5) Much more
   - (63, 46) Some more
   - (25, 49) No change
   - (0, 0) Some less
   - (0, 0) Much less

3. Since the program, how much interest has the participant taken in his or her subordinates?
   - (26, 5) Much more
   - (67, 49) Some more
   - (7, 46) No change
   - (0, 0) Some less
   - (0, 0) Much less

---

of the interview determined changes related to each of the six topics discussed in the program. The reader should note that all responses in Exhibit 15.2 and Tables 15.1 through 15.8 are given in percentages. When two figures are given, the first is the percentage response from participants, and the second is the percentage response from their immediate supervisors.

One question asked, on an overall basis, To what extent has the participant's job behavior changed since the program? Table 15.1 shows the responses in regard to changes in performance and attitude. Positive changes were indicated in all nine areas, with the greatest improvement occurring in attitudes.

To the question, What results have occurred since the program? Table 15.2 shows the responses from participants and immediate supervisors. Positive results were observed in all eight categories. In four areas, one or two supervisors observed negative results. And one participant (2 percent) indicated that employee attitudes and morale were somewhat worse.

Table 15.1. Change in Behavior

Supervisory areas	Much better	Somewhat better	No change	Somewhat worse	Much worse	Don't know
Giving orders	25, 12	70, 65	5, 14	0, 0	0, 0	0, 9
Training	22, 17	56, 39	22, 39	0, 0	0, 0	0, 5
Making decisions	35, 14	58, 58	7, 23	0, 0	0, 0	0, 5
Initiating change	21, 9	53, 53	26, 30	0, 0	0, 0	0, 7
Appraising employee performance	21, 7	50, 42	28, 36	0, 0	0, 0	0, 12
Preventing and handling grievances	12, 7	42, 40	46, 46	0, 0	0, 0	0, 7
Attitude toward job	37, 23	37, 53	26, 23	0, 0	0, 0	0, 0
Attitude toward subordinates	40, 7	42, 60	19, 30	0, 0	0, 0	0, 2
Attitude toward management	42, 26	26, 35	32, 37	0, 0	0, 0	0, 2

Table 15.2. Results

Performance benchmarks	Much better	Somewhat better	No change	Somewhat worse	Much worse	Don't know
Quantity of production	5, 5	43, 38	50, 50	0, 2	0, 0	0, 5
Quality of production	10, 7	60, 38	28, 52	0, 0	0, 0	0, 2
Safety	21, 7	28, 37	49, 56	0, 0	0, 0	0, 0
Housekeeping	23, 14	32, 35	42, 46	0, 5	0, 0	0, 0
Employee attitudes and morale	12, 7	56, 53	28, 32	2, 5	0, 0	0, 2
Employee attendance	7, 2	23, 19	67, 77	0, 0	0, 0	0, 0
Employee promptness	7, 2	32, 16	58, 81	0, 0	0, 0	0, 0
Employee turnover	5, 0	14, 16	79, 79	0, 5	0, 0	0, 0

It is interesting to note that, in nearly all cases, participants were more likely than supervisors to indicate that positive changes had taken place. There is no way of telling who is right. The important

Table 15.3. Giving Orders

	Much more	Somewhat more	No change	Somewhat less	Much less	Don't know
Since the program, is the participant taking more time to plan his orders?	17, 23	58, 60	16, 12	9, 0	0, 0	0, 5
Since the program, is the participant taking more time to prepare the order receiver?	24, 17	71, 57	5, 19	0, 0	0, 0	0, 7
Since the program, is the participant getting more voluntary cooperation from his employees?	26, 0	37, 56	37, 23	0, 0	0, 0	0, 21
Since the program, is the participant doing more in the way of making sure the order receiver understands the order?	51, 21	44, 44	5, 7	0, 0	0, 0	0, 28
Since the program, is the participant taking more time to make sure the order receiver is following instructions?	21, 16	60, 58	19, 12	0, 0	0, 0	0, 14
Since the program, is the participant making more of an effort to praise his employees for a job well done?	24, 30	50, 22	8, 7	0, 0	0, 0	0, 41
Since the program, is the participant doing more follow-up to see that his orders were properly carried out?	37, 21	39, 42	24, 26	0, 0	0, 0	0, 11

fact is that both participants and supervisors saw positive changes in both behavior and results.

Tables 15.3 to 15.8 show the responses to the questions asked on each of the six topics that the program covered. The responses are uniformally positive.

Table 15.4. Training Employees

Questions	Yes	No	Not sure	No new or transferred employees
Since the participant attended the program, are his or her new or transferred employees better trained?	63, 46	9, 0	23, 43	6, 11

Questions	Participant always	Participant usually	Participant sometimes	Participant never
Before the program, who trained the workers?	16, 13	42, 45	34, 31	8, 11
Since the program, who trained the workers?	15, 18	45, 42	32, 29	8, 11

Questions	Does not apply	Much more	Somewhat more	No change	Somewhat less	Much less	Don't know
Since the program, if someone else trains the employees, has the participant become more observant and taken a more active interest in the training process?	14, 11	22, 16	40, 27	24, 30	0, 0	0, 0	0, 16
Since the program, if the participant trains the employees, is he or she making more of an effort in seeing that the employees are well trained?	8, 5	42, 24	42, 42	8, 18	0, 0	0, 0	0, 11
Since the program, is the participant more inclined to be patient while training?	8, 11	24, 5	47, 50	21, 20	0, 3	0, 0	0, 11
Since the program, while teaching an operation, is the participant asking for more questions to ensure understanding?	8, 21	27, 14	46, 46	9, 8	0, 0	0, 0	0, 11
Since the program, is the participant better prepared to teach?	8, 11	29, 18	47, 52	16, 8	0, 0	0, 0	0, 11
Since the program, is the participant doing more follow-up to check the trainees' progress?	0, 0	41, 21	38, 49	21, 14	0, 0	0, 0	0, 16

Table 15.5. Appraising Employees' Performance

Is the participant required to complete appraisal forms on his or her subordinates?

	Yes	No
	62, 69	38, 31

	Does not apply	Much more	Large extent	Some extent	Little		Don't know
Before the program, if the participant conducted appraisal interviews, to what extent did he or she emphasize past performance?	48, 40		10, 5	40, 12	2, 14		0, 29
Before the program, to what extent did the participant try to determine the goals and objectives of his or her employees?	—		5, 15	65, 52	30, 30		0, 3
Before the program, to what extent did the participant praise the work of his or her employees?	—		8, 12	77, 52	15, 18		0, 18

	Does not apply	Much more	Somewhat more	No change	Somewhat less	Much less	Don't know
Since the program, is the participant doing more follow-up to see that the objectives of the appraisal interview are being carried out?	48, 40	10, 5	24, 21	14, 19	2, 0	0, 0	0, 14
Since the program, during an appraisal interview, is the participant placing more emphasis on future performance?	48, 40	24, 7	17, 10	10, 14	0, 2	0, 0	0, 26
Since the program, is the participant making more of an effort to determine the goals and objectives of his or her employees?	—	22, 15	60, 50	18, 18	0, 0	0, 0	0, 18
Since the program, how much does the participant praise his or her employees?	—	22, 10	40, 38	38, 38	0, 2	0, 0	0, 12

Table 15.6. Preventing and Handling Grievances

Do participant's employees belong to a union?

Yes	No
69, 69	31, 31

Who usually settled/settles grievances?	Participant always	Participant usually	Participant sometimes	Participant never
Before the program, if an employee had a grievance, who usually settled it?	10, 12	64, 38	24, 43	2, 5
Since the program, who usually settles employee grievances?	10, 12	69, 48	21, 38	0, 2

	Always defended management	Usually defended management	Acted objectively	Usually defended employees	Always defended employees	Don't know
Before the program, to what extent did the participant defend management versus the employees in regard to grievance problems?	34, 17	22, 39	44, 20	0, 10	0, 0	0, 15

	Much more	Somewhat more	No change	Somewhat less	Much less	No union	Don't know
Since the program, is the participant more inclined to the management viewpoint regarding grievances and complaints?	19, 14	31, 29	48, 48	2, 0	0, 0	0, 0	0, 9
Since the program, has there been a change in the number of grievances in the participant's department?	2, 5	7, 14	81, 71	10, 5	0, 0	0, 0	0, 5
Since the program, has the degree of seriousness of grievances changed?	0, 0	2, 2	74, 74	24, 12	0, 7	0, 0	0, 5
Since the program, has the participant been better able to satisfy employee complaints before they reach the grievance stage?	17, 7	31, 52	26, 24	0, 0	0, 2	26, 14	

Table 15.7. Making Decisions

	Yes	No	Don't know
Participants only: Since the program, is the participant making better decisions?	88	2	10

	Much better	Somewhat better	No change	Somewhat worse	Much worse	Don't know
Supervisors only: Since the program, is the participant making better decisions?	12	68	10	0	0	10

	Frequently	Sometimes	Hardly ever	Don't know
Before the program, how often did the participant's boss involve or consult him or her in the decision-making process in the participant's department?	40, 65	45, 30	15, 5	
Before the program, to what extent did the participant involve or consult employees in the decision-making process?	24, 26	57, 38	19, 24	0, 10

Continued

149

Table 15.7. Making Decisions (*continued*)

	Much more	Somewhat more	No change	Somewhat less	Much less	Don't know
Since the program, how often does the participant's boss involve him or her in the departmental decision-making process?	13, 23	25, 17	60, 55	3, 3	0, 3	0, 0
Since the program, how often does the participant involve employees in the decision-making process?	26, 0	38, 43	33, 33	3, 7	0, 3	0, 14
Since the program, does the participant have less tendency to put off making decisions?	0, 0	0, 0	36, 33	36, 40	28, 22	0, 5
Since the program, is the participant holding more group meetings with employees?	12, 5	26, 17	62, 55	0, 0	0, 0	0, 24
Since the program, does the participant have more confidence in the decisions he or she makes?	29, 19	60, 60	12, 21	0, 0	0, 0	0, 0
Since the program, is the participant using a more planned approach to decision making (taking more time to define the problem and develop an answer)?	40, 14	50, 71	10, 7	0, 0	0, 0	0, 7
Since the program, does the participant take more time to evaluate the results of a decision?	24, 3	60, 62	14, 12	3, 0	0, 0	0, 24

Table 15.8. Initiating Change

	Frequently	Sometimes	Hardly ever
Before the program, when the need for change arose, how often did the participant ask his or her subordinate for suggestions or ideas regarding the change or need for change?	21, 21	64, 52	14, 21
Before the program, how often did the participant inform his or her employees of the change and the reason for it?	50, 26	36, 55	14, 14

	Much more	Somewhat more	No change	Somewhat less	Much less	Don't know
Since the program, is the participant doing more follow-up to the change process to make sure it is going in the right direction?	38, 17	50, 60	12, 12	0, 0	0, 0	0, 12
Since the program, how often has the participant involved his or her subordinates by asking them for suggestions or ideas?	17, 2	43, 40	40, 38	0, 7	0, 0	0, 12
Since the program, is the participant doing more in the way of informing employees of impending change and the reasons for it?	33, 10	38, 45	29, 26	0, 2	0, 0	0, 17

Summary and Conclusions

Because this program is repeated a number of times a year, it was worthwhile to spend the time and money that it takes to do a detailed evaluation. It was rewarding to find such positive responses from both the participants and their immediate supervisors. Because it was not possible to measure behavior and results on a before-and-after basis, the evaluation design took the alternative approach: to determine how behavior and results after the program differed from what they had been before the program.

The important thing for the reader of this case study is not what the researchers found out as a result of the research but what they did. You can borrow the design and approach and use it as is or modify it to meet your own situation. For example, you may want to add another set of interviews with subordinates of the participant and/or others who are in a position to observe the behavior of participants. You may even want to use a control group to eliminate other factors that could have caused changes in either behavior or results. In any case, consider evaluating in terms of behavior and even results, especially if the program is going to be repeated a number of times in the future.

Chapter 16

Evaluating a Leadership Training Program

This case illustrates an organized approach to evaluating a leadership training program at all four levels. Forms and procedures are included as well as the results of the evaluation. The approach can be adapted to any type of organization.

Gap Inc.

Don Kraft, Manager, Corporate Training
Gap Inc., San Bruno, California

Introduction: Why Leadership Training?

In 1994 the need for leadership training was identified for the store manager level for the Gap, GapKids, Banana Republic, and International divisions of Gap Inc. The focus was on supervisory and leadership skills—how to influence and interact with store employees.

The program selected to meet this need was Leadership Training for Supervisors (LTS). By providing store managers the opportunity to attend LTS, managers would not only improve their performance with supervisory and leadership skills, but job satisfaction would also increase.

As one manager shared after attending LTS, "This was the most rewarding experience I've had with the company in my four years as a manager." Equally important, LTS would also provide managers with the necessary tools for developing people so the business could remain competitive and continue to grow.

Getting to Level 4 Evaluation

Program

The LTS program was developed through a partnership between Blanchard Training and Development (BTD) and Gap Inc. Corporate Training Department. The content and delivery were customized to be applicable to the needs of the company. The three-day program focuses on the Situational Leadership® II model, as well as communication skills, goal setting, action planning, monitoring performance, giving feedback, and providing recognition.

The program continues, and training occurs throughout all divisions of the organization. The widespread use of one program connects employees at Gap Inc. by providing a shared philosophy and common language.

Audience

In 1994, the program roll-out began and included general managers, area managers, district managers, and regional managers for Gap, Gap-Kids, Banana Republic, and International divisions. In 1995 and 1996, LTS was rolled out to store managers. The program continues today, focusing on new store managers and the additional participation of general managers from Gap Inc.'s division, Old Navy.

Evaluation Strategy

From the onset of planning the 1995 roll-out to store managers, Gap Inc. Corporate Training Department was committed to evaluating the effectiveness of the LTS program. The evaluation strategy included measuring the program's effectiveness on four levels:

1. *Level 1: Evaluating Reaction.* Determining participants' initial *reactions* to the LTS program: Were they satisfied with the program?
2. *Level 2: Evaluating Learning.* Determining if participants *learned* the fundamental concepts of Situational Leadership® II during the program: What new knowledge was acquired as a result of attending the program?
3. *Level 3: Evaluating Behavior.* Determining participants' *change in behavior* since attending the LTS program: How has the program affected on-the-job performance?
4. *Level 4: Evaluating Organizational Results.* Determining the *impact* of the LTS program on the company: How has the program contributed to accomplishing company goals?

Evaluation Methods

Level 1: Evaluating Reaction

Participant reaction was evaluated both qualitatively and quantitatively using the LTS Program Evaluation form. Each participant completed an LTS program evaluation at the end of the program. See Exhibit 16.1 for the LTS Program Evaluation questionnaire, grouped with the other exhibits at the end of the chapter.

Level 2: Evaluating Learning

Participant learning was evaluated using the LTS Questionnaire. The LTS Questionnaire is a "fill-in-the-blank" test with fifty-five possible answers (see Exhibit 16.2). A sample of 17 percent of total participants completed the questionnaire at the end of the LTS program. The questionnaire was completed anonymously. While completing the questionnaire, participants were not permitted to use any notes or program materials. Results were then aggregated by division.

The facilitators who delivered the program received detailed written and verbal instructions on how to administer the questionnaire. Participants were told on the first day of the training that a questionnaire would be administered to determine the effectiveness of the LTS program.

The LTS Questionnaire was scored on a percentage basis by the number of correct answers. Each blank was equal to one point. All questionnaires were scored by Gap Inc. Corporate Training Department.

Level 3: Evaluating Behavior

Short-Term Behavior Change. Behavior change was measured quantitatively by interviewing participants and their direct reports using the LTS Post-Program Survey. A random sample of 17 percent of total participants from each division was selected for this evaluation method. See Exhibits 16.3 and 16.4 for LTS Post Program Surveys.

The LTS Post-Program Survey is an absolute rating scale survey of twelve questions. There are two versions of the survey. A store manager version was completed by interviewing the managers who attended the program no less than three months prior to the interview. A second version, with the same question content, was completed by interviewing two to three of the store managers' direct reports. The results of the survey determined managers' perception of changes in behavior since attending LTS as well as perceptions of their direct reports.

Division facilitators completed the survey by conducting telephone interviews without recording participants' or direct reports' names. Results were aggregated by division, not by individual. No names or store numbers were used in the results. All completed interview surveys were mailed to Gap Inc. Corporate Training Department.

Long-Term Behavior Change. Leadership skills assessments were administered to store managers' direct reports prior to the training as well as six to nine months after attendance. Quantitative results were determined by comparing the pre–leadership skills assessment score with the post–leadership skills assessment score. See Exhibit 16.5 for the Leadership Skills Assessment questionnaire.

This evaluation method measured the percent of change between pre- and postassessment, specifically for eight skill areas—directing, coaching, supporting, delegating, goal setting, observing performance, providing feedback, and communication.

Level 4: Evaluating Organizational Results

To investigate the impact LTS had on organizational results, Gap Inc. Corporate Training Department, in partnership with Blanchard Training and Development, conducted an impact study to determine if improvement in leadership and supervisory skills had a positive impact on areas such as store sales, employee turnover rates, and shrinkage.

Sales. It was assumed that if the leadership skills of store managers improved, employee performance would improve, customers would be served better, and sales would increase.

Employee Turnover Rates. Studies indicate that recruitment, hiring, and on-the-job training costs are about 1.5 times the first-year salary for a job. Therefore, any training intervention that reduces turnover contributes directly to the bottom line.

Shrinkage. It was also assumed that by improving store managers' effectiveness, shrinkage as a percent of sales should go down.

Interpreting LTS Results

Level 1: Reaction

When reviewing the averages from the LTS program evaluation (Exhibit 16.1), use the following ranges as guidelines for responses to *expectations, relevance, facilitator's presentation,* and *overall program.*

Range	Interpretation
1–2	Participants had serious concerns about the training.
Low–mid 3	Training provided some value, but could have been better.
High 3–4	Participants found real value in the training and indicated a positive reaction.
High 4–5	Outstanding! Participants indicated strong positive reaction.

Use the following ranges as guidelines for responses to *appropriate for skill level.*

Range	Interpretation
1–2	Participants' reactions indicated the material of the program was entirely too elementary.
2–3	Participants' reactions indicated the material of the program was somewhat elementary.

3	Participants found the material "just right" for their skill level.
3–4	Participants' reactions indicated the material was somewhat advanced.
4–5	Participants' reactions indicated the material was entirely too advanced.

Use the following ranges as guidelines for responses to *pace of program*.

Range	*Interpretation*
1–2	Participants' reactions indicated the pace of the program was entirely too quick.
2–3	Participants' reactions indicated some sections were covered too quickly.
3	Participants' reactions indicated the pace was "just right."
3–4	Participants' reactions indicated certain sections were covered too slowly.
4–5	Participants' reactions indicated the pace of the program was entirely too slow.

Figure 16.1 shows the results of LTS Program Evaluation. Table 16.1 shows a breakdown of these results. Store managers attending the LTS program responded to the training with incredible enthusiasm. They reacted favorably; their expectations were met and the training

Figure 16.1. LTS Program Evaluation Results (all sessions)

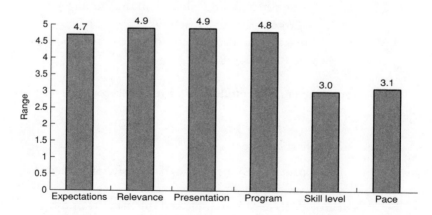

Table 16.1. LTS Program Evaluation Results, by Division

Category	All divisions	Gap	GapKids	Banana Republic	Canada	UK
Average of expectations	4.7	4.7	4.7	4.7	4.7	4.6
Average of relevance	4.9	4.9	4.9	4.9	4.9	4.8
Average of presentation	4.9	4.9	4.8	4.9	4.8	4.7
Average of program	4.8	4.8	4.7	4.7	4.8	4.6
Average of skill level	3.0	3.0	2.9	3.0	3.0	3.0
Average of pace	3.1	3.1	3.2	3.2	3.2	3.2

was relevant to the job. Reaction was also extremely positive to the overall program and the facilitators' presentation of the material.

As regards appropriateness of material for store manager skill level and the overall pace of the program, store managers responded overwhelmingly positively, with "just right" to both questions.

Interpreting Level 2: Learning

Although store manager reaction was extremely positive, the question to ask was, Did they *learn* while attending the session? The following guidelines were used to interpret learning scores from the LTS sessions:

Range	Interpretation
Less than 50%	More than half of the participants did not increase their knowledge.
50–60%	Little over half the participants improved their knowledge.
60–80%	The majority of participants gained new knowledge as a result of the training.
80–100%	Outstanding! Almost all participants gained new knowledge.

The results from the LTS Questionnaire shown in Figure 16.2 indicate that significant learning did occur during the program. *The average score for all divisions from the LTS Questionnaire was 87 percent.* Store managers were unfamiliar with LTS concepts before attending the session. The score of 87 percent indicates that new learnings were used to successfully complete the LTS Questionnaire.

Figure 16.2. LTS Questionnaire Results

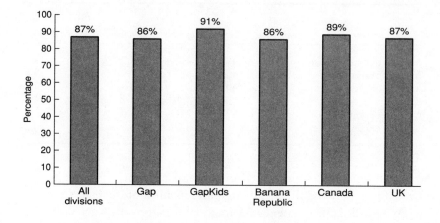

Interpreting Level 3: Change in Behavior (Short Term)

Store managers' reactions were positive, and significant learning occurred during the training. Now the question to ask was, Did the
managers *change* their behavior on the job as a result of the training?

The LTS Post-Program Survey measured the degree to which
managers' behaviors changed in twelve skill areas, according to their
own perceptions as well as their direct reports' perceptions. Each of
the survey questions focuses on a skill from the LTS program. Following are the skills surveyed:

Skill	*Interpretation*
1. Diagnosing	The ability to look at a situation and assess the developmental needs of the employee involved.
2. Leadership styles	The patterns of behavior a leader uses as perceived by others.
3. Flexibility	The ability to use a variety of leadership styles comfortably.
4. Direction	What supervisors use to build an employee's knowledge and skills with accomplishing a task.
5. Support	What supervisors use to build an employee's commitment, both confidence and motivation.

6. Contracting   The ability to communicate with employees and reach agreement about which leadership style to use to help them develop competence and commitment to achieve a goal or complete a task.

7. Receiver skills   Supervisors in this role can make communication effective by encouraging dialogue, concentrating, clarifying, and confirming a sender's message.

8. Sender skills   Supervisors in this role can make communication effective by analyzing their audience, being specific, and using appropriate body language and tone.

9. Goal setting   A function of leadership for ensuring standards are clarified. A clear goal creates a picture of what good performance looks like.

10. Positive feedback   Positive feedback focuses on the employee's positive behavior.

11. Constructive feedback   Constructive feedback focuses on the employee's behavior that needs improvement.

12. Providing recognition   Reinforcing desired performance by acknowledging progress and celebrating accomplishments.

When looking over the results of the Post-Program Survey shown in Tables 16.2 and 16.3, the following ranges can be used as guidelines:

Range	*Interpretation*
Less than 4	No improvement. In fact, since attending LTS the participant's leadership behavior has changed for the worse.
4–5	Some measurable improvement did take place back in the stores. Store managers are somewhat better with using the skill since attending LTS. This is a positive change in behavior.
Greater than 5	Any rating in this range is very positive and indicates the store manager improved dramatically in using the skill they learned since attending LTS.

Table 16.2. LTS Post-Program Survey Results (all interviews)

Skill	Store managers	Assistant/associate managers
1. Diagnosing	5.3	5.0
2. Leadership style	5.1	5.0
3. Flexibility	4.9	4.9
4. Direction	5.1	4.9
5. Support	5.2	5.0
6. Contracting	4.8	4.9
7. Receiver skills	5.1	5.0
8. Sender skills	4.9	4.8
9. Goal setting	5.0	4.9
10. Positive feedback	4.9	4.9
11. Constructive feedback	5.0	4.9
12. Providing recognition	5.0	5.0

As seen in Table 16.3, store managers believe they have become "somewhat better" to "much better" in using all of the leadership skills included in the program. Specifically, store managers believe they have significantly improved their leadership skills in four areas:

1. *Diagnosing* the development level of their employees
2. Using the correct *leadership style* with each development level
3. Providing *direction* to employees when needed
4. Providing *support* to employees when needed

Table 16.3 also illustrates associate and assistant managers' perceptions of their store manager. All responses indicate a dramatic improvement in leadership skills since the managers attended LTS. In fact, five out of the twelve questions asked have an average score of five.

Interpreting Level 3: Change in Behavior (Long Term)

As store managers continued to focus on developing their supervisory and leadership skills, measurement of their ongoing success continued. In 1996, store managers participated in the post–leadership skills assessment.

Table 16.3. LTS Post-Program Survey
Results (all interviews), by Division

	Store Managers						Associate/Assistant Managers					
Skill	All	Gap	GapKids	Banana Republic	Canada	UK	All	Gap	GapKids	Banana Republic	Canada	UK
Diagnosing	5.3	5.5	5.1	5.1	5.0	5.7	5.0	5.1	5.0	5.0	4.6	4.9
Leadership styles	5.1	5.3	5.0	4.9	5.0	5.3	5.0	5.1	5.0	5.0	4.8	5.1
Flexibility	4.9	4.9	4.9	4.9	4.3	5.0	4.9	5.0	4.8	4.9	4.3	4.7
Direction	5.1	5.2	4.9	4.9	5.0	5.2	4.9	5.0	4.8	4.9	4.3	5.0
Support	5.2	5.3	4.9	5.0	5.3	5.2	5.0	5.1	5.0	5.0	4.6	5.0
Contracting	4.8	4.9	4.6	4.7	4.5	4.9	4.9	4.9	4.9	4.8	4.4	4.9
Receiver skills	5.1	5.1	5.1	5.1	5.0	5.2	5.0	5.1	5.2	4.8	4.9	4.9
Sender skills	4.9	5.0	4.9	4.9	4.5	5.2	4.8	4.8	4.9	4.7	4.9	4.9
Goal setting	5.0	5.0	4.7	5.1	4.5	5.3	4.9	4.9	4.8	4.8	4.6	4.7
Positive feedback	4.9	5.0	4.8	5.0	4.0	5.0	4.9	4.9	4.8	4.7	4.6	5.1
Constructive feedback	5.0	5.1	4.9	4.9	5.0	5.1	4.9	5.0	4.7	5.0	5.0	4.7
Providing recognition	5.0	4.9	5.2	4.9	4.8	4.9	5.0	5.1	5.1	4.8	4.9	4.7

A comparison of all pre- and posttraining leadership skills assessment (LSA) results indicated that according to store employees, store managers had improved in all skill areas measured by the LSA—namely, directing, coaching, supporting, delegating, goal setting, observing and monitoring performance, feedback, and communication. In fact, seven of the eight skill areas included in the assessment showed improvement at a statistically significant level. In other words, the odds of the increased effectiveness occurring by chance were highly improbable, or less than 50 in 1,000. In summary, this important information indicated that store managers had actually changed their behavior as a result of the training.

Interpreting Level 4: Evaluating Organizational Results

Store managers' reactions were positive, new learnings occurred during the training, and behaviors changed on the job since attending LTS. The next question was, How has the training contributed to organizational results?

Recent statistical analyses have revealed positive correlation between improved LSA scores and increased sales, decreased turnover, and increased loss prevention in stores from which managers attended the training. The study examined stores with increased sales, reduced turnover, and reduced shrinkage that had the same managers in place one year prior to the training and one to one and a half years after attending LTS.

For each month, quarter, or year of store performance data examined, the number of managers with increased sales, reduced turnover, and reduced shrinkage was compared with the number of managers with increased LSA scores and increased performance on these three measures. Of the stores with increased sales, reduced turnover, and reduced shrinkage, 50 to 80 percent of the time managers had also increased their LSA scores. In other words, store managers increased their leadership effectiveness and had a positive impact on store performance.

Over time (one to two years after training), the trend in the data is also very positive; the percentage of store managers with improved LSA scores and positive business results steadily increases.

Summary

On four levels of evaluation, LTS was a success. Store managers

1. Had a positive reaction to the LTS program
2. Learned new skills and knowledge while attending the program
3. Used those learnings to improve their performance as leaders on the job
4. Impacted their stores' business

Exhibit 16.1. LTS Program Evaluation

Please help us evaluate the Leadership Training for Supervisors Program by answering the following questions. Give the completed evaluation to your facilitator(s), who will then forward your comments to the Training Department. Your candid feedback will be key in creating a strategy for future roll-out of the program and in improving its facilitation.

	Entirely ineffective			*Very effective*	
1. Rate how well this program met your expectations. Comments:	1	2	3	4	5
2. Rate the relevance of the program to your job. Comments:	1	2	3	4	5
3. Rate how helpful the *Participant's Workbook* was as an in-class tool. Comments:	1	2	3	4	5
4. Do you think you will refer to the *Participant's Workbook* at a later time? If Yes, how?	Yes			No	

5. What three key skills will you apply immediately?

   a.

   b.

   c.

6. What is the most significant thing(s) you learned about:

   • Leadership

   • Coaching and developing employees

   • Communication

   • Goal setting and action planning

   • Monitoring performance

   • Problem solving and decision making

   • Recognizing accomplishments

Exhibit 16.1. LTS Program Evaluation *(continued)*

---

7. Overall, was the material appropriate for your skill level? Select the best response.

_____ Entirely too elementary

_____ Somewhat elementary

_____ Just right

_____ Somewhat advanced

_____ Entirely too advanced

Please comment:

8. Overall, how was the pace of the program? Select the best response.

_____ Entirely too quick

_____ Some sections were covered too quickly

_____ Just right

_____ Certain sections were covered too slowly

_____ Entirely too slow

Please comment:

	Entirely ineffective			*Very effective*	
9. How effectively did the activities (i.e., role-plays, games, and practices) reinforce the concepts discussed? Which activities did you find interesting? Dull? Challenging? Overly simple? Please comment:	1	2	3	4	5

10. How would you improve this program?

	Poor	*Good*	*Excellent*		
11. Overall, how do you rate this program?	1	2	3	4	5
12. Overall, how do you rate the facilitator's presentations?	1	2	3	4	5

13. Additional comments:

Exhibit 16.2. LTS Questionnaire

Check your division: Gap _____   GapKids _____   Banana Republic _____

UK _____   Canada _____

Check your manager level: District manager _____   Store manager _____

General manager _____   Area manager _____

Complete the following questions by filling in the blanks.

1. What are the three skills that situational leaders use when working to develop people to eventually manage themselves?

    1. _____

    2. _____

    3. _____

2. A person at D2 (Disillusioned Learner) has _____ competence and _____ commitment.

3. Diagnose the development level of the individual in this situation.

    Eric has begun working on a merchandising project that is important to his store. He has successfully completed previous merchandising projects in the past but feels there is some pressure on him. He is already involved in other projects and is beginning to feel discouraged because of the time crunch.

    Eric's development level on this project is _____ .

4. Competence is a measure of a person's _____ and _____ related to the task or goal at hand.

5. Describe what a style 4 leader (Delegating) does. List three behaviors/actions you would see a style 4 leader take.

    1. _____

    2. _____

    3. _____

6. A person at D4 (Peak Performer) has _____ competence and _____ commitment.

7. In order to listen well, a supervisor must concentrate. What are two examples of concentration techniques?

    1. _____

    2. _____

8. Commitment is a measure of a person's _____ and _____ with regard to the task or goal at hand.

9. Describe what a style 2 leader (Coaching) does. List three behaviors/actions you would see a style 2 leader take.

    1. _____

    2. _____

    3. _____

Exhibit 16.2. LTS Questionnaire *(continued)*

---

10. Define "leadership."

11. Who takes the lead in goal setting, feedback, decision making, and problem solving in leadership styles 1 and 2?

12. A person at D1 (Enthusiastic Beginner) has _____ competence and _____ commitment.

13. Define the acronym for a SMART goal.

    S _____

    M _____

    A _____

    R _____

    T _____

14. When contracting, whose perception should prevail if a supervisor and employee do not agree on the same development level?

15. Describe what a style 3 leader (Supporting) does. List three behaviors/actions you would see a style 3 leader take.

    1. _____

    2. _____

    3. _____

16. To create a positive interaction with an employee, a supervisor's attention must be focused on _____ and _____ .

17. List four examples of what you see someone doing or hear someone saying to be a good listener.

    1. _____

    2. _____

    3. _____

    4. _____

18. When monitoring performance, supervisors reinforce performance standards by using three methods of giving feedback. They are _____ , _____ , and _____ .

19. Suppose you have a sales associate, Becky, who needs to improve her listening skills. Create a goal for improving Becky's listening skills using the formula for a clear goal.

20. Encouraging dialogue means using attentive body language. What are two examples of attentive body language?

    1. _____

    2. _____

Exhibit 16.2. LTS Questionnaire *(continued)*

---

21. Interactions a supervisor has with an employee that have a positive or negative impact on that person's performance and satisfaction are called

    _____ .

22. A person at D3 (Emerging Contributor) has _____ and _____ commitment.

23. Describe what a style 1 leader (Directing) does. List three behaviors/actions you would see a style 1 leader take.

    1. _____

    2. _____

    3. _____

24. When communicating, a sender sends a message three ways:

    1. _____

    2. _____

    3. _____

25. Who takes the lead in goal setting, feedback, decision making, and problem solving in leadership styles 3 and 4?

Exhibit 16.3. LTS Post-Program Survey: Store Manager Version

Store Manager _____ Division _____

This survey is designed to describe your experiences with your employees since completing the LTS program. Please answer the questions by identifying the number that corresponds to your response.

	Much better	Somewhat better	No change	Somewhat worse	Much worse	Don't know

Since attending the LTS program,

1. How would you describe your ability to look at a situation and assess the development level of your employees? (e.g., skills, knowledge, past experience, interest, confidence level, etc.)

	6	5	4	3	2	1

   Comments:

2. How effective are you with choosing the most appropriate leadership style to use to develop your employees' skills and motivation?

	6	5	4	3	2	1

   Comments:

3. How would you describe your ability to use a variety of the four leadership styles comfortably?

	6	5	4	3	2	1

   Comments:

4. How is your ability to provide direction? (e.g., setting clear goals, training, setting priorities, defining standards, etc.)

	6	5	4	3	2	1

   Comments:

5. How is your ability to provide support? (e.g., praising, trusting employees, explaining why, listening, allowing mistakes, encouraging, etc.)

	6	5	4	3	2	1

   Comments:

6. How is your ability to reach agreement with your employees about the leadership style they need from you in order to complete a task or goal?

	6	5	4	3	2	1

   Comments:

Exhibit 16.3. LTS Post-Program Survey: Store Manager Version *(continued)*

	Much better	Somewhat better	No change	Somewhat worse	Much worse	Don't know
7. To what extent have your listening skills changed? (e.g., encouraging dialogue, concentrating, clarifying, and confirming) Comments:	6	5	4	3	2	1
8. How would you describe your ability to communicate information in a clear and specific manner? Comments:	6	5	4	3	2	1
9. How are your skills with creating clear goals with your employees? Comments:	6	5	4	3	2	1
10. How would you describe your ability to provide timely, significant, and specific *positive* feedback? Comments:	6	5	4	3	2	1
11. How would your describe your ability to provide timely, significant, and specific *constructive* feedback? Comments:	6	5	4	3	2	1
12. To what extent have you changed with providing recognition for employee accomplishments? Comments:	6	5	4	3	2	1

Exhibit 16.4. LTS Post-Program Survey:
Associate/Assistant Manager Version

Associate/Assistant Manager_____ Division _____

This survey is designed to describe your experiences with your store manager since their completing the LTS program. Please answer the questions by identifying the number that corresponds to your response.

	Much better	Somewhat better	No change	Somewhat worse	Much worse	Don't know

Since your store manager attended
the LTS program,

1. How would you describe their ability
   to look at a situation and assess your skills,
   knowledge, past experience, interest,
   confidence level, etc.?

   | | 6 | 5 | 4 | 3 | 2 | 1 |

   Comments:

2. How effective have they been with
   helping you develop your skills
   and motivating you?

   | | 6 | 5 | 4 | 3 | 2 | 1 |

   Comments:

3. How would you describe their ability
   to use a "different strokes for different
   folks" approach when helping you
   accomplish a task or goal?

   | | 6 | 5 | 4 | 3 | 2 | 1 |

   Comments:

4. How would you describe their ability
   to provide you direction when needed?
   (e.g., setting clear goals, training, setting
   priorities, defining standards, etc.)

   | | 6 | 5 | 4 | 3 | 2 | 1 |

   Comments:

5. How would you describe their ability
   to provide you support when needed?
   (e.g., praising, trusting, explaining
   why, listening, allowing mistakes,
   encouraging, etc.)

   | | 6 | 5 | 4 | 3 | 2 | 1 |

   Comments:

6. How is their ability to reach agreement
   with you about what you need in order
   to complete a task or goal?

   | | 6 | 5 | 4 | 3 | 2 | 1 |

   Comments:

Exhibit 16.4. LTS Post-Program Survey:
Associate/Assistant Manager Version *(continued)*

	Much better	Somewhat better	No change	Somewhat worse	Much worse	Don't know
7. To what extent do they listen to what you say? Comments:	6	5	4	3	2	1
8. How would you describe their ability to communicate information that is clear and specific? Comments:	6	5	4	3	2	1
9. How have their skills changed with creating clear goals with you? Comments:	6	5	4	3	2	1
10. How would you describe their ability to provide timely, significant, and specific *positive* feedback? Comments:	6	5	4	3	2	1
11. How would you describe their ability to provide timely, significant, and specific *constructive* feedback? Comments:	6	5	4	3	2	1
12. To what extent have they changed with recognizing your accomplishments? Comments:	6	5	4	3	2	1

Exhibit 16.5. Situational Leadership® II
Leadership Skills Assessment

Directions: The purpose of the Situational Leadership® II Leadership Skills Assessment is to provide feedback to your immediate supervisor or manager on his/her use of Situational Leadership® II. Because your responses will be used by your supervisor or manager in his/her professional development, your honest and accurate evaluations are crucial.

The information you and others provide will be analyzed by computer, and the results will be provided to your manager in summary form so that no individual responses are identified. To ensure confidentiality, *do not put your name* on the questionnaire, but make sure that your *manager's name* is on the LSA questionnaire.

Assume that the person who gave you this questionnaire is the supervisor/manager described in each of the thirty situations. For each situation, mark the point on the scale that you think best describes your supervisor's/manager's recent behavior. Mark *only one* choice. *Please answer all questions. Do not leave any blank.* Choose the answer that is closest to how you believe your manager would respond. Be sure to read each question carefully.

At most, this questionnaire should take twenty-five minutes to complete. Once you have completed the questionnaire, put it in the envelope and mail it back to Blanchard Training and Development, Inc., today.

Manager's or supervisor's name: _____ Date: _____

Mail by: _____

	Never	Rarely	Sometimes	Frequently	Almost always	Always
1. When I am able to perform a task and am confident in my ability to do so, I am given the flexibility to determine the best way to accomplish it.	1	2	3	4	5	6
2. When I am new to a particular task and learning how to do it, my manager provides me with enough direction.	1	2	3	4	5	6
3. If I am making progress but become discouraged in learning a new task, my manager tends to encourage me.	1	2	3	4	5	6
4. When I know I have the skills to complete a task but feel apprehensive about an assignment, my manager listens to my concerns and supports my ideas.	1	2	3	4	5	6
5. When I begin to learn how to complete a task and develop some skill with it, my manager listens to my input on how to better accomplish the task.	1	2	3	4	5	6

Exhibit 16.5. Situational Leadership® II
Leadership Skills Assessment *(continued)*

	Never	Rarely	Sometimes	Frequently	Almost always	Always
6. If I have shown I can do a job, but lack confidence, my manager encourages me to take the lead in setting my own goals.	1	2	3	4	5	6
8. When I have demonstrated expertise in my job but am not confident about making a particular decision, my manager helps me problem-solve and supports my ideas.	1	2	3	4	5	6
9. If I have not performed at an acceptable level while learning a new task, my manager shows and tells me once again how to do the job.	1	2	3	4	5	6
10. When I get frustrated while learning a new task, my manager listens to my concerns and provides additional help.	1	2	3	4	5	6
11. My manager delegates more responsibility to me when I have demonstrated the ability to perform at a high level.	1	2	3	4	5	6
12. When I begin to learn new skills and become discouraged, my manager spends time with me to know what I am thinking.	1	2	3	4	5	6
13. When I am new to a task, my manager sets goals that tell me exactly what is expected of me and what a good job looks like.	1	2	3	4	5	6
14. To encourage me, my manager praises my work in areas where I have skills and experience but am not totally confident.	1	2	3	4	5	6
15. When I have shown I can do my job well, my manager spends less time observing and monitoring my performance.	1	2	3	4	5	6
16. When I am new to a task, my manager tells me specifically how to do it.	1	2	3	4	5	6
17. When I have developed some skill with a task, my manager asks for input on how he/she wants me to accomplish it.	1	2	3	4	5	6
18. Once I have learned a task and am working more independently, my manager encourages me to use my own ideas.	1	2	3	4	5	6

Exhibit 16.5. Situational Leadership® II
Leadership Skills Assessment *(continued)*

	Never	Rarely	Sometimes	Frequently	Almost always	Always
19. When I am confident, motivated, and have the skills, my manager only meets with me once in a while to tell me how well I am doing.	1	2	3	4	5	6
20. When I am learning a new task, my manager frequently observes me doing my job.	1	2	3	4	5	6
21. When I am performing a task well, my manager lets me set my own goals.	1	2	3	4	5	6
22. When I am learning how to do a new task, my manager provides me with timely feedback on how well I am doing.	1	2	3	4	5	6
23. When I feel overwhelmed and confused with completing a new task, my manager is supportive and provides me with enough direction to proceed.	1	2	3	4	5	6
24. My manager observes my performance closely enough in areas where I have skills so if I lose confidence or interest, he/she is there to help me.	1	2	3	4	5	6
25. When communicating information or feedback to me, my manager is clear and specific.	1	2	3	4	5	6
26. When talking to me, my manager's tone is positive and respectful.	1	2	3	4	5	6
27. If my manager is unsure of what I am saying, he/she asks questions to clarify my message.	1	2	3	4	5	6
28. When I talk to my manager, he/she listens to me and does not get distracted.	1	2	3	4	5	6
29. During conversations, my manager restates and asks questions about what I said to avoid miscommunication.	1	2	3	4	5	6
30. My manager is able to communicate with me in a way that gets his/her message across while keeping my self-esteem intact.	1	2	3	4	5	6

Source: Reprinted with permission by Blanchard Training and Development, Inc., Escondido, CA.

Chapter 17

Evaluating a Training Program on Problem Solving

This program was conducted at the City of Los Angeles and was evaluated at levels 1 and 3. Of special interest will be the recommendations for improvements in evaluating future programs. For example, specific suggestions are offered on how to conduct a patterned interview to measure level 3.

City of Los Angeles

Selwyn Hollins, Personnel Department,
City of Los Angeles

Jane Holcomb, On-Target Training,
Playa Del Rey, California

Purpose

The Personnel Department of the City of Los Angeles was given a large sum of money to develop training for city employees. The population includes forty city departments and 40,000 employees. The city hired an outside consulting firm to do an extensive needs assessment, which included interview, focus groups, and surveys. The needs assessment identified eight topics or areas for development that were relevant, important, and needed by city employees. Since the city has only four people in the Personnel Training Department, all of the programs were contracted to external consultants.

Jane Holcomb, a consultant with expertise in evaluation, was hired to work with Selwyn Hollins from Personnel to evaluate the eight programs. They decided to do a level 1 evaluation for all of the programs and choose one program on which to do a level 3 evaluation. The purpose of the level 1 evaluation was to determine the effectiveness of the program and help the external consultants improve their programs based on feedback from the participants. In one case, the decision was made to replace a consultant, based on the level 1 evaluation results. The purpose of the level 3 evaluation was to gather data to determine to what extent the ideas and concepts learned in training were used by participants back on the job. This would be communicated to the City Council.

Level 1 Evaluation

The level 1 evaluation asked questions regarding the curriculum and the instructor that were quantifiable on a Likert scale from 1 through 5. Exhibit 17.1 is a copy of the reaction sheet that was used, including the reactions, comments, and suggestions from the participants.

Level 3 Evaluation

The level 3 evaluation was used on the Analytical Skills Program, which is a five-day program covering research and analysis, data compilation, and problem solving. We chose the Problem-Solving class for the pilot evaluation. The Problem-Solving class was divided into groups of five to six people working together. Each person submitted a problem idea to their group. They chose one problem to work on as a team. The rest of the day was focused on how to solve problems, with each team working on their selected problem.

To conduct our level 3 evaluation, we did a telephone interview with each person whose problem was used. That meant interviewing four to five people from each class. The interviews were done three to four months after the program.

A phone call was made to the selected participants by the program evaluator, who was an objective outsider. Each telephone interview took about thirty minutes. The interviewer asked, "Do you remember the Problem-Solving class you attended on September 10th? I'm calling to follow up on that training program to find out if the training is making a difference on the job. I understand from your instructor that your team chose to work on your problem. Could you tell me about it and what happened since you left class?"

Recommendations

As a result of the pilot evaluation, we plan to do the following:

- Evaluate all eight programs.
- Continue to evaluate level 1 with each class using the same reaction sheet.
- Create a simple one-page test for level 2 evaluation to determine understanding of main concepts.
- Conduct interviews via telephone three to four months after the program.
- Interview six participants from each class. This will be a 20 percent representation.
- Create and use a more structured interview (patterned interview) so that the answers can be quantified.

For the patterned interview, Kirkpatrick suggests that the following questions be directly related to program objectives:

1. To what extent have you applied the knowledge and skills taught in the program? (refer to specific subject matter)
   _____ To a great extent   _____ To some extent
   _____ Not at all
2. If you answered "to a great extent" or "to some extent" on item 1, please describe how you have applied this knowledge/skills.
3. If you answered "not at all" to item 1, please say why you haven't applied the knowledge and skills that were taught. So

that we can be more effective in accomplishing program objectives, please indicate which of the following conditions apply:

_____ I didn't really learn anything I can apply.

_____ I haven't had the opportunity.

_____ I have been too busy—too many higher priorities.

_____ My boss has prevented or discouraged me from changing.

_____ Any other reason? Please specify.

4. Do you plan to use some of the knowledge and skills in the future? If yes, please be specific.

5. As you think back on the program, what would have made it more helpful for you?

It is important that the tone of this interview is geared toward improving future programs, not to put participants on the defensive.

Exhibit 17.1. Training Program Evaluation

Program Title: Analytical Skills Program
Instructor: Linda Mundel, CDSNet, Inc.

Module: Problem Solving and Decision Making
Date: September 10, 1997

	Total respondents	High 5	4	Medium 3	2	Low 1	Average rating
Curriculum							
1. The program's goals and objectives were clearly stated.	20	6 / 30%	7 / 35%	6 / 30%	1 / 5%	0 / 0%	3.9
2. The topics discussed were relevant to my current job responsibilities.	21	8 / 38%	5 / 24%	7 / 33%	1 / 5%	0 / 0%	4.0
3. The course materials contributed to the learning process and will serve as a valuable resource.	20	7 / 35%	7 / 35%	4 / 20%	2 / 10%	0 / 0%	4.0
4. The program enhanced my knowledge and understanding of problem solving and decision making.	20	7 / 35%	8 / 40%	5 / 25%	0 / 0%	0 / 0%	4.1
5. The course met my expectations.	16	3 / 19%	5 / 31%	5 / 31%	3 / 19%	0 / 0%	3.5
Instruction							
6. The instructor was able to competently answer participants' questions.	20	8 / 40%	9 / 45%	3 / 15%	0 / 0%	0 / 0%	4.3
7. The method of instruction was appropriate for this program.	21	7 / 33%	7 / 33%	6 / 29%	1 / 5%	0 / 0%	4.0
8. The instructor made the subject matter interesting.	21	8 / 38%	7 / 33%	5 / 24%	1 / 5%	0 / 0%	4.0
9. The instructor encouraged participant involvement.	21	14 / 67%	5 / 24%	2 / 10%	0 / 0%	0 / 0%	4.6

Exhibit 17.1. Training Program Evaluation (continued)

	Total respondents	High 5	4	Medium 3	2	Low 1	Average rating
10. The instructor was professional and demonstrated a thorough knowledge of the subject.	21	9 43%	9 43%	3 14%	0 0%	0 0%	4.3
11. Please provide your overall evaluation of this training.	25	12 48%	7 28%	6 24%	0 0%	0 0%	4.2

12. If you answered Low (1 or 2) to any of the above, please explain.

"A single project 'walk through' by the instructor would have been a more effective demonstration of the techniques provided for problem solving. The small self-led groups were too prone to stumble and miss parts of the presentation."

"The instructor didn't follow some course material—however, her explanation was fine. More explaining concepts and going into it as a class would be helpful. Subject matter was more interesting than the first courses in this series."

	Total respondents	High 5	4	Medium 3	2	Low 1	Average rating
Total Averages	21	39%	34%	23%	4%	0%	4.1

Work Experience

	Total respondents	Quantity 0–5	6–10	11–15	16–20	21–25	26+
13. How many years have you worked for the city?	21	2 10%	7 33%	4 19%	7 33%	0 0%	1 5%

	Total respondents	1	2	3	4	5	6+
14. How many different departments have you worked in?	21	3 14%	8 38%	3 14%	5 24%	1 5%	1 5%

	Total respondents		Yes			No	
15. Have you had training like this in the past?	21		8 38%			13 62%	

Exhibit 17.1. Training Program Evaluation *(continued)*

16. Which topics or strategies did you find most helpful?
    "Problem-solving/decision-making outline."
    "None."
    "Brainstorming techniques."
    "Approaching a problem."
    "The brainstorming for potential solutions strategy was particularly helpful."
    "Steps of problem solving."
    "The combining of tasks and the process of 'bubble up, bubble down' as a
        method of prioritizing action to be taken."
    "Brainstorming. Making lists of symptoms/hard facts vs. soft facts."
    "Everything."
    "Determining worst possible outcome of each possible solution tried."
    "When you decide on solving a problem, look at the total cause without being
        one-sided on just seeing a problem from your view only."
    "The ideas about problem solving and brainstorming; class involvement
        was great."
    "The participation of group."
    "Data collection methods. Work groups."
    "Brainstorming, focusing on the actual problem, then the symptom, then the
        suggested solutions."

17. Which topics or strategies did you find least helpful?
    "None." (4)
    "All were interesting."
    "Sometimes topics to be discussed in group settings were unclear; led to
        discussions off-track."

18. Based on your work experience, what topics do you think should be added to
    the curriculum?
    "None." (3)
    "In-depth solutions to the problem."
    "Using statistics analysis for collected data, then solving the problems or reaching
        the solution."
    "I would like to have had name placards, and I would like to have known more
        about the instructor's background."
    "Most of the time, the time available to solve problems is scarce and the time
        factor could be addressed."
    "More handout directed, going over them one by one, good material and
        information but should cover them a little more."
    "Positive reinforcement techniques and methods."

19. How will you use the information presented?
    "I am going to sit down with my supervisor and explain how I am affected by
        not meeting the time frame re this procedure."
    "Probably will not."
    "Apply to difficult problems in the workplace, home, and church management."
    "Deal with a problem more objectively."
    "I will use it to deal with problems I am facing in profession *and* personal situations."
    "In future work."

Exhibit 17.1. Training Program Evaluation *(continued)*

"To problem-solve in my workplace. Additionally, I am an instructor for my
    department and I can pass on much of what I learned today in some
    of those courses."
"At work on current assignments, at school, anywhere applicable."
"If I have enough time, I'll use the methods learned to solve problems."
"Apply strategies."
"To view problems and solve them."
"The information to solve problems."
"Practice what was learned."
"To solve problems at work."
"To improve communications in my unit—morale/responsibility."

Chapter 18

Evaluating a Corporatewide Performance Improvement System

U nder the direction of Eric Freitag, evaluation is a continuous and integrated ingredient of training programs at Intel. This case study illustrates evaluation at all four levels. It begins with level 4, results, which is the reason for the training. The approach is very structured and measured in terms of objective data. The study describes specific forms and procedures that can be adapted to organizations serious about evaluation.

Intel Corporation

Eric Freitag, Manager
Intel University, Chandler, Arizona

Michael Harris, Training Evaluation Manager
Intel University, Chandler, Arizona

Introduction

In today's high-tech industries, innovations have life cycles of only a few years. At Intel, training is a key strategic tool that ensures the corporation meets the challenges of this very competitive environment.

Intel delivers an average of forty-five hours of training to each of its 60,000 employees. New employees (10,000+ hired in each of the last three years) are trained to ensure that Intel's strong culture stays alive. Engineers are trained (their knowledge base is outdated approximately every eighteen months) to guarantee that the next generation of microprocessors are designed and developed. Factory workers are trained and factories are set up in record times and with increasingly sophisticated equipment. Managers are trained in how to make correct strategic business decisions.

The importance of continuously training all employees has risen dramatically with the need for cycle-time reductions and therefore so has the need for improving our training through the use of evaluation. To meet Intel's business goals, training needs to be evaluated and continuously improved. Intel invests hundreds of millions of dollars per year in training. Currently, about 300,000 students attend one or more of the 43,000 sessions offered through Intel University. Given this great investment of time and money, senior management expectations are high that all training products and services will be provided at the lowest costs, the highest quality, and in the most timely manner.

Kirkpatrick has provided a model that is the basis for Intel's evaluation of its 3,000 courses. The data gathered from the evaluations are used to improve not only course content and instructor performance but also the overall systems and processes that support training. The evaluation system covers training in the areas of orientation, management, general skills, and technical expertise. Below we describe how for the past four years Intel has applied Kirkpatrick's model at the systems level to improve impact, cost, quality, and timeliness across all training programs. Because we believe it is important to start with the end in mind, we begin by first discussing level 4 evaluation.

Level 4: Decreasing Costs and Increasing Impact

Preparing for Success

One of the six key values espoused by Intel's leadership is "results orientation." Application of Kirkpatrick's fourth level of evaluation has allowed the corporate university to better demonstrate return on investment. There are many complex algorithms available for determining ROI, but it basically boils down to two things: decreasing costs and increasing desired impact.

A process has been developed to apply evaluation as both an up-front assessment tool and tail-end evaluation process. These evaluations are done because the most opportune time to impact cost and quality is prior to course release and also because the data are necessary for successful level 4 evaluation. The course release process is similar to the document control process used in the factories. Course cost, quality, and desired outcomes are examined before courses are deployed through Intel University. Key questions are asked and documented during the release process and include:

- What are the courses' business goals/indicators and objectives?
- Is the course redundant with other training already available?
- What is the intended audience for the course?
- Who is the course owner? Does the owner know of the need to drive course quality improvements throughout the life cycle of the course?

Cost is also examined before course implementation. For example, all costs of supplier-developed training are examined by our purchasing group. Purchasing ensures the lowest total cost for training. Figure 18.1 shows a total cost model used to analyze the total cost of training. The model examines cost of training in the analysis, design, development, implementation, and maintenance phases of training. These data are used to help negotiate lower costs of training with our training suppliers. The total cost data are also used to help make decisions around media selection (for example, computer-based versus instructor-led training).

The up-front questions defined in Intel's course release process are valuable both for driving the quality of the course and in providing the baseline information necessary for level 4 evaluation. For example, if you do not have well-defined objectives, you can not effectively evaluate a course at any of the four levels of evaluation. If you do not know what indicators you are trying to impact before the course is implemented, it makes little sense to define these indicators after the implementation.

Teaming Up and Conducting the Evaluation

Table 18.1 provides some examples of level 4 indicators. Even when training is an appropriate intervention, it is often insufficient to

Figure 18.1. Total Cost Model

Learning activity name				Developer					
				Sponsor					
Target population year 1		Total target population		Life expectancy					
Analysis, Design and Development									
	No.	T-Comp	Time	Airfare	Lodging	Meals	Other	Total	Comment
Developer/designer(s)								0.00	
Vendor/consultant(s)								0.00	
Manager								0.00	
Content expert(s)								0.00	
Media support								0.00	
Subtotal personnel								0.00	
Materials and Other									
	No.	Unit Cost	Description					Total	
Materials								0.00	
Other								0.00	
Subtotal								0.00	
								0.00	
Implementation and Maintenance									
	No.	T-Comp	Time	Airfare	Lodging	Meals	Other	Total	Comment
Instructor(s) year 1								0.00	
Evaluator(s) year 1								0.00	
Participants year 1								0.00	
Administrative year 1								0.00	
Subtotal year 1								0.00	
Materials and Other									
	No.	Unit Cost	Description					Total	
Materials								0.00	
Other								0.00	
Subtotal								0.00	
								0.00	
Summary									
		Total	Additions to Total		Subtractions to Total		Adjusted Total		
Total cost year 1 (A + B)									
Total cost per student									
Total cost years 2–3									
Total cost per student									
Total cost									
Total cost per student									

achieve desired results on its own. Other environmental supports may be needed as well. Environmental supports include things like management backing, rewards and recognition, and the appropriate equipment.

Table 18.1. Training, Indicators, Costs, and Results

Learning activity	Indicator	Cost per student	Result
Safety training	Decrease accidents by 5%	$135	Accidents decreased by 6%
Training developers/ workshops	Decrease development time by 2%	$90	Decreased by 5%
Management training	Increase employee satisfaction by 5%	$1,000	Increased by 2%
Handling wafers	Decrease misprocessing by 1%	$850	Decreased by 3%
Equipment reliability and maintenance ability	Reduce mean time between failures by 2%	$300	Decreased by 2%

Rather than dismiss or try to explain away the other factors that impact business outcomes, performance technologists should attempt to identify all key factors that will help improve business results. Training is just one part of the performance improvement intervention. For example, when designing Intel's new-hire orientation program, training personnel worked with management and the other human resource support groups to ensure successful impact to the business. The nontraining components of the intervention included the following:

1. A corporatewide employee reward (bonus) was offered for successful attainment of the integration goals.
2. Management was provided clear expectations on what they needed to do to support their new employees. This was done by providing a checklist of required activities for a new hire's first nine months.
3. Staffing helped design improved processes before the new employee was hired. This included a prehire orientation package and video.
4. The information technology group worked to ensure that new hires' offices were set up before they arrived.

The outcome was higher reported satisfaction among new hires regarding their indoctrination and ability to contribute in a timely fashion. Over 95 percent of the new hires participated in all the required learning activities (a 10 percent increase). Satisfaction with the integration experience increased by over 8 percent. This desired outcome was achieved not just through training, but through a comprehensive set of interventions.

Another key insight when examining level 4 evaluation is that a series of courses often impact the same indicator. The designers may or may not have realized this fact when designing the courses. For example, Intel has many courses in the area of safety. When examining the organizational impact of these courses, it makes sense to look at how the courses tie together from a program perspective. For example, such courses as Introduction to Safety, Handling Dangerous Chemicals, and Advanced Safety are best evaluated together. Looking for common indicators across courses helps the training function to demonstrate its contribution at a higher level and ties results to the company's strategic business objectives.

Summary of Level 4 Key Learnings

The following were key learnings gained from the level 4 evaluation:

- Success indicators and cost considerations should be defined before the training intervention is implemented and then reexamined after implementation.
- In almost all cases, successful training is just one of many factors contributing to level 4 indicator changes. To achieve desired outcomes, management and other change agents in the organization need to team up.
- Multiple courses often impact the same indicator. Therefore, courses should be positioned and evaluated not in isolation but as part of a curriculum.

Level 4: Intel's Results

By applying the processes listed above and in conjunction with the level 1 through 3 processes described below, Intel has documented savings of over $15 million dollars in direct costs over a three-year period and reduction of over 1,500 courses that were redundant, of poor quality, or outdated.

Level 3: Processes Used to Capture Transfer of Training

Capturing Level 3 Data

Intel has developed level 3 processes to capture data across all of its courseware. Given the large volumes, these methods typically begin with the most cost-effective means of data collection: the administration of a self-report survey. Based on the feedback on the questionnaire, the analysis may be followed up with interviews, direct observation, or analysis of documented performance against action plans. Level 3 provides another opportunity to identify and address barriers to behavior transfer. Of most value in self-report data are reports in which respondents indicate that they are not applying the skills to their jobs and explain why. This feedback lends itself to action.

Exhibit 18.1 (grouped with the other exhibits at the end of the chapter) shows a generic level 3 questionnaire. Intel University works with the course owner to tailor the survey to each of the courses that are taught. The level 3 instrument collects data on the respondents' perceptions of both posttraining intervention behavior and the training influences of the work environment.

Based on an analysis of approximately one hundred courses, it was found that the most common reported reason for lack of transfer, from a student's perspective, was that students had not had an opportunity to use the skills they were taught in the course (see Figure 18.2). The reasons students gave for not having an opportunity to use the skills were the timing of the course and lack of planning for how the skills would be used on the job. Based on these findings, Intel University has increased emphasis on improving timing of the sessions and encouraging employees to attend courses based on a defined development plan created by the employee and the manager.

Summary of Level 3 Key Learnings

The following key learnings were gained from the level 3 evaluation:

- The value of collecting self-report data at level 3 regarding behavior transfer is to answer the question, "If not, why not?"
- Timing of the course is a significant factor in training transfer.
- One of the greatest barriers to transfer is poor planning on the part of the manager and student in terms of how the skills will be applied to the job.

Figure 18.2. Graph of Reported Reasons Why Training
Did Not Transfer from Level 3 Surveys

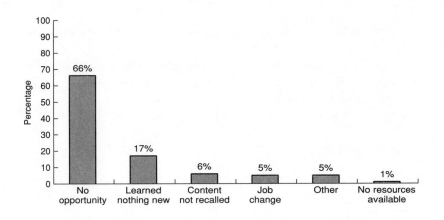

Level 3: Intel's Results

By applying the processes listed above, the number of courses that met the transfer rate standard (80 percent of respondents' self-reporting skills and knowledge transferred back to the job) increased by 30 percent.

Level 2: Getting Testing Data When Needed

Level 2 evaluation at Intel is not currently conducted with great frequency for general skills courseware. Level 2 assessment is applied, however, to a large percentage of technical skills training courses taught in the factories. The assessments are mostly conducted using behavioral checklists or computer-based tests. The results are used to determine whether participants should be certified on a piece of equipment or area within the factory and also as part of the instructional strategy to validate the training materials.

All certifications are tracked on an automated system, and tests are validated for job-relatedness. The instructional designer ensures that the assessment matches the instructional objectives, which match the required performance. The individual test results are kept anonymous or confidential.

Summary of Level 2 Key Learnings

Level 2 learnings were as follows:

- Performance checklists are a very effective way to determine if technical skills have been mastered.
- Level 2 evaluations should follow legal guidelines when used for certification or other job-related reasons. In addition, the results should be kept confidential.
- Well-written objectives are critical for level 2 evaluation.

Level 2: Intel's Results

During the past three years, over 10,000 technicians and other factory workers have been certified using validated checklists and other assessment techniques.

Level 1: Capturing a Wealth of Information

Ongoing level 1 evaluations are conducted on every course delivered by Intel University by using standardized surveys. The use of standardized instruments allows for the development of norms and comparisons across courses and curriculums. Both students and instructors provide feedback regarding training. The cumulative data (both quantitative and qualitative) are fed to course owners and administrators for analysis. Instructors also receive a level 1 scorecard for each session taught. Based on those data, improvements are driven on the administration, material and content, and instruction for the course.

Like level 3, level 1 evaluation provides an excellent opportunity to identify environmental barriers previously unknown. Ideally, these are uncovered during the needs assessment, but in a rapidly changing environment new barriers may develop between the time of the upfront analysis and course deployment. The standard students' critique used by Intel University asks respondents to identify potential barriers (see item 3, Exhibit 18.2).

Although developers are required to describe the intended target audience prior to course release, training programs tend to take on a life of their own in large, decentralized, global corporations. It is not uncommon for students to enroll in programs that were not intended for them and for which neither they nor the company will reap much benefit. Instructors' perceptions are one method used for monitoring the appropriateness of the program for the attending audience (see item 2, Exhibit 18.3). As discussed earlier, employee-supervisor planning is one key to identifying appropriate development opportunities and positively influencing skills application to the work environment. At Intel, low reported transfer rates at level 3 can often be tied to low levels of development planning as reported on the level 1 instrument (see item 1, Exhibit 18.2). This combination of results serves as another indication that a course might no longer be finding its intended target audience.

Summary of Level 1 Key Learnings

The following level 1 learnings were gained:

- Standardized surveys are useful for comparative purposes and the development of norms.
- Level 1 is generally the first opportunity to identify holes (new or previously undiscovered barriers) in the needs assessment.
- High student satisfaction may mean little if the intervention is delivered to the wrong population.

Level 1: Intel's Results

For the previous year, the percentage of positive student responses to items in the three major categories described (administration, material/content, and instruction) were 94, 95, and 97 percent, respectively.

Conclusion and Recommendations

Training at Intel has become more accountable for demonstrating its contribution to the bottom line. Given this, it is recommended that no intervention be initiated without first determining and documenting desired organizational outcomes. Evaluation begins not with level 1, but rather with level 4. The easiest time to decrease cost and increase desired impact is before a training product is released. When relying on self-report feedback, the data of greatest value are those that identify courses that are definitely not working as intended; these are the courses that require attention first. The notion of applying these standardized methodologies to such large volumes may seem daunting at first glance. Intel supports these efforts with surprisingly few resources by applying current technologies to data processing and report distribution.

While examples of some specific data collection tools have been provided here, no attempt was made to recommend one or more tools over others. The point being made is the value of developing and applying a standardized evaluation framework to all courseware. Applying common indicators enables the development of norms and enforcement of standards. Not only can action be taken to improve (or delete) individual training interventions at the course level, systemwide barriers that challenge whole curriculums or whole populations can also be identified and resolved. By definition, an evaluation or performance improvement system should allow stakeholders to drive improvements at a systemic level. Kirkpatrick's four-level model was instrumental in the development of Intel's corporatewide evaluation system.

Exhibit 18.1. Generic Level 3 Survey

During the past few months you attended the CMS 000269, ROI Customer Service training class. Please take a few moments to answer the following questions to the best of your ability. We are attempting to evaluate the training we are providing to you. Your input will greatly help us to improve this and other courses offered in the future.

Please Reply by Friday, October 31.

1. After returning from training I was able to use the skills/knowledge I learned in the class.
   (1) Immediately
   (2) Within a week
   (3) Within a month
   (4) 2–3 months after class
   (5) 3–6 months after class
   (6) Have not used yet
   Please enter your response here >>
   Comments:

   Please enter your response here >>

2. My supervisor and I discussed my objectives for going to this course prior to training.
   (1) Agree
   (2) Disagree
   Please enter your response here >>
   Comments:

   Please enter your response here >>

3. The skills/knowledge-related resources that were used in the class are available for use on the job (e.g., reference manuals, tools).
   (1) Agree
   (2) Disagree
   Please enter your response here >>
   Comments:

   Please enter your response here >>

4. Situations have arisen in which I have been able to apply my newly learned skills/knowledge.
   (1) Strongly agree
   (2) Agree
   (3) Disagree
   (4) Strongly disagree
   Please enter your response here >>
   Comments:

   Please enter your response here >>

Exhibit 18.1. Generic Level 3 Survey *(continued)*

---

5. I am currently applying the skills/knowledge on my job.
   (1) Strongly agree
   (2) Agree
   (3) Disagree
   (4) Strongly disagree
   Please enter your response here >>
   Comments:

   Please enter your response here >>

6. There are some issues that are keeping me from being able to use my new skills/knowledge properly.
   (1) Strongly agree
   (2) Agree
   (3) Disagree
   (4) Strongly disagree
   Please enter your response here >>

   If you rated question 6 as Strongly agree or Agree, then please answer question 7.

7. The reason(s) that I have been unable to use my new skills/knowledge properly. Please enter "X" for each applicable response below. Enter the "X" between the ">>" and "–" symbols:
   >>   – Haven't had the opportunity
   >>   – Job changed
   >>   – Manager doesn't support
   >>   – Resistance to change (self)
   >>   – Resistance to change (group)
   >>   – Didn't learn anything new
   >>   – Don't recall content
   >>   – Resources not available
   >>   – Other
   Comments:

   Please enter your response here >>

Exhibit 18.2. Example of Level 1 Scorecard from Student Survey

Personal Profile	Yes	No
1. Was this training part of your development plan, training plan, or redeployment plan?	132 (88%)	18 (12%)
2. As a customer, did this course meet your requirements/needs?	143 (99%)	2 (1%)
3. Are there any barriers that might prevent you from using the concepts and skills gained in this course back on the job?	8 (5%)	141 (95%)

Course Availability	Later	Right now	Earlier
4. I needed to take this course:	3 (2%)	118 (80%)	26 (18%)

Quality Rating

Course Duration	Too long	Just right	Too short
5. The duration of this course was:	5 (3%)	142 (95%)	3 (2%)

Instructor	Poor	Fair	Good	Superior	N/A	No. of responses	Mean	Percentage score of 3's and 4's
6. Kept to stated objective(s)	0	1	44	105		150	3.69	99%
7. Knew subject matter well	0	4	52	92	1	148	3.59	97
8. Encouraged participation	0	8	56	75	8	139	3.48	94
9. Presented subject matter clearly	0	4	54	89		147	3.58	97
10. Answered students' questions	0	3	51	85	8	139	3.59	98
Material and Content								
12. Content supported objective(s)	0	3	49	93		145	3.62	98
13. The student material was useful	5	14	54	69	5	142	3.32	87
14. Activities supported objectives	0	8	54	74	11	136	3.49	94

Exhibit 18.2. Example of Level 1 Scorecard from Student Survey (*continued*)

Pacing

	Too fast	Too slow	Just right
15. The level of pacing was:	0 (0%)	7 (5%)	137 (95%)

Difficulty

	Too fast	Too slow	Just right
16. The level of difficulty was:	0 (0%)	11 (8%)	133 (92%)

Administration

	<-------- Ratings -------->					No. of responses	Mean	Percentage score of 3's and 4's
	Poor	Fair	Good	Superior	N/A			
18. Enrollment process convenient	1	4	32	101	4	138	3.69	96%
19. Room setup conducive to learning	3	3	39	94	1	139	3.61	96

	Yes	No	N/A
20. Req'd course materials available	131 (98%)	3 (2%)	4
21. Received verification/reminders	97 (88%)	13 (12%)	30
22. Received preassignment	44 (92%)	4 (8%)	92

Summary of averages	Mean	Percentage scores of 3's and 4's
Instructor Score	3.59	97%
Material and Content Score	3.48	93
Administration Score	3.65	96
Total Critiques Processed	151	
Total Classes Processed	14	

Exhibit 18.3. Example of Level 1 Scorecard from Instructor's Survey

Course Title: Effectiveness Listening Workshop   CC: Instructor File Developer

Course Code: GEN000495   Time Frame: Quarterly—Q3 1997

Sites: AZ   Session Dates: 6/29/97–9/27/97

Instructor Information

Site

AZ	DP	FM	NM	OR	SC
5	0	0	0	0	0

IR	MN	PG	PR	APAC	EURO	IS	Other
0	0	0	0	0	0	0	0

Preparation for instruction of class:

<1 hr	1–3 hrs	>3 hrs
1 (25%)	1 (25%)	2 (50%)

Means by which certification took place:

Train-the-trainer course	Audited the course	Both	Neither
0 (0%)	1 (33%)	1 (33%)	1 (33%)

| Content | *Ratings* | | | | Number of responses | Mean | Percentage of 3's and 4's |
	Strongly disagree	Disagree	Agree	Strongly agree			
1. Content supported objectives.	1	1	3	0	5	2.40	60%★
2. Content was applicable to audience.	0	0	3	2	5	3.40	100
3. Course content was up to date.	0	2	1	2	5	3.00	60★
4. Level of difficulty was aligned to skills.	0	0	5	0	5	3.00	100
5. Length of course was appropriate.	0	2	3	0	5	2.60	60★

Exhibit 18.3. Example of Level 1 Scorecard from Instructor's Survey *(continued)*

| | <--------- Ratings ---------> | | | | | | |
Design	Strongly disagree	Disagree	Agree	Strongly agree	Number of responses	Mean	Percentage of 3's and 4's
6. Delivery method was most conducive.	0	0	4	1	5	3.20	100%
7. Delivery was easy to implement.	0	0	4	1	5	3.20	100
8. Student materials were useful during session.	0	2	1	2	5	3.00	60*
9. Course design allowed for adequate student interaction.	0	0	3	2	5	3.40	100
Instructor Guide							
10. Guide was easy to refer to.	1	1	2	1	5	2.60	60*
11. Guide gave sufficient background knowledge.	0	2	2	1	5	2.80	60*
12. Guide provided sufficient examples.	0	2	1	2	5	3.00	60*
Administration							
13. Advanced notice was given to teach.	0	0	3	2	5	3.40	100%
14. Administrator was available for requests.	0	0	1	4	5	3.80	100
15. Room setup was conducive to learning.	0	2	1	2	5	3.00	60*
16. All required course materials were available.	0	2	1	2	5	3.00	60*
17. Course materials were up to date.	0	0	4	1	5	3.20	100
18. Necessary learning tools were available.	0	0	2	3	5	3.60	100

Exhibit 18.3. Example of Level 1 Scorecard from Instructor's Survey (*continued*)

Other	<------------ Ratings ------------>				Number of responses	Mean	Percentage of 3's and 4's*
	Strongly disagree	Disagree	Agree	Strongly agree			
19. I have received sufficient training/coaching to be effective.	0	1	1	3	5	3.40	80%*
20. Intel's money was well spent on training.	0	1	2	2	5	3.20	80*

Summary of Averages	*Mean*	*Percentage score of agree or strongly agree*
Content Score	2.88	76%*
Design Score	3.20	90*
Instructor Guide Score	2.80	60*
Administration Score	3.33	87*
Other Score	3.30	80*
Total Critiques Processed: 5		

*These items did not meet Intel University standards for course ratings, which is that no less than 90 percent of responses are Strongly agree or Agree.

Chapter 19

Evaluating an Outdoor-Based Training Program— a Search for Results

This is a revision and update of the case study that appeared in the first edition of this book. The evaluators have used a sophisticated approach in an attempt to evaluate at all four levels. Statistics are used to measure the effectiveness of the program. This case study will be of particular interest to organizations that want to measure program effectiveness on an objective basis.

St. Luke's Hospital

Richard Wagner, Associate Professor of Management
University of Wisconsin–Whitewater

Robert Wiegand, Director of Organizational Development
St. Luke's Hospital, Bethlehem, PA

Faced with increasing competition from nearby hospitals and the need to improve efficiency and cost control, St. Luke's Hospital began to look for innovative ways to improve its training of management personnel. In 1990 St. Luke's Training Department, supported by top management, introduced the concept of outdoor-based training. While outdoor-based training programs are a relatively recent phenomena for training managers, they have been found to be effective in improving interdepartmental communications, increasing the level of trust among employees, and empowering employees at all levels by reducing existing boundaries between departments.

St. Luke's Experiential Training Program

St. Luke's Hospital, a 435-bed medical complex located in the Lehigh Valley of Pennsylvania, began using outdoor-based training as a technique for training management personnel in 1990. While those who attended the early programs expressed a great deal of satisfaction with them, no formal evaluation of these programs had been conducted.

The use of outdoor-based training programs at St. Luke's was supported by top management primarily as a means of improving interdepartmental communications. This included making interdepartmental communications more direct and increasing the honesty and openness of these communications. Additional goals of the program were to increase the level of trust among employees, empower employees at all levels by encouraging increased sharing, and reduce the boundaries that exist between departments within the hospital.

The outdoor-based experiential training program was conducted in three phases of one day each at a remote location called Stony Acres. Program participants were management employees from areas throughout the hospital, including Human Resources, Accounting, Engineering, and a number of medical departments. All participants were volunteers. A key feature of the program was that each of the groups traveled to and from the training site in a bus together. This served to increase the informal interaction and communication among group members.

In phase 1 of the training program the focus was on the participants getting to know each other better as individuals, beginning to improve interpersonal communication, and working on trust issues. Morning program activities were "low-ropes" activities and included (1) the wall—the group has to climb a twelve-foot-high wall using only their own resources; (2) the spider's web—the group has to pass all members through a rope web without disturbing the "spider"; and (3) the blind trust walk—group members are blindfolded and led on a walk through the woods. In the afternoon the group was led through three "high-ropes" activities—that is, the events took place from ten to twenty feet above the ground. The overall mix of activities for the program was approximately 60 percent low elements and 40 percent high elements.

Phase 2 took place after phase 1 and focused on building trust and group support by increasing the level of challenge for the participants. The morning session began with a warm–up session to get the participants ready for the rest of the day. The morning also focused on building trust and developing a "challenge-by-choice contract" so that no one felt pressured to participate in the high-ropes activities. The afternoon was devoted to the high-ropes activities and building group trust through group support. The mix for this phase of the program was approximately 40 percent low elements and 60 percent high elements.

Phase 3 took place after phase 2 and focused on individual development and increasing group support. The mix for this phase of the program was about 25 percent low ropes and trust building and 75 percent high ropes and individual development.

The processing or debriefing of each activity by a skilled facilitator has been found to be a key element in the effective transfer of training material to the work setting. In order to maximize transfer of training, it was decided to use two debriefing periods: debriefing by the facilitator after each activity during the program and additional debriefing during a follow-up program after each phase had been completed. The feeling of group spirit and togetherness was further fostered by the use of group T-shirts and group slogans.

Evaluating the St. Luke's Program

In 1991 an effort to evaluate the effectiveness of this type of training was undertaken by Robert Weigand, St. Luke's manager of Training and Development, and Richard J. Wagner, associate professor of Management at the University of Wisconsin–Whitewater. As manager of Training and Development, Bob Weigand had directed the design of the outdoor-based program and was the primary facilitator of the program. Dick Wagner is a former corporate training director and currently serves as a consultant to a number of major organizations in evaluating their experiential training programs. The initial evaluation program that was designed for St. Luke's combined the unique features of St. Luke's program and the quantitative evaluation format used previously by Wagner and his associates. As the need for more sophisticated analysis has evolved, so has the evaluation process evolved from a focus on level 3 (behaviors) to a focus on level 4 (results).

Part 1 of the evaluation program was designed to develop a "theory" of what the Stony Acres program accomplished for those who had participated in the original program. While the goals of the program had been established by St. Luke's top management, there was no way to be sure that these goals were all that this type of program was accomplishing. Since a group of previous participants (subject matter experts) existed, we felt that they could offer some unique insights into the program before we began evaluating new participants. Due to the geography of the evaluation, we used a nondirectional questionnaire to gather these data. This questionnaire asked the participants to tell us what they had personally gotten out of the Stony Acres program and how it had changed their behaviors at work.

The results of this survey suggested that a number of behavioral changes not anticipated by the program designers were being impacted. An analysis of these surveys by a four-member panel of the research team indicated that these behaviors could be placed in the following four categories: communications, team spirit, willingness to try new ideas, and interpersonal relations. A questionnaire was then developed to allow the researchers to evaluate future participant responses regarding the program.

In part 2 of the evaluation program, the instrument developed in part 1 was given to participants in the second program. The participants completed the evaluation instrument at three time periods: as a premeasure before attending phase 1, as a postmeasure three months after training, and as a second postmeasure six months after the program. In an effort to improve the precision of the evaluation and to focus on the actual results of the program, at the three-month postmeaasure the participants completed a "behavioral style" open-response questionnaire to behaviorally justify any changes they felt took place after the program. Since this postquestionnaire was tied directly to the program, it was felt that three months was both long enough for the posttraining "euphoria" to be reduced and short enough that participants would remember the specifics of the Stony Acres program. (A copy of the three-month postquestionnaire is found in Exhibit 19.1, grouped with the other exhibits at the end of the chapter).

Part 3 of the evaluation consisted of a prequestionnaire and a six-month postquestionnaire. Both the pre- and the postquestionnaires used items developed during previous research in similar programs. Since these items are all behavioral, a six-month postmeasure was chosen to allow us to evaluate the long-term impact of outdoor training on these behaviors. In addition to the scale developed specifically for the Stony Acres program, the following behaviors were also measured:

1. *Group trust*—measured the extent that one is willing to assign good intentions to, and have confidence in, the words and actions of one's coworkers
2. *Self-esteem*—assessed whether one has a positive or negative view of oneself (a measure of participant self-confidence)
3. *Group awareness*—measured the feeling among the group members that each member of the group recognizes the differences in abilities among the individual members of the group and understands and is committed to the goals of the group
4. *Group effectiveness*—the best measure of the overall functioning of the group, including the level of cooperation, effectiveness of communication, and goal clarity of the unit
5. *Group bonding*—a broad measure of group cohesiveness, including group stimulation, group commitment, and group compatibility

In addition to the above behaviors, we also measured participants' attitude toward the Stony Acres program. Attitude was defined as participants' general feeling toward the program and what they would tell other people about the program if asked. (A copy of this questionnaire is found in Exhibit 19.2.)

Results of the Behavioral Evaluation

A total of sixteen managers completed the Stony Acres program, including seven males and nine females. The average age of the participants was 39.8 years old, with the youngest being 25 and the oldest being 61 years old. Six were high school graduates, four had some college, and the remaining six were all college graduates.

St. Luke's Theory Measures

The results of the empirical evaluation of the behavioral changes from the St. Luke's theory measures at three months showed statistically significant changes in all four behaviors (communications, team spirit, willingness to try new ideas, and interpersonal relations). At the six-month postmeasure, a significant change was found only in communications. (The statistics are found in Table 19.1.)

Table 19.1. St. Luke's Theory Measures

Measure	Time (1) mean/S.D.	Time (3) mean/S.D.	Change 1 (T3 – T1)	Change 2 (at T2)
Communications	4.33 (1.267)	5.42 (1.475)	+1.08★	+2.73★
Team spirit	5.17 (.835)	5.33 (1.231)	+.17	+2.00★
Willingness to try new ideas	4.42 (1.676)	5.08 (1.730)	+.67	+2.47★
Interpersonal relations	4.81 (.912)	4.89 (1.301)	+.08	+2.42★

★$p < .05$ (a statistically significant change occurred).
Note: N = 16.

Behavioral Justifications

The results of the behavioral justification questionnaires suggest that the participants could link the training program to specific actions at work. (The actual behavioral justifications from the participants are summarized by category in Exhibit 19.3.)

Previous Research Measures

The results of the empirical evaluation of reactions to the program at the six-month postmeasure showed that the overall attitude toward the program was more favorable than it was before the program (remember, they all volunteered) but that the increase was not significant. Of the five behaviors that were evaluated, only one (group effectiveness) showed a significant improvement. (The statistics are found in Table 19.2.)

Table 19.2. Previous Research Measures

Measure	Pre (Time 1) mean/S.D.	Post2 (Time 3) mean/S.D.	t	p-value
Attitude toward program	5.18 (.960)	5.64 (1.214)	1.20	.257
Trust in group members	5.78 (.780)	5.77 (.875)	0.06	.957
Self-esteem	2.10 (1.068)	2.38 (1.408)	0.79	.445
Group awareness	5.90 (.754)	5.97 (.807)	0.48	.643
Group effectiveness	4.06 (.473)	5.81 (1.212)	6.26	.000★
Group bonding	4.62 (.851)	4.99 (1.106)	0.85	.413

★$p < .05$ (a statistically significant change occurred).
Note: N = 16.

Conclusion

The results of the questionnaire administered three months after the program suggest that significant changes have occurred in the behaviors identified in part 1. It was not surprising that at the three-month postmeasure participants reported strongly positive behavior changes resulting from the program. Anecdotal evidence strongly suggests that participants, in general, really enjoy programs such as Stony Acres. Thus, posttraining euphoria would suggest that participants in this type of program, when asked directly, would say that it was a very effective program.

However, the behavioral justifications the participants gave for their behavior change ratings strongly support the direction (if not the magnitude) of the behavior change ratings they gave in part 2. In the area of communications, ten of the sixteen participants gave a specific example of a positive change that had occurred after the program. Only one participant had a concern—namely, that the participant did not interact with the other group members on a regular basis.

In the area of team spirit, nine of the sixteen participants described a specific positive change in their behaviors. In the area of trying new ideas, only five of the sixteen participants referred to a specific behavioral change that had occurred, but all of these were positive. Finally, in the area of interpersonal relations all sixteen participants referred to specifics. One was negative, and the remaining fifteen were strongly positive. In fact, almost half of the participants described more than one specific behavioral change they experienced after the program.

By asking participants to rate only their behaviors, not their behavior changes, the questionnaire administered six months after training was subject to little, if any, posttraining euphoria and can be viewed as a more "conservative" estimate of the effectiveness of the Stony Acres program. After six months, only communications showed a statistically significant improvement. While a relatively large (.67) improvement was also found in the willingness to try new ideas, this change was not significant, primarily due to the small (N = 16) sample size.

The results of evaluation after six months indicate only one statistically significant change—in group effectiveness. A large positive change was also found in group bonding, but the small sample size (N = 16) kept this change from being statistically significant.

A Search for Results

While the results of the reaction and behavior evaluations were interesting and encouraging, both the researchers and St. Luke's management continue to ask the question, Was the training program really worth the investment? Unfortunately, as most trainers have found, this decision is not easily made. However, by taking a relatively unique approach, we have begun moving in the direction of actually measuring the organizational results of the behavior changes we have identified.

We began our work by interviewing most of the participants in the original training program. While many of these people had moved into new and more responsible positions within St. Luke's, they were still able to identify a number of specific work behaviors they felt had improved because of their training experiences. The specific behaviors that were identified were

- Employees listen and communicate more effectively.
- Work load is distributed more equitably.
- Teamwork is better.
- Associates observe RNs to learn approaches to dealing with patients.
- RNs teach organizational skills to associates.
- RNs trust and respect associates and do not check up on them.
- Work is done quicker and better and the staff is less stressed.
- Employees recognize the needs of different people.
- Employees recognize different needs of patients.
- There is increased employee accountability.
- Room cleaning is more timely.
- Clinical coordinators problem-solve.
- Treatment times have improved.
- Patients are transported to other units in a more timely fashion.
- Clinical and support associates help licensed staff.

From Behaviors to Results

We then used these behaviors as a framework to meet with many managers at St. Luke's with one purpose: to find out if any of these behaviors could be specifically identified as resulting in cost saving or revenue enhancement for St. Luke's. For example, does improving treatment times have any positive results in terms of revenue or costs? In this example, we identified the following positive organizational consequences that could result from this behavior change:

- Able to increase revenue since more patients can be treated
- Able to reduce payroll and benefit costs
- Increased revenue due to higher return rate for satisfied patients
- Increased revenue due to referrals from satisfied patients

Using a similar format we were able to identify some specific organizational consequences for many of the behaviors and then were able to link these to the following organizational consequences:

1. Increases in efficiency and teamwork improve employee satisfaction with their job, which consequently decreases job turnover.
2. Increases in efficiency reduce waste and result in lower indirect expenses for the hospital (materials, utility bills, equipment, and so on).
3. Unitization of fewer employees saves on payroll and benefits costs.
4. On-the-job training saves training and development dollars as well as reducing direct costs—for example, increasing productivity (output) and reducing labor costs.
5. Delegation saves money by freeing up higher-salaried employees to do more of the important tasks, since lower-salaried employees can perform the more routine jobs.
6. Cross-training increases employee job flexibility, which makes employees more valuable, since they can perform tasks that were previously done only by specialists.
7. Employees experience reduced stress, are less burned out, and work together better, all of which results in lower costs due to reduced costs for health care coverage, lost time from work, and disability claims.
8. Greater patient occupancy means more revenue for the hospital.
9. Satisfied patients recommend St. Luke's to others, which leads to increased revenue.

The Organizational Consequences Model for Level 4

While the identification of specific organizational consequences is a significant first step in moving toward level 4 evaluation, it is only a first step. In most cases, St. Luke's was able to provide the data needed to complete a level 4 evaluation. The ability to generate the data to support these efforts is clearly critical to being able to evaluate the results of any training program.

As important to generating the data is being able to use our "organization consequences" methodology to complete a level 4 evaluation for all training programs at St. Luke's and eventually at any organization. To do this, we are working on developing a series of questions that can be applied to any training intervention to identify the organization consequences that result. We are also working with other organizations to produce a model that can be generalized to other organizations.

Exhibit 19.1. St. Luke's Theory Questionnaire

Please answer each of the following questions using the following scale. After you have rated this question using the scale below, briefly describe a *specific situation* that justifies your rating.

1   Increased strongly after outdoor training
2   Increased moderately after outdoor training
3   Increased slightly after outdoor training
4   Did not change after outdoor training
5   Decreased slightly after outdoor training
6   Decreased moderately after outdoor training
7   Decreased strongly after outdoor training

1. I find this group to be very friendly. _____
    Justification:

2. I think that the communications in this group needs a lot of help. _____
    Justification:

3. There is a lot of team spirit in this group. _____
    Justification:

4. This is a very informal and relaxed group to be with. _____
    Justification:

5. The members of this group are very willing to help each other solve problems. _____
    Justification:

6. As a group, we communicate really well with each other. _____
    Justification:

7. The members of this group really know each other as individuals. _____
    Justification:

8. I am more willing to try new ideas because I know that the members of this group will help me if I need it. _____
    Justification:

9. The members of this group carefully guard their "territory." _____
    Justification:

10. The members of this group are open and easy to get to know. _____
    Justification:

Exhibit 19.2. St. Luke's Attitude/Behavioral Questionnaire

Sex: Male   Female   (Circle one)

Age: _____

Education: High school grad   Attended some college

            College grad   Tech school grad

            Graduate degree   No high school diploma

            (Circle the highest level completed)

General Instructions

This survey contains a number of questions about you and your job. All of the questions ask that you choose the one number that best matches the description of how you feel about the question. Please mark only *one*.

The following statements concern your perceptions of the Outdoor-Based Training Program (OBT) that you will attend shortly. How much do you agree or disagree with each of the following?

1   Disagree strongly
2   Disagree moderately
3   Disagree slightly
4   Neither agree nor disagree
5   Agree slightly
6   Agree moderately
7   Agree strongly

I understand completely the objectives of the OBT.   1   2   3   4   5   6   7

I can see no potential value in the OBT.   1   2   3   4   5   6   7

I have no idea what you do in the OBT.   1   2   3   4   5   6   7

I am very much looking forward to participating   1   2   3   4   5   6   7
in the OBT.

I would strongly prefer not to participate in the OBT.   1   2   3   4   5   6   7

I think that the OBT is a great idea for improving   1   2   3   4   5   6   7
effectiveness at my organization.

I have heard good things about the OBT.   1   2   3   4   5   6   7

Please circle the one that best describes you at *work*.

Successful   1   2   3   4   5   6   7   Not successful

Important   1   2   3   4   5   6   7   Not important

Doing my best   1   2   3   4   5   6   7   Not doing my best

Happy   1   2   3   4   5   6   7   Not happy

Exhibit 19.2. St. Luke's Attitude/Behavioral Questionnaire *(continued)*

How much do you agree or disagree with each of the following statements?

1   Disagree strongly
2   Disagree moderately
3   Disagree slightly
4   Neither agree nor disagree
5   Agree slightly
6   Agree moderately
7   Agree strongly

If I get into difficulties at work, I know that my workmates would try to help me out.	1	2	3	4	5	6	7
I can trust the people with whom I work to lend me a hand if I need it.	1	2	3	4	5	6	7
Most of my workmates can be relied on to do as they say they will do.	1	2	3	4	5	6	7
I have full confidence in the skills of my workmates.	1	2	3	4	5	6	7
Most of my fellow workers would get on the job even if supervisors were not around.	1	2	3	4	5	6	7
I can rely on other workers not to make my job more difficult by careless work.	1	2	3	4	5	6	7
I recognize that members of my work group vary widely in skills and abilities.	1	2	3	4	5	6	7
I recognize that my work group contains members from widely varying backgrounds.	1	2	3	4	5	6	7
My work group knows exactly what things it has to get done.	1	2	3	4	5	6	7
Each member of my work group has a clear idea of the group's goals.	1	2	3	4	5	6	7
I feel that I am really a part of my work group.	1	2	3	4	5	6	7
I look forward to being with the members of my work group each day.	1	2	3	4	5	6	7
To what extent does your work group plan together and coordinate efforts?	1	2	3	4	5	6	7
To what extent does your work group make good decisions and solve problems well?	1	2	3	4	5	6	7
To what extent do persons in your work group know what their jobs are and know how to do them well?	1	2	3	4	5	6	7
To what extent is information about important events and situations shared within your work group?	1	2	3	4	5	6	7
To what extent does your work group really want to meet its objectives successfully?	1	2	3	4	5	6	7
To what extent is your work group able to respond to unusual work demands placed upon it?	1	2	3	4	5	6	7
To what extent do you have confidence and trust in the persons in your work group?	1	2	3	4	5	6	7

Exhibit 19.2. St. Luke's Attitude/Behavioral Questionnaire *(continued)*

Please answer the following questions about your feelings toward the group with which you attended OBT.

1   Disagree strongly
2   Disagree moderately
3   Disagree slightly
4   Neither agree nor disagree
5   Agree slightly
6   Agree moderately
7   Agree strongly

I have influenced what the group talked about and did.	1	2	3	4	5	6	7
I have felt excited in this group.	1	2	3	4	5	6	7
I think about the group between sessions.	1	2	3	4	5	6	7
I am included by the group in the group's activities.	1	2	3	4	5	6	7
I have regretted joining this group.	1	2	3	4	5	6	7
I would not mind missing future training sessions with this group.	1	2	3	4	5	6	7
I think that the group should meet more often.	1	2	3	4	5	6	7
I want to remain in the group.	1	2	3	4	5	6	7
I would like the opportunity to dissuade members if most of the members decided to dissolve the group by leaving.	1	2	3	4	5	6	7
Most of the members fit what I feel to be the idea of a good group member.	1	2	3	4	5	6	7
I find the activities in which I participate as a member of the group to be enjoyable.	1	2	3	4	5	6	7
The group is composed of people who fit together.	1	2	3	4	5	6	7
I like the group that I am in.	1	2	3	4	5	6	7

Please answer the following questions about your feelings toward the group with which you attended OBT.

1   Disagree strongly
2   Disagree moderately
3   Disagree slightly
4   Neither agree nor disagree
5   Agree slightly
6   Agree moderately
7   Agree strongly

I find this group to be very friendly.	1	2	3	4	5	6	7
I think that the communication in this group needs a lot of help.	1	2	3	4	5	6	7
There is a lot of team spirit in this group.	1	2	3	4	5	6	7
This is a very informal and relaxed group to be with.	1	2	3	4	5	6	7
The members of this group are very willing to help each other solve problems.	1	2	3	4	5	6	7

Exhibit 19.2. St. Luke's Attitude/Behavioral Questionnaire *(continued)*

As a group, we communicate really well with each other.	1	2	3	4	5	6	7
The members of this group really know each other as individuals.	1	2	3	4	5	6	7
I am more willing to try new ideas because I know that the members of this group will help me if I need it.	1	2	3	4	5	6	7
The members of this group carefully guard their "territory."	1	2	3	4	5	6	7
The members of this group are open and easy to get to know.	1	2	3	4	5	6	7

Exhibit 19.3. Behavioral Justifications

Communications

- Communication with certain individuals I interact with frequently improved, but I only interact with some group members.
- Being physically close during training improved communication.
- After Stony Acres we are more relaxed around each other and communicate better. Less formality makes communications easier.
- We had communication problems on one activity but learned from it.
- After the program I feel comfortable speaking to upper management.
- Each activity saw communication improve as defenses came down, each member gave input, and we learned to listen better.
- Open communications have continued into the work setting.
- Some people now communicate with me more at work than before training.
- A few challenges really helped improve communication.
- We are more confident in speaking with each other on issues that affect us.
- Everyone could express an opinion *without* criticism.

Team spirit

- Follow-up meeting was fun. We worked together to design our T-shirts.
- The procedures for each challenge built this up.
- As the day went on the group became more relaxed with each other and had more fun being together.
- I am amazed at how positively people react to this type of training.
- Going over the wall really increased our team spirit.
- Best example was going over the wall.
- We could see it grow throughout the day, even if it started high (2).
- The challenge of completing the spider web really brought everyone together.

Try new ideas

- This increased due to collaborative problem solving.
- We all became committed to doing the best that we can with the support of the others.
- Absolutely, because I *trust* them.
- During training I got to know some upper managers better and would now consult them for help.

Interpersonal relations

- Positive hallway interaction.
- During training everyone distanced themselves from the work hierarchy.
- After training people are free to visit other people's territory.
- Training allowed people to be more informal.
- At work we are more open with each other.
- When different levels of management are out of the office setting they are able to interact and joke around with each other.
- Now everyone says hello to each other.
- Some members still guard their territory very closely.
- The ride to the site was in their "clique," but not the ride home.

Exhibit 19.3. Behavioral Justifications *(continued)*

- At the end of the day everyone could relax and laugh about the comments made about you—both positive and negative.
- Met new people and got to know old acquaintances better.
- Secret friend discussing made me feel more open with others.
- Territorial boundaries have come down.
- Talking and laughing really helps.
- Lunch was very relaxed. Everyone shared food.
- Learned individual fears.
- Relations with other group members improved during the session and have continued to get better since that time.
- Group worked together to complete each challenge.
- Apprehensive group members were more willing to help each other by the end of the day.
- Formal barriers have been reduced and even eliminated.

Chapter 20

Evaluating a Safety Training Program for Managers

T his case describes evaluation at levels 1, 2, and 3 in a government
agency. Specific forms and procedures are described that can be
used and/or adapted for evaluating programs in other organizations.

Fluor Daniel Hanford, Inc.

Edwin A. Keeney, Michael L. Fox, and JoKay Haberstok
Senior Training Evaluation Consultants
Fluor Daniel Hanford, Inc., Training,
Richland, Washington

Introduction

Fluor Daniel Hanford (FDH), Inc., is the management contractor for
the Project Hanford Management Contract for the Department of
Energy–Richland Operations(DOE RL) Office. The Central Training Organization within FDH provides cross–cutting training services
for its own personnel as well as for six subcontractors and six enterprise companies performing project work across the 560 square miles
of the Hanford site near Richland, Washington.

Manager Safety Training has been presented by the Environmental
Safety and Health Training (ES&HT) team to managers, supervisors,
team leaders, and other personnel across the Hanford site for over four

years. The training is intended to heighten the awareness of management toward both identified (via accident/injury reports) and potential safety issues and concerns. Managers need to be aware of their responsibilities and to know where to go and who to contact (for example, company manuals or facility safety representatives) for additional information. At the conclusion of each training session, students are asked to complete a level 1 evaluation (Kirkpatrick model) and this feedback is reviewed by the instructors. Commonly, revisions to the course content and presentation format are made solely by the ES&HT instructors and their manager each year. Exhibit 20.1 (grouped with the other exhibits at the end of the chapter) shows the level 1 evaluation form.

In 1996, this approach to training evaluations and course revisions began to change. When revising the course, the instructional team updated the level 1 instrument to specifically ask some open-ended questions, including (1) How would you improve this training? (2) What topics/issues do you feel would most benefit you in managing safety?

Process

In October of 1996, ES&HT embarked on a level 3 evaluation of Manager Safety Training. The purpose of the level 3 evaluation was to determine the degree to which students transfer course objectives and the training received into workplace performance. Working with company consultants from the Hanford Training Assessment Center (HTAC), an internal FDH training team that assists in the development and conduct of training evaluations, a task team composed of two ES&HT team members and an HTAC consultant was formed. The team and the ES&HT manager completed the HTAC design document to determine the focus of the evaluation. This four-page document was designed to obtain as much up-front information as possible about the evaluation. Questions about the course, level 1 and 2 instruments, measurements of success, and decisions to be made were some of the factors discussed in a one-hour design document meeting. With the involvement and concurrence of the ES&HT manager, the team agreed on the following purposes for conducting this level 3 evaluation:

- To determine whether Manager Safety Training is effective
- To identify the best approach to use for updating this training each year
- To determine what the focus of this training should be in 1997

To answer these and other important questions, the team designed a survey that included ten questions and encouraged write-in comments as well. A letter was sent from the ES&HT manager to the managers to inform them of the evaluation purpose and to encourage their participation. Surveys were sent to a randomly selected sampling of 99 students who had completed Manager Safety Training between March 1 and September 30, 1996. Of those, 55 forms were completed, returned and analyzed as part of the level 3 process. In addition, the level 1 student feedback forms from classes during the selected time frame were reviewed.

Following initial analysis of the survey results, the team conducted telephone interviews with 25 of the students who had indicated their willingness to participate in a follow-on interview. These interviews, while time-consuming (trying to schedule 15 minutes to talk with busy managers is no easy feat!), provided valuable additional information and insight into what students felt should be emphasized in the 1997 Manager Safety Training course.

In December 1996, a facilitated focus group meeting was held with five managers from various areas of the Hanford site. These managers were ones who had also indicated on the surveys that they would be willing to spend four to eight hours of their time to help determine the content and format of the 1997 training. This group brainstormed ideas for the format and table-top (hands-on) exercises for the course.

Results

Armed with the level 3 final report and copious telephone and meeting notes, the ES&HT team designed the Manager Safety Training course, which is currently being implemented.

The previous year's training had focused on accident investigation and case management—in other words, how to respond or react when an accident or injury occurs. From the level 3 evaluation, it was determined that most managers felt that it would be more beneficial to focus on being proactive when it comes to safety.

The recommendations were that the 1997 training course should:

1. Provide the "foundation" for safety. Managers need to be aware of the company procedures, policies, and programs they are responsible for following and implementing in the workplace.
2. Provide tools for safety success. With the foundation in place, managers need tools in order to effectively build on that foundation. Managers need ideas to help them implement good communication, teamwork, and a team spirit when it comes to safety. They need to understand how to perform comprehensive prejob safety meetings with their team. They need ideas for presenting interesting safety meetings.

With a good foundation and the right tools and materials, managers can be successful in reaching their safety goals. As well as company safety goals, most work teams have set their own internal safety goals, such as reducing or eliminating injuries/accidents or increasing awareness of safety requirements and how to meet those requirements.

The 1997 Manager Safety Training follows the same format as the company's safety procedure manuals and will be updated as changes occur in the policies and procedures. The student handout includes highlights from these manuals as well as copies of many of the forms used regularly in the workplace. The handout also includes reference information, including a listing of the company's industrial safety and industrial hygiene points of contact, examples of workplace housekeeping and safety inspection checklists, and directions for accessing safety "lessons learned" from the company's internal web site. In addition, photos taken at actual work site locations are used for identification of both positive examples (What's right with this picture? Would you take the time to recognize a team member in this area for working safely?) and areas needing improvement (Do you see any potential safety hazards here? What would you do if you came across this situation?).

Another change to the 1997 course was the addition of a pretest. Because managers' responsibilities for safety are so important, at the beginning of the training session students are asked to complete a thirty-question, mostly multiple-choice pretest. (This was shortened from forty to thirty questions after the pilot class.) Exhibit 20.2 presents the MST pretest. The questions and answers are then discussed as part of the overall learning experience. While some managers are initially taken aback at being required to "take a test," almost all agree that this has helped them to realize that they don't know all the answers. The average number of missed questions on the pretest is eleven. "I was surprised at the answers to some of the questions that I really thought I knew," said one student. "The test showed me that I should pay attention and actively participate in the rest of the course."

ES&HT has received positive feedback from managers completing the 1997 Manager Safety Training. (All students are asked to complete a level 1 evaluation form at the completion of each training session, and the instructors explain to students at the beginning of the course why the team asks for their feedback and how it is reviewed and used to make improvements in future sessions.) The following comments are a representative sampling of student responses to question 9 on the level 1 evaluation (see Exhibit 20.1) from the eight class sessions of Manager Safety Training conducted in FY 1998 (the new version of the course):

- Pretest format/discussion was excellent lead-in.
- Like the format of using the quiz and going over the questions and answers. I thought this was very effective.
- The pretest helped get mind set for class and reminded me of a number of areas I had been previously trained in but was rusty on details and requirements.
- Technique of up-front "exam," then discussion of each item was very effective.
- Quiz was good discussion tool.
- Preexam is excellent learning tool.
- Good awareness activity. Manual is useful.
- Good information and student interaction.
- Good discussion and examples.
- Beneficial lessons learned passed on during class.
- Lessons learned from actual accidents are most effective.
- Thank you for eliminating the practical group situation exercises; they used time but I learned little.

Comments from some managers who participated in the telephone interviews and the focus group meeting have made the results of the level 3 worthwhile to all involved, for example: "I was happy to make the time to be involved in this. And I'm thrilled to see that my ideas were actually listened to and incorporated into this year's training!" Although the survey results indicated most would prefer a "cafeteria-style" offering of training, the telephone interviews did not strongly confirm this. In addition, due to time and budget constraints, the ES&HT team decided not to make a change to a cafeteria-style format.

Exhibit 20.3 is a "sanitized" copy of the final evaluation report that HTAC usually provides their customers.

Exhibit 20.4 lists the survey questions used to determine application on the job (level 3).

Exhibit 20.5 provides the Manager Safety Training survey results for calendar year 1996.

Exhibit 20.1. Manager Safety Training 1997, Level 1 Course Evaluation

Instructor(s) name(s): _____ Course date: _____

Please "✓" your level of agreement with each of the following statements as they relate to this course:	Strongly Disagree 1	Disagree 2	Neutral 3	Agree 4	Strongly Agree 5

1. The objectives for the course were adequately explained.

2. The course was well-organized.

3. The participant handout will be a useful reference on the job.

4. The instructor(s) was knowledgeable in the subject matter.

5. The presentation portion of the course increased my awareness of *my* responsibilities regarding safety.

6. There was sufficient opportunity for discussion and student interaction.

7. The classroom activities/exercises helped me identify potential safety hazards.

8. Overall, I feel that the time I spent in this class was worthwhile.

9. This year's Manager Safety Training course was designed and developed based on input from students who completed the 1996 training. Please provide additional comments and/or suggestions regarding safety topics/issues that you feel would benefit you most.

Your name (optional): _____

Environmental Safety and Health Training
thanks you for your participation today!

Exhibit 20.2. Manager Safety Training Pretest

The following questions were taken from the WHC-CM-1-10 *Safety Manual* and the WHC-CM-1-11 *Industrial Hygiene Manual*. Please choose the *most correct* answer to these questions based on your knowledge of these manuals.

Quiz # _____   Name _____   Date _____

1. The WHC-CM-1-10 *Safety* and the WHC-CM-1-11 *Industrial Hygiene* manuals apply to which group(s)?
   a. Fluor Daniel Hanford, Inc.
   b. Fluor Daniel Hanford, Inc., and the contractors working "within the fence"
   c. All PHMC employees

2. Management is responsible to ensure that safety meetings are conducted, attended, and documented according to the established attendance requirements. Complete each statement with the designated requirement.
   a. Construction forces personnel are required to attend safety meetings every _____ .
   b. Plant force personnel (operations, maintenance, radiation control) are required to attend safety meetings every _____ .
   c. Administrative personnel are required to attend safety meetings every _____ .

3. Management is to document field assessments of work areas and facilities. Fill in the minimum time requirement for each of the following types of activities.
   a. _____ for construction work (may be documented in the supervisor's log).
   b. _____ for oversight of construction contractors.
   c. _____ for shops and storage areas.
   d. _____ prior to new occupancy for plant facility buildings and offices.

4. A job-related "lost work day case/restricted work activity" occurs when the employee is not able to be in the work environment during the normal work shift. If the employee is at work but not able to perform all normal duties, it will not count as a "lost work day case/restricted work activity."
   a. True
   b. False

5. The construction manager has the ability to enforce nonpaid work stoppages if a construction contractor refuses to comply with project safety and health requirements.
   a. True
   b. False

6. What form should a manager use to communicate hazard information for routine work activities and verbal work requests to the affected workers?
   a. The computer-based qualitative job hazard analysis (QJHA)
   b. Use of a job-specific JHA/JSA
   c. Use of an existing job JHA/JSA

7. Per shift, how many personnel are required to hold a current first-aid certificate to provide emergency first aid?
   a. One
   b. Two
   c. Three

Exhibit 20.2. Manager Safety Training Pretest *(continued)*

---

8. A person who locks out and tags out machines, equipment, or systems to perform servicing or maintenance on the machine or equipment is identified as a/an _____ .
    a. Affected worker
    b. Authorized worker
    c. Control worker

9. Which of the following correctly identifies the topic(s) that must be covered when providing training for employees on the proper use of PPE?
    a. Determination of level of protection required
    b. How to correctly apply the PPE
    c. Methods for keeping the equipment in usable condition
    d. All of the above

10. Who is responsible for confirming and documenting that all valves on the water supply to the eyewash and/or safety shower are locked in the open position before personnel are assigned to work in an area with significant potential for injury due to splashing hazardous chemicals?
    a. Facility plumber
    b. Facility pipefitters
    c. Facility management

11. All electrically powered tools will be equipped with a constant pressure switch that will shut off power when pressure is released by the operator.
    a. True
    b. False

12. To separate incompatible or combustible materials, compressed gas cylinders are to be stored isolated from any incompatible or combustible materials storage by a barrier at least 5 feet high with a minimum fire resistance rating of 3/2 hour and/or
    a. A minimum of 10 feet from any incompatible or combustible material
    b. A minimum of 20 feet from any incompatible or combustible material
    c. A minimum of 30 feet from any incompatible or combustible material

13. Who is the "authority having jurisdiction" for interpretation and application of worker electrical safety requirements at the Hanford site?
    a. Maintenance Management Board
    b. National Electric Code
    c. Hanford Workplace Electrical Safety Board
    d. 29 CFR 1910 Subpart S and 29 CFR 1926 Subpart K

14. When should a worker check electrical test equipment for proper operation when verifying that circuits are deenergized?
    a. At the beginning of the shift
    b. At the end of the shift
    c. Immediately prior to the verification
    d. Immediately after the verification
    e. Immediately prior to and after the verification

15. A stairway, ladder, ramp, or other safe means of egress must be provided in trenches that are 4 feet or more in depth. Spacing of exits must not cause employees to travel more than _____ feet (lateral travel) to exit.
    a. Ten (10)
    b. Fifteen (15)
    c. Twenty (20)
    d. Twenty-five (25)

Exhibit 20.2. Manager Safety Training Pretest *(continued)*

16. Prior to construction or maintenance activities on roofs of mobile offices and other maintained structures with no known structural defects, an assessment may be performed by one safety inspector for compliance.
    a. True
    b. False

17. When the danger of falling cannot be engineered out of an activity, at what height is the use of personal protective equipment, such as a full body harness, required?
    a. Four feet
    b. Six feet
    c. Eight feet
    d. Ten feet

18. Any portable ladder purchased for the Hanford site must be ANSI approved and be rated either _____ .
    a. Type I or IA
    b. Type II or IIB
    c. Type III or IIIC

19. A registered professional engineer must be used to inspect all scaffolds (and their components) in use before the start of each work shift and following any occurrence that could affect the unit's structural integrity.
    a. True
    b. False

20. When is it appropriate to transport personnel in the back of a pickup truck?
    a. Never
    b. When driving a short distance
    c. When there is a declared emergency

21. Employees are not to work continuously for more than (fill in the blank) _____ hours in any 24-hour period.

22. If a condensation-induced water hammer occurs, or is suspected of having occurred during steam system operation, what five steps must be taken?
    1. _____
    2. _____
    3. _____
    4. _____
    5. _____

23. List the four characteristics that cause a confined space to be a permit-required confined space.
    1. _____
    2. _____
    3. _____
    4. _____

24. When is it appropriate for a confined-space attendant to enter the confined space for a rescue attempt?
    a. Life-threatening conditions exist
    b. The confined-space worker has lost consciousness
    c. The attendant is trained to use retrieval systems
    d. Never

Exhibit 20.2. Manager Safety Training Pretest *(continued)*

---

25. Who will help line management in determining the potential exposure hazards portion of the employee job task analysis (EJTA)?
    a. Facility/project industrial hygienist
    b. Employee
    c. Human Resources
    d. Medical contractor

26. Line management must request assistance from Industrial Hygiene in conducting a noise exposure assessment and quantify noise exposures when historical monitoring data, type of operation, or duration of work in noisy areas indicate employee exposures may equal or exceed _____ dba.
    a. 60
    b. 75
    c. 80
    d. 85

27. Identify the circumstance that triggers annual lead (Pb) worker training.

    _____

28. For general industry, when is biological monitoring required for workers exposed to lead (Pb) hazards?
    a. Always
    b. Never
    c. When exposure has occurred above the action level
    d. When exposure has occurred at or above the action level for 30 days or more a year

29. If an employee is a respirator wearer, when must they receive a medical evaluation?
    a. Within 6 months of job assignment
    b. Within 6 months of respiratory protection training
    c. Annually and with any new job assignment
    d. Prior to respiratory fit testing

30. The temperature using the WBGT formula is 29.4°C (85°F), and your employee is performing some heavy work in one pair of Anti-C's. From WKH 16 (provided), identify the appropriate percent ratio of work/rest per hour.
    a. 75/25
    b. 50/50
    c. 25/75
    d. 0/100

Exhibit 20.3. HTAC Executive Summary and Evaluation Report

Executive Summary

I. Overview: Per request of the manager or Environmental Safety and Health Training (ES&HT), the Hanford Training Assessment Center (HTAC) assisted that organization in conducting an evaluation (Kirkpatrick model, level 3) of Manager Safety Training.

II. Evaluation purposes: To determine whether this training is effective, to identify the best approach to use for updating this training each year, and to determine what the focus of this training should be in 1997.

III. Evaluation scope: As stated in paragraph II above.

IV. Evaluation constraints: Fifty-five (55) of 99 students completed and returned surveys for analysis. Confidence in the survey data is 73.3 percent. Readers are cautioned that the survey results provide evidence, not proof, to support any observations, recommendations, and conclusions stated in this report.

Summary of Survey Results

Items 1–3, 7, and 8 are grouped based on use of Yes/No response options.	*Yes*	*No*
1. Do you use this training on your job?	33.3%	66.7%
2. Is a structured Manager Safety Training program needed?	79.6	20.4
3. Is annual or follow-on training needed?	72.7	27.3
7. Are you willing to be interviewed regarding this training?	62.3	37.7
8. Are you willing to participate in a focus group meeting to help determine course content?	25.9	74.1

4. Which do you prefer?

Cafeteria-style offering in which you complete two modules of your choosing each year	52.8%
Standard, core course, and a specific module as a follow-on, if needed/desired	17.0
Standard, core course	11.3
Other	09.4
None	09.4

5. Rank order topic preferences

Management responsibilities	34.0%
Hazards recognition/awareness	25.0
Accident investigation/case management	19.2
Voluntary protection program	09.4
Ergonomics	09.4
Behavior-based safety training	06.0

6. List any topics more important than those in item 5.	Ten responses, no pattern noted

9. To what extent are you familiar with the FDH Zero Accident Program?

Those who said Somewhat	25
Those who said Not at all	20
Those who said the Accident goal = 0.	2

Exhibit 20.3. HTAC Executive Summary and Evaluation Report *(continued)*

---

10. What do you see as your role in the FDH Zero Accident Program?

    Leadership   31
    Don't know yet   5
    Other   3
    Nothing   2

V. Conclusion: Managers want a structured course emphasizing their responsibilities, hazards/recognition awareness, and accident investigation/case management. Moreover, the specificity of their many comments provides a wide array of topics applicable to the majority of site managers.

VI. Overall recommendation: Implement the ES&H Training Team strategy (focus group meeting with customers), stated in paragraph III, to improve this training. It appears to be the right approach and will give them a sense of ownership.

Evaluation Report

I. Background Information

   a. The terms "employees," "members," "people," "personnel," "respondents," "students," and "survey respondents" may be used interchangeably in this report.

   b. Manager Safety Training (Course 004005) has been offered annually for the past four years. It is driven by the Voluntary Protection Program and Best Management Practices. Each year, Subject Matter Experts conducted an annual Table Top Analysis to determine the course content. Based on analysis results, annual offerings consisted of primary safety issues and concerns identified by the analysis group. For 1996, the training consisted of discussion and a directed team activity in which participants worked through a likely workplace safety scenario, including identifying the point at which a manager would intervene with the hypothetical employee who was involved. Accident investigation and case management steps were also reviewed as a key part of this course. Participant learning is informally measured (level 2, Kirkpatrick model) during class activities, and there is a level 1 evaluation component.

   c. Evaluation constraints: See paragraph IV, Executive Summary.

   d. Guidance from ES&H Training Management: ES&H Training is best positioned to determine the meaning of collected evaluation data and any courses of action that should be pursued so this training has greater impact for line organizations. Therefore, the HTAC consultants conducted a limited analysis of the evaluation data and is providing limited commentary regarding Observations, Recommendations, and Conclusions.

   e. Strategy: Level 3 evaluation data were gathered through a combination of surveys and interviews. Survey data were collected and analyzed and the results provided to the ES&H Training Team. The team used the results to develop questions that were asked of past students during telephone interviews. Data from both sets of information may be used to help determine the content of Manager Safety Training for 1997.

Exhibit 20.3. HTAC Executive Summary and Evaluation Report *(continued)*

II. Description of the Evaluation

    a. Evaluation methodology: In a joint undertaking, the HTAC and the ES&H Team completed the level 3 Evaluation Design Document. Recipients were provided advance notification of the evaluation. Survey data were collected October 16 through October 28, 1996.

    b. Review of level 1 and level 2 evaluation process:
        (1) <u>Level 1:</u> Students' satisfaction with this training is measured each class. The data are compiled with feedback from other sessions, periodically analyzed, and training changes made when appropriate.
        (2) <u>Level 2:</u> Learning is informally measured (level 2, Kirkpatrick model) during class activities.

    c. Evaluation purposes: See paragraph II, Executive Summary.

    d. Types of information needed:
        (1) If employees value this training.
        (2) If this training is used on the job, and if not, why not.
        (3) If this training has limited or no application on the job.

III. Evaluation Results Strategy: The ES&H Training Team intends to use the results of this evaluation to determine the direction and content of a customer focus group meeting to be held in the near future. The participants will provide input for the content and format of Manager Safety Training for calendar year 1997. Asking customers what they need and/or want leads to their involvement, buy-in, and, ultimately, satisfaction. This is a good idea.

Exhibit 20.4. Manager Safety Survey Questions

---

1. Since completing this training, have you applied any of it on your job? If yes, explain. If no, why not?

2. Do you believe a structured Manager Safety Training program of some type is needed at Hanford?

3. If you answered yes to question 2 above, do you believe some type of annual refresher or follow-on training is needed once a manager completes an initial Manager Safety Training course?

4. Which do you prefer?

5. Based on participants' reactions to the Manager Safety Training presented in 1996, the topics listed below were most often suggested for inclusion in Manager Safety Training for 1997. Please rank these items in order of importance to you. A ranking of 1 is most important, a ranking of 6 is least important.

6. If there is a more important topic to cover in 1997 than what is listed in 5 above, please tell us what it is.

7. Are you willing to participate in a short (10–15 minute) interview to discuss your responses to this survey?

8. Are you willing to participate in a focus group meeting to determine the content of the 1997 Manager Safety Training?

9. To what extent are you familiar with Fluor Daniel Hanford's Zero Accident program?

10. What do you see as your role in Fluor Daniel Hanford's Zero Accident program?

Exhibit 20.5. Survey Results—Manager Safety Training

---

1. Do you use this training on your job?

   33.3% (18)—Yes
   66.7% (36)—No

   Observation 1-1: Comments supporting yes responses were about evenly split between managers taking measures to prevent safety incidents and actions taken subsequent to incidents occurring. Assuming that reacting to safety incidents shows an absence of preventive measures may be unwarranted. Perhaps the individual(s) involved failed to follow established procedures. It may also be inappropriate to assume preventive measures precluded occurrence of an incident —maybe there were no measures and the person's common sense took over.

   Recommendation 1-1: None.

   Observation 1-2: Of the thirty-six people who responded no to this item, twenty-eight provided explanations, eighteen of which were "not yet needed." Two conclusions that may be drawn from the responses to this item are:
   1. Those who responded "not yet needed" intend to apply the training when the need does arise.
   2. For some managers, not applying this training until it is needed may mean reacting to an incident.

   Recommendation 1-2: Continue encouraging managers to implement proactive safety measures. As the saying goes: "An ounce of prevention . . ."

2. Do you believe a structured Manager Safety Training program of some type is needed at Hanford?

   79.6% (43)—Yes
   20.4% (11)—No

   Observation 2-1: The thirty-six written comments that support the yes responses provided specific ideas for consideration. They range from "address those issues . . . causing current workplace problems" to "not . . . at the elementary level."

   Recommendation 2-1: None. The ES&H Training Team's strategy to determine the content and format of the 1997 Manager Safety Training should provide the greatest benefit to the majority of recipients.

   Observation 2-2: Some thoughts expressed in the no responses to this item were that facility-specific training, weekly and monthly safety training, manager and employee participation in said training, and daily involvement with safety on the job may be perceived as adequate.

3. If you answered yes to question 2 above, do you believe some type of annual or follow-on training is needed once a manager completes an initial Manager Safety Training course?

   72.7% (32)—Yes
   27.3% (12)—No

Exhibit 20.5. Survey Results—Manager Safety Training *(continued)*

Observation 3-1: Respondents provided almost two dozen thoughts regarding this item. Many were repeats from item 2 above, but with preferences stated regarding differences in content between initial and annual/follow-on training.

Recommendation 3-1: Same as 2-1 above.

Observation 3-2: There were no patterns/trends in the no responses. Four people said annual training is enough.

Recommendation 3-2: None.

4. Which do you prefer?

   11.3% (6)—Standard, core course
   17.0% (9)—Standard, core course, and a specific module as a follow-on, if
   needed/desired
   52.8% (28)—Cafeteria-style offering in which you complete two modules of
   your choosing each year
   9.4% (5)—Other
   9.4% (5)—None

   Observation 4-1: No patterns or trends were noted in the narrative responses. Managers seemed content to let their preferences speak for them.

   Recommendation 4-1: None.

5. Topics listed below were most recommended for inclusion in Manager Safety Training 1997.

   34% (17)—Management responsibilities
   25% (13)—Hazards recognition/awareness
   19.2% (10)—Accident investigation and case management
   9.4% (5)—Voluntary protection program
   9.4% (5)—Ergonomics
   6% (3)—Behavior-based safety training

   Observation 5-1: None.

   Recommendation 5-1: None.

6. If there is a more important topic to cover in 1997 than what is listed in 5 above, please give us a brief description.

   • Overview of what like organizational entities do better at safety, and why that is so.
   • Individual martyrs who come to work sick and make the workplace unsafe by spreading their disease.
   • I believe that more time should be spent on the changes that have occurred in the *Safety Manual*.
   • An awareness of nationally recognized programs, innovative ideas, methods, and safeguards.
   • Recognizing safety as a value—where it fits among other life values.
   • Supplemental guidance on the Zero Accident program.

   Observation 6-1: Written responses were quite diverse. No patterns/trends were noted.

   Recommendation 6-1: None.

Exhibit 20.5. Survey Results—Manager Safety Training *(continued)*

7. Are you willing to participate in a short telephone interview (10 to 15 minutes) to discuss your responses to this survey?

62.3% (33)—Yes
37.7% (20)—No

Observation 7-1: The ES&H Training Team called those who responded yes, to (1) obtain additional information they may wish to share, (2) thank them for inputs, and (3) inform them the next step will be conducting a focus group meeting to determine course content for 1997. Frequent communication such as this improves relations, along with the probability that next year's training will meet stakeholders' needs. *This is a good idea.* The manager of ES&H Training routinely informs customers of training improvements.

Observation 7-2: None.

Recommendation 7-2: None.

8. Are you willing to participate in a focus group meeting to determine the content of the 1997 Manager Safety Training? This meeting may require 4-8 hours of your time.

25.9% (14)—Yes
74.1% (40)—No

Observation 8-1: None.

Recommendation 8-1: None.

9. To what extent are you familiar with Fluor Daniel Hanford's Zero Accident program?

(2) That all accidents or injuries are avoidable so the actual goal is for 0.
(20) Not at all . . . Zero . . . Never heard of it.
(25) Just introduced . . . Somewhat . . . Just what I've read in the company newsletter.

Observation 9-1: None.

Recommendation 9-1: None.

10. What do you see as your role in Fluor Daniel Hanford's Zero Accident program?

• Providing a safe working environment for my employees and empowering them to work as a team.
• My role is to continue my lifestyle of safe thinking and safe actions at work and at home.
• Personal accountability for my safety and responsibility to help others be safe.
• A leadership role, promoting the policies and procedures of the program.
• Making sure my organization and I continue to concentrate on safety.

Observation 10-1: None.

Recommendation 10-1: None.

Conclusion: Managers want a structured course emphasizing their responsibilities, hazards/recognition awareness, and accident investigation/case management. Moreover, the specificity of their many comments provides a wide array of topics applicable to the majority of site managers.

Chapter 21

Evaluating a Training Program on Stress Management for Intact Work Teams

This case study begins by describing how the needs for training were determined. It then describes how the training program was evaluated at all four levels. The comprehensive approach includes the use of the StressMap® to measure learning as well as the use of control groups. In evaluating level 4, a description is included of how ROI was measured. The specific forms and procedures make the case study of practical value for organizations that are serious about evaluating at all four levels.

Midwest Electric, Inc.

Jack J. Phillips, President
Performance Resources Organization,
Birmingham, Alabama

Patricia F. Pulliam, Chief Operating Officer
Performance Resources Organization,
Birmingham, Alabama

Background

Midwest Electric, Inc. (MEI), is a growing electric utility serving several midwestern states. Since deregulation of the industry, MEI has been on a course of diversification and growth. Through a series of acquisitions,

MEI has moved outside of its traditional operating areas and into several related businesses.

MEI has been experiencing significant workplace changes as it is transformed from a bureaucratic, sluggish organization into a lean, competitive force in the marketplace. These changes have placed tremendous pressure on employees to develop multiple skills and perform additional work. Employees, working in teams, must constantly strive to reduce costs, maintain excellent quality, boost productivity, and generate new and efficient ways to supply customers and improve service.

As with many industries in a deregulated environment, MEI detected symptoms of employee stress. The safety and health function in the company suggested that employee stress lowered productivity and reduced employee effectiveness. Stress is also considered to be a significant employee health risk. Research has shown that high levels of stress are commonplace in many work groups and that organizations are taking steps to help employees and work groups reduce stress in a variety of ways. The vice president of Human Resources at MEI asked the Training and Education Department, with the help of the Safety and Health Department, to develop a program for work groups to help them alleviate stressful situations and deal more productively and effectively with job-induced stress.

Needs Assessment

Because of its size and sophisticated human resource systems, MEI has an extensive database on employee-related measures. MEI prides itself as being one of the leaders in the industry in human resources issues. Needs assessments have been routinely conducted at MEI, and the HR vice president was willing to allow sufficient time for an adequate needs assessment before proceeding with the Stress Management program.

The overall purpose of the needs assessment was to identify the causes of a perceived problem. The needs assessment would:

- Confirm that a problem does exist and provide an assessment of the actual impact of this problem
- Uncover potential causes of the problem within the work unit, company, and environment
- Provide insight into potential remedies to correct the problem

The sources of data for the needs assessment include company records, external research, team members, team leaders, and managers. The assessment began with a review of external research that identified factors usually related to high stress and the consequences of high stress in work groups. The consequences uncovered specific measures that could be identified at MEI.

This external research led to a review of several key data items in company records, including attitude surveys, medical claims, EAP utilization, safety and health records, and exit interviews. The attitude survey data represented the results from the previous year and were reviewed for low scores on the specific questions that could yield stress-related symptoms. Medical claims were analyzed by codes to identify the extent of those related to stress-induced illnesses. Employee Assistance Plan (EAP) data were reviewed to determine the extent to which employees were using provisions and services of the plan perceived to be stress-related. Safety records were reviewed to determine if specific accidents were stress-related or that causes of accidents could be traced to high levels of stress. In each of the above areas, the data were compared to the previous year to determine whether stress-related measures were changing. Also, where available, data were compared to expected norms from the external research. Finally, exit interviews for the previous six months were analyzed to determine the extent to which the stress-related situations were factors in an employee's decision to voluntarily leave MEI.

During MEI's needs assessment process, a small sample of employees (ten team members) was interviewed to discuss their work-life situations and uncover symptoms of stress at work. Also, a small group of managers (five) was interviewed with the same purpose. To provide more detail on this input, a 10 percent sample of employees received a questionnaire to explore the same issues. MEI has 22,550 employees, with 18,220 nonsupervisory team members.

Summary of Findings

The needs assessment process uncovered several significant findings:

- There was evidence of high levels of stress in work groups caused by MEI's deregulation, restructuring, and job changes.

In essence, the change in the nature of work induced high levels of stress in most work groups.

- Stress has led to a deterioration in several performance measures, including medical costs, short-term disability, withdrawals (absenteeism, turnover), and job satisfaction.
- Employees were often not fully aware of stress factors and the effect that stress had on them and their work.
- Employees had inadequate skills for coping with stress and adjusting to, managing, and eliminating highly stressful situations.
- Managers had more insight into the causes of stress but did not have the skills or mechanisms to deal with most stressful situations.

Program Planning and Design

Several inherent factors about work groups and data at MEI influenced the program and its subsequent evaluation. MEI is organized around teams, and groups are not usually identical. However, many teams have similar performance measures. The HR database is rich with a variety of measures and data on employees and work-unit factors. Because of the team environment and the important role of the team leader/manager, the program to reduce stress must involve the management group in a proactive way. Any efforts to reduce stress must shift much of the responsibility to participants and thus reduce the amount of time off the job. Job pressures in the deregulated environment provide fewer off-the-job opportunities for meeting and development activities.

Program Design

While several approaches could be feasible to satisfy this need, four issues surfaced that influenced program design:

- A skills and knowledge deficiency existed, and some type of learning event was necessary.
- Several stress management programs were commercially available that could prevent developing a new program from scratch.
- Managers needed to be involved in the process to the greatest extent possible.
- Because of the concerns about time away from the job, the actual classroom/formal meeting activities should be limited to one or two days.

With this in mind, the program outlined in Exhibit 21.1 was designed to meet this important need. (The exhibits are grouped at the end of the chapter.)

Why Business Results?

HR/HRD training programs usually targeted for a level 4 evaluation are those perceived to be adding significant value to the company and closely linked to the organizational goals and strategic objectives. The evaluation is then pursued to confirm the added value. Based on the results of the analysis, these programs may be enhanced, redesigned, or eliminated if the results are insufficient. Stress management can be different. If the results are inadequate, the program may not be discontinued but may be altered for future sessions, particularly if behavior changes are not identified in the level 3 evaluation.

At MEI, the Stress Management program was chosen for a level 4 evaluation for two reasons. First, the Human Resources and Training and Education Departments were interested in the accountability of all programs, including stress management. Second, positive results would clearly show management that these types of programs, which are preventive in nature, can significantly contribute to the bottom line when they are implemented and supported by management.

Because the program can be expensive if applied to the entire company, it was decided to try it on a limited basis to determine its success and then make a decision to adjust, discontinue, or expand the program to other areas in MEI. The evaluation methodology provided the best information to make that decision.

Data Collection Plan

Exhibit 21.2 shows the data collection plan for the Stress Management program. Broad objectives were established for levels 1, 2, 3, and 4 data collection. The data collection plan is comprehensive but necessary to meet all of the requirements at each of the four levels of data collection. The timing and responsibilities are detailed. For measuring learning, three tools are used. The StressMap® is one measure of learning in the awareness category. Completion of this map provides insight into stress factors and stress signals. In addition, built into the one-day program is an end-of-course self-assessment to measure learning. Finally, the facilitator has a brief checklist to indicate the extent of learning for the group.

At level 3 data collection, the completion of the twenty-one-day plan provides some evidence that participants have changed behavior to reduce stress. A conference call is planned with the facilitator, team manager, and the team twenty-one days after the course. This provides a review of issues and addresses any concerns or barriers to further implementation. A follow-up session is planned with the team, cofacilitated by the manager and facilitator, approximately one to two weeks after the one-day program to discuss changes in behavior and address barriers. To determine the extent to which the participants are using internal or external resources to address stress-related problems, records of those requests will be reviewed for approximately six months. Finally, a detailed follow-up questionnaire is planned six months after the program to collect both level 3 and 4 data. This questionnaire will capture sustained behavior changes, indicate barriers to improvement, and identify impact measures for both groups and individuals.

Group records reveal changes in medical costs, absenteeism, turnover, and productivity six months after the program. In addition, increased job satisfaction will be determined from the follow-up questionnaire, which will be administered six months after the program (that is, the same questionnaire described earlier).

Evaluation Analysis Plan

Exhibit 21.3 shows the evaluation analysis plan. For most data items, the method to isolate the effects of training will be obtained in a control group arrangement in which the performance of the group involved in the program will be compared to a carefully matched companion control group. In addition, for most of the data items, trend-line analyses will be utilized. Historical data are projected in a trend and compared with the actual data to determine the impact of the program.

The methods of converting data involve a variety of approaches, including tabulation of direct costs, using standard values and also external data, and securing estimates from a variety of target audiences. The cost categories represent fully loaded costs for the program. Expected intangible benefits from the program are based on the experience of other organizations and other stress-reduction programs. The communication target audience shows six key groups ranging from corporate and business unit managers to participants and their immediate supervisors.

Management Involvement

Management involvement has been a key issue from the very beginning and was integrated throughout the design of the program. The manager serves as the team leader for the program, although a facilitator provides assistance and conducts a one-day workshop. Exhibit 21.4 illustrates the tool used for identifying initial problems as the work group began utilizing the Stress Management program. With this brief questionnaire, the manager identifies specific problem areas and provides appropriate comments and details. This exercise allows program planning to focus on the problems and provides guidance to the facilitator and the team.

Manager responsibility and involvement for the process are illustrated in Exhibit 21.5. This handout, provided directly to the managers, details twelve specific areas of responsibility and involvement for the managers. Collectively, initial planning, program design, and detailing of responsibilities pushed the manager into a higher-profile position in the program.

Control Group Arrangement

The appropriateness of control groups was reviewed in this setting. If a stress-reduction program is needed, it would be appropriate and ethical to withhold the program for certain groups while the experiment was being conducted. It was concluded that this approach was appropriate because the impact of the planned program was in question. Although it was clear that stress-induced problems exist at MEI, there was no guarantee that this program would correct them. Six control groups were planned. The control group arrangement was diligently pursued because it represented the best approach to isolate the effects of the program, if the groups could be matched.

Several criteria were available for group selection. Exhibit 21.6 shows the data collection instrument used to identify groups for a control group arrangement. At the first cut, only those groups that had the same measures were considered (that is, at least 75 percent of the measures were common in the group). This action provided an opportunity to compare performance in the six months preceding the program.

Next, only groups in the same function code were used. At MEI, all groups were assigned a code depending on the type of work, such as finance and accounting or engineering. Thus, each experimental group had to be in the same code as the matched control group. It was also required that all six groups be spread over at least three different codes.

Two other variables were used in the matching process: group size and tenure. The number of employees in the groups had to be within a 20 percent spread, and the average tenure had to be within a two-year range. At MEI, as with many other utilities, there is a very high average tenure rate.

Although other variables could be used to make the match, these five were considered to be the most influential in the outcome. In summary, the following criteria were used to select the two sets of groups:

- Same measures of performance
- Similar performance in the previous six months
- Same function code
- Similar size
- Similar tenure

The six pairs of groups represented a total level of employment of 138 team members for the experimental groups and 132 team members and six managers for the control groups.

Program Results

Questionnaire Response

A follow-up questionnaire, Exhibit 21.7, served as the primary data collection instrument for participants. A similar, slightly modified instrument was used with the managers. In all, 73 percent of the participants returned the questionnaire. This excellent response rate is due, in part, to a variety of actions taken to ensure an appropriate response rate. Some of the most important actions were:

- The team manager distributed the questionnaire and encouraged participants to return it to the external consulting firm. The manager also provided a follow-up reminder.
- A full explanation of how the evaluation data would be utilized was provided to participants.
- The questionnaire was reviewed during the follow-up session.

- Two types of incentives were used.
- Participants were promised a copy of the questionnaire results.

Application Data

The application of the program was considered an outstanding success, with 92 percent of the participants completing their twenty-one-day action plan. A conference call at the end of the twenty-one days showed positive feedback and much enthusiasm for the progress made. The follow-up session also demonstrated success, because most of the participants had indicated changes in behavior.

The most comprehensive application data came from the six-month questionnaire administered to participants and managers. The following skills and behaviors were reported as achieving significant success:

- Taking full responsibility for one's actions
- Identifying or removing barriers to change behavior
- Applying coping strategies to manage stressful situations
- Responding effectively to conflict
- Creating a positive climate
- Acknowledging a complaint properly

Coworkers were the most frequently cited group in which relationships had improved through use of the skills, with 95 percent indicating application improvement with this group.

Barriers

Information collected throughout the process, including the two follow-up questionnaires, indicated few barriers to implementing the process. The two most frequently listed barriers were: (1) not enough time; and (2) the work environment does not support the process.

Management Support

Manager support seemed to be quite effective. The most frequently listed behaviors of managers were: (1) managers set goals for change and improvement; and (2) managers discussed how the program can apply to the work group.

Impact Data

The impact of the program was very significant with regard to both perceptions and actual values. On the follow-up questionnaire (Exhibit 21.7), 90 percent of the participants perceived this program as a good investment for MEI. In addition, participants perceived that this program had a significant influence on:

- Employee satisfaction
- Absenteeism
- Turnover
- Health care cost
- Safety and health cost

This assessment appears to support the actual improvement data outlined below. For each measure below, only the team data were collected and presented. Since managers were not the target of the program, manager performance data were not included. Instead of month 6, an average of months 5 and 6 was used consistently for the postprogram data analysis to eliminate the spike effect.

Health Care Costs. Health care costs for employees were categorized by diagnostic code; thus, it was a simple process to track the cost of stress-induced illnesses. Although there were few differences shown in the first three months after the program began, by month 5 and 6 an average difference of $120 per employee per month was identified. This was apparently due to the lack of stress-related incidents and the subsequent medical costs resulting from the stress. It was believed that this amount would be an appropriate improvement to use. The trend-line projection of health care costs was inconclusive because of the variability of the medical care costs prior to the program. A consistent trend could not be identified.

Absenteeism. There was significant difference in absenteeism in the two groups. The average absenteeism for the control group for months 5 and 6 was 4.65 percent. The absenteeism rate for the groups involved in the program was 3.2 percent. Employees worked an average of 220 days. The trend-line analysis appeared to support the absenteeism reduction. Because no other issues were identified that could have influenced absenteeism during this time period, the trend-line analysis provided an accurate estimate of the impact.

Turnover. Although turnover at MEI was traditionally low, in the past two years it had increased due to significant changes in the workplace. A turnover reduction was identified using the differences in the control group and experimental group. The control group had an average annual turnover rate for months 5 and 6 of 19.2 percent. The experimental group had an average of 14.1 percent for the same two months. As with absenteeism, the trend-line analysis supported the turnover reduction.

Productivity. Control group differences showed no significant improvement in productivity. Of all the measures collected, the productivity measure was the most difficult to match between the two groups, which may account for the inconclusive results. Also, the trend-line differences showed some slight improvement but not enough to develop an actual value for productivity changes.

Job Satisfaction. Because of the timing difference in collecting attitude survey data, complete job satisfaction data were not available. Participants did provide input on the extent to which they felt the program actually influenced job satisfaction. The results were very positive, with a significant influence rating for that variable. Because of the subjective nature of job satisfaction and the difficulties with measurement, a value was not assigned to job satisfaction.

Monetary Values

The determination of monetary benefits for the program were developed using the methods outlined in the evaluation analysis plan. The medical costs are converted directly. A $120 per month savings yields a $198,720 annual benefit. A standard value has routinely been used at MEI to reflect the cost of an absence. This value is 1.25 times the average daily wage rate. For the experimental group, the average wage rate was $123 per day. This yields an annual improvement value of $67,684. For employee turnover, several turnover cost studies are available that reveal a value of 85 percent of annual base pay. As expected, senior managers felt that this cost of turnover was slightly overstated and preferred to use a value of 70 percent, yielding an annual benefit of $157,553. No values were used for productivity or job satisfaction. The total annual benefit of the Stress Management program was $423,957. Table 21.1 reflects the total economic benefits of the program.

Table 21.1. Annual Monetary Benefits for 138 Participants

	Monthly difference	*Unit value*	*Annual improvement value*
Medical costs	$120	—	$198,720
Absenteeism	1.45%	$153.75	$ 67,684
Turnover	5.1% (annualized)	$22,386	$157,553
		Total	$423,957

The medical costs are converted directly. A $120 per month savings yields a $198,720 annual benefit. Other values are as follows:

Unit value for an absence
$123 × 1.25 = $153.75

Unit value for turnover
$31,980 × 70% = $22,386

Improvement for absenteeism
138 employees × 220 workdays × 1.45% × $153.75 = $67,684

Improvement for turnover
138 employees × 5.1% × $22,386 = $157,553

No values were used for productivity or job satisfaction.

Intangible Benefits

Several intangible benefits were identified in the study and confirmed by actual input from participants and questionnaires, as follows:

- Employee satisfaction
- Teamwork
- Improved relationships with family and friends
- Time savings
- Improved image in the company
- Fewer conflicts

No attempt was made to place monetary values on any of the intangibles.

Program Costs

Calculating the costs of the Stress Management program also follows the categories outlined in the evaluation plan. For needs assessment, all of the costs were fully allocated to the six groups. Although the needs assessment was necessary, the total cost of needs assessment, $16,500, was included. All program development costs were estimated at $95 per participant, or $4,800. The program could possibly be spread through other parts of the organization, which would ultimately be prorated across all the sessions. However, the costs were low because the materials were readily available for most of the effort and the total development cost was used

The salaries for the team members averaged $31,980, while the six team managers had average salaries of $49,140. The benefits factor for MEI is 37 percent for both groups. Although the program took a little more than one day of staff time, one day of program time was considered sufficient for cost. The total salary costs were $24,108. The participants' travel cost ($38 per participant) was very low because the programs were conducted in the area. The costs for facilitator, program coordination, and training and development overhead were estimated to be $10,800. The meeting room facilities, food, and refreshments averaged $22 per participant for a total of $3,968. Evaluation costs were $22,320. It was decided that all of the evaluation costs would be allocated to these six groups. This determination was extremely conservative, since the evaluation costs could be prorated if the program was implemented over other areas.

Table 21.2 details the Stress Management program costs. These costs were considered to be fully loaded, with no proration except for

Table 21.2. Program Costs

Cost category	Total cost
Needs assessment	$16,500
Program development	4,800
Program materials (144 × $95)	13,680
Participant salaries/benefits (based on 1 day) 138 × $123 × 1.37 and 6 × $189 × 1.37	24,108
Travel and lodging 144 × $38	5,472
Facilitation, coordination, T&E overhead	10,800
Meeting room, food, refreshments 144 × $22	3,168
Evaluation costs	22,320
Total	$100,848

needs assessment. Additional time could have been used for participants' off-the-job activities. However, it was concluded that one day should be sufficient (for the one-day program.)

Results: ROI

Based on the given monetary benefits and costs, the return on investment (ROI) and the benefits/cost ratio (BCR) are shown below.

$$\text{BCR} = \frac{\$423,957}{\$100,848} = 4.20$$

$$\text{ROI} = \frac{\$423,957 - \$100,848}{\$100,848} = 320\%$$

Although this number is considered to be very large, it is still conservative because of the following assumptions and adjustments:

- Only first-year values have been used. The program should actually have second- and third-year benefits.
- Control group differences were used in analysis, which is often the most effective way to isolate the effects of the program. These differences were also confirmed with the trend-line analysis.
- The participants provided additional monetary benefits, detailed on the questionnaires. Although they could have been added to the total numbers, these benefits were not included since only 23 of 144 participants supplied values for those questions.
- The costs are fully loaded.

When considering these adjustments, the value should represent a realistic value calculation for the actual return on investment.

Communication Strategies

Due to the importance of sharing the analysis results, a communication strategy was developed. Table 21.3 outlines this strategy. Three separate documents were developed to communicate with the different target groups in a variety of ways.

Table 21.3. Communication Strategies

Communication document	Communication target	Distribution
Complete report with appendices (75 pages)	Training and education staff Safety and health staff Intact team manager	Distributed and discussed in a special meeting
Executive summary (8 pages)	Senior management in the business units Senior corporate management	Distributed and discussed in routine meeting
General interest overview and summary, without the actual ROI calculation (10 pages)	Program participants	Mailed with letter
Brochure highlighting program, objectives, and specific results	Prospective team leaders	Included with other program descriptions

Policy and Practice Implications

Because of the significance of the study and the information, two issues became policy. Whenever programs are considered that involve large groups of employees or a significant investment of funds, a detailed needs assessment will be conducted to ensure that the proper program is developed. Also, an ROI study is conducted for a small group of programs to measure the impact before complete implementation. In essence, this influenced the policy and practice on needs assessment, pilot program evaluation, and the number of impact studies developed.

Exhibit 21.1. Stress Management for Intact Work Teams

Departments or work groups of ten or more people who are committed to improving the satisfaction and effectiveness of their teams will benefit by this more comprehensive approach to stress. The process uses the **StressMap**® tool as the starting point. Managers and representative employees will participate in focus groups to identify work satisfiers and distressors and then will collaborate on alleviating systemic sources of stress.

What Group Members Will Learn

- How to identify sources of stress and personal response to them.
- That *individuals* have the ability to make a difference in their lives.
- How to take the first steps to enhance personal health and overall performance.
- How to access resources, internally and externally, to help teach personal goals.

What the Group/Manager Will Learn/Participate In

- Group profile of sources of stress and response patterns.
- Additional information on sources of both work distress and work satisfaction will be obtained through focus groups. Themes will be identified where possible.
- New stress-reduction skills specific to the needs of the group.
- Development of recommendations for next steps to take to improve work satisfaction and productivity.

Highlights

- Through completion of a comprehensive self-assessment tool called the **StressMap**® individuals will be able to immediately score themselves on twenty-one stress scales dealing with work and home life as well as learn about their preferred coping styles and the thinking and feeling patterns that impact their ability to manage stress. Anonymous copies of each member's **StressMap**® will be compiled to create a group score.
- A **StressMap**® debriefing session of three to four hours designed to help individuals better interpret their scores will be followed by a four-hour module suited to the needs of the group (such as situation mastery, changing habits, creating climate for agreement). Total of one day.

Precourse Requirements

- Management commitment to the process. Employees to complete the **StressMap**® tool and submit a confidential copy.

Length and Format

- Lead time of three to four weeks minimum for preparation and communication.
- Consultant on site a day and a half.
- Initial follow-up one to two weeks later on site or by phone to senior management. Subsequent follow-up on impact of the initiative to occur as negotiated. Three to four hours of telephone follow-up included.

Cost

- Approximately $XXXX (plus taxes) US per group of eight to twenty-five; $XX US per set of materials. Travel and living expenses for consultant are additional.

Exhibit 21.2. Data Collection Plan

Program: _____ Responsibility: _____ Date: _____

Level	Broad program objective(s)	Data collection method	Timing of data collection	Responsibilities for data collection
I. Reaction, satisfaction, and planned actions	Positive reaction Suggestions for improvements Planned action	Standard questionnaire 21-day action plan	End of one-day course End of course	Facilitator Facilitator
II. Learning	Personal stress awareness Coping strategies Stress reduction skills	StressMap® Self-assessment Facilitator assessment	Prior to course End of course End of course	Facilitator Facilitator Facilitator
III. Job application	Change behavior to reduce stress Develop group action plan and communicate to group Access internal/external resources Application of skills/knowledge	Completion of 21-day plan Conference call Follow-up session Review records Follow-up questionnaire	21 days after course 21 days after course 1–2 weeks after one-day course 6 months after course 6 months after course	No report Facilitator Facilitator/manager Program coordinator External consultant
IV. Business impact	Reduce medical care costs Reduce absenteeism Reduce turnover Increase productivity Increase job satisfaction	Group records Group records Group records Group records Follow-up questionnaire	6 months after course 6 months after course 6 months after course 6 months after course 6 months after course	Program coordinator Program coordinator Program coordinator Program coordinator External consultant

Source: Copyright 1997 Jack J. Phillips, Ph.D., Performance Resources Organization. All Rights Reserved. P.O. Box 380637, Birmingham, AL 35238-0637 USA.

Exhibit 21.3. Analysis Plan

Program: _____   Responsibility: _____   Date: _____

Data items	Methods of isolating the effects of the program	Methods of converting data	Cost categories	Intangible benefits	Other influences/issues	Communication targets
Medical health care costs—preventable claims	Control group arrangement Trend-line analysis	Direct costs	Needs assessment Program development Program materials	Improved communication	Match groups appropriately	Program participants
Absenteeism	Control group arrangement Trend-line analysis	Supervisor estimation Standard value	Participant salaries/benefits Participant travel (if applicable)	Time savings	Limit communication with control group	Intact team/manager
Employee turnover	Control group Trend-line analysis	External study—cost of turnover in high-tech industry Management review	Facilitator Meeting facilities (room, food, beverages)	Fewer conflicts Teamwork	Check for team building initiatives during program	Senior manager/management in business units
Employee job satisfaction	Control group arrangement Management estimation	Management estimation	Program coordinator	Improvement in problem solving	Monitor restructuring activities during program	Training and education staff Safety and health staff
Employee/group productivity	Control group arrangement Trend-line analysis	Standard values Management estimation	Training and education overhead Evaluation costs		6 groups will be monitored	Senior corporate management Prospective team leaders

Exhibit 21.4. Manager Input: Potential Area for Improvement

Before you begin the Stress Reduction program for your team, it is important to capture specific concerns that you have about your work group. Some of these concerns may be stress-related and consequently may be used to help structure specific goals and objectives for your team. For each of the following potential areas of improvement, please check all that apply to your group. Add others if appropriate. Next to the item provide specific comments to detail your concerns and indicate if you think that this concern may be related to excessive stress.

☐ Employee turnover. Comments:

☐ Employee absenteeism. Comments:

☐ Employee complaints. Comments:

☐ Morale/job satisfaction. Comments:

☐ Conflicts with the team. Comments:

☐ Productivity. Comments:

☐ Quality. Comments:

☐ Customer satisfaction. Comments:

☐ Customer service. Comments:

☐ Work backlog. Comments:

☐ Delays. Comments

☐ Other areas. List and provide comments:

Exhibit 21.5. Manager Responsibility and Involvement

With the team approach, the team manager should:

1. Have a discussion with the trainer to share reasons for interest in stress reduction and the desired outcome of the program. Gain a greater understanding of the **StressMap**® and the OD approach. Discuss recent changes in the work group and identify any known stressors. This meeting could be held with the senior manager or the senior management team.

2. Identify any additional work group members for the consultant to call to gather preliminary information.

3. Appoint a project coordinator, preferably an individual with good organizing and influencing skills who is respected by the work group.

4. Send out a letter inviting the group to participate in the program, with personal endorsement and signature.

5. Allocate eight hours of work time per employee for completion of the **StressMap**® and attendance at a **StressMap**® debriefing and customized course.

6. Schedule a focus group after discussing desired group composition with the facilitator. Ideal size is ten to twenty-two participants. Manager should not attend.

7. Attend the workshop and ensure that direct reports attend.

8. Participate in the follow-up meeting held after the last workshop, either in person or by conference call. Other participants to include are the HR representative for your area, the Safety and Health representative for your area, and your management team. The trainer will provide you feedback about the group's issues and make recommendations of actions to take to reduce work stress or increase work satisfaction

9. Commit to an action plan to reduce workplace distress and/or increase workplace satisfaction after thoughtfully considering feedback.

10. Communicate the action plan to your work group.

11. Schedule and participate in a twenty-one-day follow-up call with the consultant and your work group.

12. Work with your team (managers, HR, Safety and Health, facilitator) to evaluate the success of the action plan and determine next steps.

Exhibit 21.6. Manager Input: Group Measures and Characteristics

---

To measure the progress of your team, a brief profile of performance measures for employees and your work group is needed. This information will be helpful to determine the feasibility of using your group in a pilot study to measure the impact of the Stress Management program. Changes in performance measures will be monitored for six months after the program.

Listed below are several categories of measures for your work group. Check the appropriate category and please indicate the specific measure under the description. In addition, indicate if it is a group measure or an individual measure. If other measures are available in other categories, please include them under "other."

Key Performance Measures

Department _____

Performance category	Measure	Description of measure	Group measure	Individual measure
Productivity	1.			
	2.			
Efficiency	3.			
	4.			
Quality	5.			
	6.			
Response time	7.			
	8.			
Cost control/ budgets	9.			
	10.			
Customer satisfaction	11.			
	12.			
Absenteeism	13.			
Turnover	14.			
Morale/job satisfaction	15.			
	16.			
Other	17.			
(Please specify)	18.			
	19.			
	20.			

Group Characteristics

Average tenure for group _____ years   Group function code _____

Average job grade for group _____   Average age _____

Number in group _____   Average educational level _____

Exhibit 21.7. Impact Questionnaire

Check one: ☐ Team member ☐ Team leader/manager

1. Listed below are the objectives of the Stress Management program. After reflecting on this program, please indicate the degree of success in meeting the objectives.

Objectives	*Failed*	*Limited success*	*Generally successful*	*Completely successful*
Personal				
Identify sources of stress in work, personal, and family worlds				
Apply coping strategies to manage stressful situations				
Understand to what degree stress is hampering your health and performance				
Take steps to enhance personal health and overall performance				
Access internal and external resources to help reach personal goals				
Group				
Identify sources of stress for group				
Identify sources of distress and satisfaction				
Apply skills to manage and reduce stress in work group				
Develop action plan to improve work group effectiveness				
Improve effectiveness and efficiency measures for work group				

2. Did you develop and implement a twenty-one-day action plan?

   Yes ☐   No ☐

   If yes, please describe the success of the plan. If not, explain why. _____
   _____
   _____

3. Please rate, on a scale of 1–5, the relevance of each of the program elements to your job, with 1 indicating no relevance, and 5 indicating very relevant.

   _____ StressMap® instrument   _____ Action planning

   _____ Group discussion   _____ Program content

Exhibit 21.7. Impact Questionnaire *(continued)*

---

4. Please indicate the degree of success in applying the following skills and behaviors as a result of your participation in the Stress Management program.

	1	2	3	4	5	No
					Very	*opportunity*
	No	*Little*	*Some*	*Significant*	*much*	*to use skills*

  a. Selecting containable
     behavior for change

  b. Identifying measures
     of behavior

  c. Taking full responsibility
     for your actions

  d. Selecting a buddy to help
     you change behavior

  e. Identifying and removing
     barriers to changing behavior

  f. Identifying and using enablers
     to help change behavior

  g. Staying on track with the
     21-day action plan

  h. Applying coping strategies
     to manage stressful situations

  i. Using control effectively

  j. Knowing when to let go

  k. Responding effectively
     to conflict

  l. Creating a positive climate

  m. Acknowledging a complaint
     properly

  n. Reframing problems

  o. Using stress talk strategies

5. List three behaviors or skills you have used most as a result of the Stress Management program.

_____

_____

---

6. When did you first use one of the skills from the program?

  _____ During the program

  _____ Day(s) after the program (indicate number)

  _____ Week(s) after the program (indicate number)

Exhibit 21.7. Impact Questionnaire *(continued)*

---

7. Indicate the types of relationships where you have used the skills.

- ☐ Coworkers
- ☐ Manager or supervisor
- ☐ MEI employee in another function
- ☐ Spouse

- ☐ Child
- ☐ Friend
- ☐ Other (list)

_____

Personal Changes

8. What has changed about your on-the-job behavior as a result of this program? (positive attitude, fewer conflicts, better organized, fewer outbursts of anger, etc.)

_____

_____

9. Recognizing the changes in our own behavior and perceptions, please identify any specific personal accomplishments/improvements that you can link to this program. (time savings, project completion, fewer mistakes, etc.)

_____

_____

10. What specific value in U.S. dollars can be attributed to the above accomplishments/improvements? While this is a difficult question, try to think of specific ways in which the above improvements can be converted to monetary units. Use one year of data. Along with the monetary value, please indicate the basis of your calculation. $ _____

Basis _____

_____

_____

11. What level of confidence do you place on the above estimations? (0% = no confidence, 100% = certainty) _____%

12. Other factors often influence improvements in performance. Please indicate the percent of the above improvement that is related directly to this program. _____%

Please explain _____

_____

_____

Group Changes

13. What has changed about your work group as a result of your group's participation in this program? (interactions, cooperation, commitment, problem solving, creativity, etc.)

14. Please identify any specific group accomplishments/improvements that you can link to the program. (project completion, response times, innovative approaches)

Exhibit 21.7. Impact Questionnaire *(continued)*

15. What specific value in U.S. dollars can be attributed to the above accomplish-
ments/improvements? While this is a difficult question, try to think of specific
ways in which the above improvements can be converted to monetary units.
Use one year of values. Along with the monetary value, please indicate the basis
of your calculation. $ _____

    Basis _____

    _____

16. What level of confidence do you place on the above estimations? (0% = no
confidence, 100% = certainty) _____ %

17. Other factors often influence improvements in performance. Please indicate the
percent of the above improvement that is related directly to this program. _____%

    Please explain _____

    _____

18. Do you think this program represented a good investment for MEI?
Yes ☐   No ☐

    Please explain _____

    _____

19. What barriers, if any, have you encountered that have prevented you from
using skills or knowledge gained in this program? Check all that apply. Please
explain, if possible.

    ☐ Not enough time
    ☐ The work environment doesn't support it
    ☐ Management doesn't support it
    ☐ The information is not useful (comments)
    ☐ Other _____

    _____

20. Which of the following best describes the actions of your manager during the
Stress Management program.

    ☐ Very little discussion or reference to the program
    ☐ Casual mention of program with few specifics
    ☐ Discussed details of program in terms of content, issues, concerns, etc.
    ☐ Discussed how the program could be applied to work group
    ☐ Set goals for changes/improvements
    ☐ Provided ongoing feedback on the action plan.
    ☐ Provided encouragement and support to help change behavior
    ☐ Other (comments) _____

    _____

Exhibit 21.7. Impact Questionnaire *(continued)*

21. For each of the areas below, indicate the extent to which you think this program has influenced these measures in your work group.

	No influence	Some influence	Moderate influence	Significant influence	Very much influence
a. Productivity					
b. Efficiency					
c. Quality					
d. Response time					
e. Cost control					
f. Customer service					
g. Customer satisfaction					
h. Employee turnover					
i. Absenteeism					
j. Employee satisfaction					
k. Health care costs					
l. Safety and health costs					

Please cite specific examples or provide more details. _____
_____
_____

22. What specific suggestions do you have for improving the Stress Management program? Please specify.
    ☐ Content
    ☐ Duration
    ☐ Presentation
    ☐ Other _____

23. Other comments: _____
_____
_____

Chapter 22

Developing an Effective
Level 1 Reaction Form

Reaction forms come in all sizes and shapes. And the information generated may or may not be used to improve training programs. This case study describes a thorough process of developing a form to evaluate the significant aspects of the program. Emphasis is on items that relate directly to job performance and desired results.

Duke Energy Corporation

W. Derrick Allman,
Plan, Manage, and Procure Training Services
Duke Energy Corporation, Charlotte, North Carolina

Duke Energy is a world leader in the development, collection, distribution, and production of energy-related services. The company conducts business in the global marketplace through national and international offices, having have two primary corporate locations: Charlotte, North Carolina, and Houston, Texas. The company employs 23,000 individuals worldwide.

Evaluation processes at Duke Energy Corporation have taken many turns through the years. As we enter the era of aggressive competition in the energy services market, we are increasing our interest in determining the value that learning and development contribute to the business. An essential element in the valuation of learning and development is the gathering and analysis of evaluation data associated with learning events. The following case tracks the history and development of an electronic level 1 evaluation process used by the company for a more rigorous evaluation at levels 1 and 3 of Kirkpatrick's model. Included is background information to assist in understanding the initial factors in implementing a more rigorous level 1 process. Methods applied in gathering levels 1 and 3 evaluation data are very important. Therefore, the case includes a discussion of how Duke Energy is working to refine the process through collaboration with an international benchmarking organization.

Duke Energy's roots are well established in serving the electrical needs of customers of central North and South Carolina for nearly ninety years. During that time, the company invested heavily in the development, construction, and operation of generating facilities. Three nuclear stations were constructed during the 1970s and 1980s. Experience gained in this highly regulated side of the business demonstrated the need for exhaustive training and education programs to ensure the safe operation of those nuclear units. In addition, particular focus on the training and education of nuclear industry employees developed during the late 1970s.

Eagerness to ensure competency in an employee's ability to perform resulted in extensive investment of resources in a systematic approach to training using job–task analysis, training program development, evaluation of lessons learned, and demonstration of competency. Through the experience gained in the years following this focused effort, the company gained insight into human performance through level 2 and level 3 evaluations. Many of the process lessons learned eventually spread from being used solely in the nuclear environment to other training areas of the corporation.

It was not until 1994 that Duke Energy sought to quantify the value of learning taking place and trend the experiences in order to monitor continuous improvement in programs. At that time, the initiating queue did not come from within the Training and Education function. In the early 1990s, Duke Energy had a strong focus on continuous improvement and quality performance measures. As a result, criteria for pursuing the Malcolm Baldrige Award (MBA) was adopted as a standard from which all corporate programs would be measured. It was thought that the use of the Baldrige criteria should be used for several reasons: (1) standardization—the award criteria was viewed as a standard by which we could directly compare our performance with other corporations across the country; (2) availability—a systematic process for evaluating programs was well established, including a network of examiners that would allow us to perform self-evaluations; and (3) success–it was viewed that compliance with Baldrige criteria would naturally result in excellence; it was later realized that excellence in all aspects of the business—and not the use of artificial criteria with which we were attempting to align practices—allows the corporation to succeed.

As a result of this effort, the Training and Education function was asked to produce reports in response to four areas of training. Later we learned that the four areas outlined in the MBA were actually the four levels of evaluation posed in Kirkpatrick's model for evaluating training and education. As proposed in the MBA, the four levels where a response and supporting data would be required were (1) reaction, (2) learning, (3) transfer to job, and (4) business results.

We immediately knew how to respond to the first of the four. Our "smile" sheets had been used for years to gauge end-of-class reaction to a course and instructor. However, as we began to learn more about the Kirkpatrick model of evaluation, we learned that our "smile" sheets were not capturing data adequate to demonstrate continuous improvement in the reaction to learning. The result of this awareness led to the development of a spreadsheet to begin capturing data from Corporate Training–sponsored events. Two weeks into the project, we discovered that an electronic spreadsheet would be incapable of providing the robust analysis necessary for continuous monitoring and improvement of programs, courses, instructors, and so on. Immediately, a project was chartered to construct a database system to perform these duties. At the center of this project were four criteria: (1) develop standard questions to apply across the enterprise, (2) develop a process for electronic gathering of data to reduce the human interface required, (3) secure the data in a manner so as to prevent any bias or tampering with results, and (4) be able to report the results of any event based on criteria important to the management of the Training and Education function. Within six weeks of the initial request, we had an operational database program capable of gathering data using an electronic scanner; analyzing data by course, instructor, location; and generating general and confidential reports for management.

When Duke Energy Training set about the development of standard level 1 reaction sheets, we knew that by their nature they would be very subjective. That is, they indicate the mood of participants as they leave training. The goal of level 1 evaluations is to "measure participant's perception (reaction) to learning experiences relative to a course, content, instructor, and relevancy to job immediately following the experience in order to initiate continuous improvement of training experiences." As a result, our project established three primary objectives:

1. Questions developed for the reaction level evaluation *must* measure the course, content, instructor, and relevancy to the job. These are four areas considered essential to successful training programs.
2. The form and delivery of the level 1 evaluation must communicate a link between quality, process improvement, and action. Participants *must* be made to feel as though their individual response is a factor in the continuous improvement process.
3. Action plans should be initiated to address identified weaknesses without regard to owner, political correctness, or other bias. If the results indicate poor quality, then appropriate corrective action should be taken. If excellence is indicated in an unlikely place, then reward and celebration should be offered commensurate with the accomplishment.

In addition to the primary objectives, several other objectives evolved. First was the need to identify the prerequisite processes that must be accomplished with each learning event. It became evident that the success of the level 1 process is directly linked to the proper completion of prerequisites for a course. Second, postmeasurement activities should be addressed by subsequent teams. During the initial database design, the team knew that certain reports would be required and others desired. Most reports were prepared during the first phase of development.

The initial computer project deliverables included the following:

- Proposed questions to be included on the level 1 evaluation
- Proposed measures from which management would determine actions to be taken when analyzing evaluation results

- Recommendations for deployment of the process within Corporate Training and Education, including roles and responsibilities
- Guideline for data collection, cycle times, reports, and analysis of data
- Schedule for developing, delivering, and measuring responsiveness of participants (generic level 1 assessment)
- Database and input program for manually gathering data
- Plans and scope document detailing a second (phase 2) project for automating the data acquisition process (This document should include plans for using data collected in multiple ways— that is, requirements that header data be used to confirm enrollment/attendance, automated course completion, level 1 automated analysis and reporting, and so on.)

Along with the development of the computer program, a team worked on drafting an initial set of questions for the standard level 1 reaction sheets. These questions included the following:

1. Overall, my impression of this course was excellent.
2. The course objectives were clearly stated and used understandable terms.
3. This course met the defined objectives.
4. Both the facility and equipment used met *all* needs of the class/course. *Note:* Please describe any facility or equipment needs that did not meet your expectations.
5. The course materials were both useful and easy to follow. *Note:* Please describe any material that was not useful or easy to follow.
6. The instructor(s) demonstrated thorough knowledge and understanding of the topic. *Note:* The instructor(s) would be the facilitator(s) of any video, CBT, or audiotape.
7. The instructor(s) presented information in a clear, understandable, and professional manner. *Note:* The instructor(s) would include the facilitator(s) of any video, CBT, or audiotape.
8. The amount of time scheduled for this course was exactly what was needed to meet the objectives.
9. This course relates directly to my current job responsibilities.
10. I would recommend this course to other teammates.

These were measured using a five-point Likert scale with a value of 5 being assigned to "strongly agree" and a value of 1 being assigned to "strongly disagree."

A test period from November through December of 1995 was used to shake down the system and remove any "bugs" found. On January 1, 1996, the first electronic level 1 evaluation instruments were formally used. During the first month, less than 200 level 1 reaction sheets were returned for processing. In the ensuing months, acceptance and use of the questions as a basis for illustrating the effects of training grew. All of Corporate Training began using the level 1 reaction sheet to gather end-of-class data by March of 1996; volume grew to nearly 1,000 evaluation sheets per month. By the end of 1996, Corporate Training at Duke Energy had recorded over 12,000 evaluations on the reaction to training. By the end of 1997, the number using the standardized level 1 reaction sheet grew to over 25,000 participants. Analysis of the data began to reveal some very interesting trends. The growth also revealed the need to adjust the Corporate Training unit.

As we analyzed the data and produced reports, training management came to the realization that "the reaction to training and education is directly linked to the operation and business management aspects of the training unit." This led to the formation of a team to monitor business management and education quality. In theory, we concluded that the two are inseparable in (1) determining areas of continuous improvement, (2) measuring the success of programs and program participants, and (3) ensuring that corporate investments in training are providing an appropriate return on investment.

Along with full implementation of the level 1 process in March of 1996 came our joining of a national benchmarking organization composed of sixty member companies. In the fall of that year, the first sub-team of this forum was commissioned to determine areas for which standardized performance metrics could be established. After two meetings, it was determined that standardized level 1 and level 3 evaluation questions should be developed. This team worked on the draft and completion of a standardized level 1 evaluation through the spring of 1997 and presented this to the larger body for use in April of 1997. We immediately set about the task of piloting the standard questions within our companies and continue to gather data for comparison at this time. In addition, the team is now completing work on the development of level 3 questions for use by the members. As a result of this effort, for the first time a standard set of data will be able to be analyzed in gauging the success of programs that literally span the globe. In doing so, the lessons learned from similar experiences will help in identifying successful practices and in avoiding the pitfalls others experience. Sometime in 1998 this information will be published and made available for other corporations to use.

Duke Energy Training stands at the threshold of a new era in evaluating the effectiveness of training. As we continue to analyze the reactions people have toward training, we are beginning to see indications that suggest a direct correlation between reaction (level 1) and transfer to the job (level 3). If this correlation is correct, the use of sophisticated techniques for analyzing participant reaction will be warranted. On the other hand, if all we are able to glean from the data are indications of areas needing improvement, then we will still be able to implement corrective actions in programs. When used effectively, analysis of level 1 evaluation data can help in the early detection of areas that need improvement or support the conclusion that a good result was achieved.

Chapter 23

Evaluating a Training Program at All Four Levels

This case study from Cisco Systems illustrates how an organization can evaluate a program at all four levels. The study was done jointly by an internal training professional and an outside consultant. The first step was to identify the desired business results. From this basis, the training program was planned and implemented.

Cisco Systems, Inc.

Peg Maddocks, Manager of Training
for WorldWide Manufacturing
Cisco Systems, Inc., San Jose, California

Ingrid Gudenas, President
Effective Training Solutions, Fremont, California

Background

Silicon Valley–based Cisco Systems, a worldwide leader in the highly competitive networking industry, is a rapidly growing company with a critical goal to keep costs down and profits high. Cisco manufactures computer networking equipment and had revenue of $6.8 billion in fiscal year 1997, with a 189 percent increase in new jobs from 1996–1998, bringing the total number of employees to about 11,000. Cisco is recognized for its profitability and low operating expenses. A key strategy in staying profitable is its emphasis on frugality in every activity while enhancing productivity through the use of information systems business tools.

Manufacturing can be a source of high operating costs, while inventories are kept up to ensure delivery to the customer and where hiring costs sometime outpace revenues. Cisco Manufacturing balances the need to hire and the cost of hiring more people by implementing tools to increase the productivity of existing employees. Often, reengineering a process and eliminating "paper trails," can have a tremendous effect on the bottom line. The challenge has always been how to train hundreds of people simultaneously to correctly use a new work process when it changes virtually overnight.

The Challenge

One example of this challenge was the new return-to-vendor (RTV) process, which was costing Cisco a significant percentage of its operating expenses in write-offs and loss of productivity. The write-offs were financial losses we incurred every quarter that cut into our profitability. Cisco manufactures routers and switches, which consist of a chassis and a set of printed circuit boards. Often the boards in the plant need to be returned to the vendor for a variety of reasons, including simply updating the components on them. This process was completely manual, with every returned circuit board being tracked using a paper process and being physically handed off to five separate work groups. Production workers would reject a board and forward it with a paper rejection request to the plant materials group. Then an engineer and buyer would determine whether to return it to the supplier. Cost Accounting would get involved as an "inspector" to ensure paperwork was properly filled out. Finally, the board would be shipped back to the vendor from the dock. Often, when it came time to receive the credit from the supplier, there were scattered records of the board being sent or received or the paperwork would be so inaccurate that Cisco could not be reimbursed.

Traceability is always a challenge in a manual process. For each board returned—and there are thousands over the course of a year—at least five departments were involved, some RTV cases were open for 30 to

120 days while people retraced the return process, and the average time to return the boards lasted five to seven days. Worst was the expense of the write-offs Cisco experienced every quarter due to untraceable returns.

Implementing the Training Project

Cost Accounting drove this project with a goal to reduce write-offs, eliminate at least one head count, and increase the speed of returning boards and receiving the credit. The Information Systems Department worked with a representative from each of the groups involved to reengineer and automate the process. Once redesigned, the paper process would be completely computer-based and all of the sign-offs could be done on line. Tracking would be accurate and timely, and the write-offs would be eliminated. On completion of the programming, the Cost Accounting Department gave the plant three weeks to train over 130 people in the new process. All process participants needed to start using the approach simultaneously for it to work, and the paper process would be "turned off."

Up to that point our Training Department had not been involved. When Cost Accounting asked us for help, we agreed, on the condition we use a training approach we knew would guarantee a successful implementation. In the past, new process training had been done by a series of department meeting demos and a question-and-answer process. Once implemented, experts would spend many hours a day answering questions and fixing problems until everyone was proficient. This could take months, depending on the complexity of the procedure.

The first step in the training project was to identify the business results that would prove that the training had been successful and that the business problem had been solved. This was fairly easy, because the Cost Accounting Department had identified overall performance measures for the business and had preexisting data. In addition, our Information Systems Department had implemented a reporting process a few months back that tracked performance by buyer and by product line, which helped us measure more specific results. We identified five distinct level 4 measures and targets and two level 3 measures and targets, which we will explain later in this case study.

100% Proficiency™ Training Method

We decided to use the 100% Proficiency™ training method, which was developed by Effective Training Solutions (ETS), a California-based training and consulting firm. Through years of training work with high-tech manufacturers, other companies, and government agencies, ETS found that traditional classroom teaching methods were not workable when applied to the demand for rapidly developed proficiency that exists in today's high-tech industry.

The 100% Proficiency™ training method is not classroom training. It is self-paced, yet its structure, its guided supervision by a trained facilitator, and its unique study and training facilitation tools distinguish it from other self-paced learning. This training system is taught to client organizations, which then apply it to their particular training needs. The method of learning results in employees who are fully proficient and who:

- Have all the necessary knowledge to do their jobs well
- Are fully able to rapidly and correctly execute the actions called for in their jobs
- Are able to use good judgment when necessary

The 100% Proficiency™ training system is based on research conducted by L. Ron Hubbard in the 1960s and published as a lecture series. This research showed that training could be improved by shifting responsibility for and control of learning to the student. By setting the standard at 100 percent and giving the student relevant learning skills, the trainer's role shifted from a teacher or trainer to one of coaching and verifying proficiency. This system has demonstrated level 4 results for manufacturing as well as software training.

The core of this system is the "checksheet," which provides a road map for the trainee to follow, with an exact sequence of steps, including study of work procedures and other documents as well as practical exercises that orient an employee to equipment or to the software application. The checksheet also ensures that students practice or "drill" with hands-on exercises sufficiently to become fully proficient *during* training. This is different than traditional training in which students are expected to become fully proficient *after* training. In Cisco's situation, this difference was critical.

Inherent in the 100% Proficiency™ system is that students are given reference material in the form of documents, work procedures, or specifications and are provided with instruction on how to learn so that they can succeed in self-paced learning. (Without this instruction, students can have a difficult time with the self-paced nature of this approach.) The training materials for the RTV process consist of the checksheets, written by the Training Department, and the procedures and work instructions, written by three subject matter experts (SMEs) who designed the new process (a cost accountant, a buyer, and a materials coordinator from the plant). To implement the training, the SMEs provided a train-the-trainer to a trainer/coach from every department. A demo of the new process was provided; then the trainers worked through the checksheet and practiced the new process in a lab or at their desks over a week's time. The department trainers used the same approach to train their department over the next two weeks. All trainers attended a training course on coaching skills for the 100% Proficiency™ training approach.

During the training itself, these trainers were available to answer questions and to help students as needed. An important responsibility for the trainers was to provide students with "trainer checkouts." The checksheet indicated to a student when a "trainer checkout" was required, but the student would ensure that he or she was ready for the checkout prior to requesting it. During the trainer checkout the trainer verified that the student was fully proficient by watching the student perform the exact task. This was the level 2 measure throughout the program. There was no pretest because students were being taught skills they previously did not have; thus, a pretest would have been irrelevant. During the checkout, a trainer signed off only after the student demonstrated full proficiency, thereby verifying the acquisition of the skill being taught.

These trainer checkouts were interspersed throughout the checksheet; there was one final trainer checkout at the end of each checksheet in which students had to put everything together and demonstrate that they were able to do the whole task rapidly and accurately. In other words, full proficiency was required in order for a student to complete a checksheet and be signed off by the trainer. This level 2 measure on the actual task to be performed on the job removed any mystery about level 3. Students had been so thoroughly measured regarding proficiency *during* their training that we expected they would have few training-related difficulties in using these new skills on the job *after* training.

Once the training was complete, the paper process was "turned off." In other words, Cost Accounting would no longer accept manually written shipping authorizations, and the product could not return to the vendor without the on-line process being complete.

Training Measures

We were able to implement all four levels of evaluation for this project. For level 1, we conducted a survey three weeks after the training program via e-mail (see Exhibit 23.1). Students were asked how they liked the training, what they learned, and how to improve it next time. We also conducted a focus group in which we asked users to evaluate the effectiveness of the new work process, the training and support materials, the training effectiveness, and the logistics of the training (that is, the demo, labs, and "at-my-desk" practice). Trainers also received informal solicited and unsolicited feedback about training effectiveness.

Level 2 was imbedded in the training process, as discussed above, because students were "tested" by their trainer as they performed the activities on the system.

Level 3 was measured in the following two ways:

1. Trainers observed students over a week-long period after they had signed off their checksheets but before the new process went "live" to see how quickly they were performing the RTV process and how many errors they were making. They also tracked the volume and cycle time of RTVs being processed by each buyer and then coached those who were having trouble.
2. Trainers and the Cost Accounting Department noted a stunning and immediate reduction in the number of questions asked about how to do RTVs and were rarely asked to solve process problems anymore. The buyers were clearly implementing the new process.

Exhibit 23.1. Survey for Level 1

To: Mfg-buyers
From :   Peg Maddocks <pmaddock@cisco.com>
Subject: Sock it to us—we need your opinion
Cc:
Bcc:
X-Attachments:

Hello,

Recently you were trained in the new Auto SA/RTV process. The method we used was called High Performance Training, in which a coach assigned to your department was first trained and then in turn trained you. Ideally, you were given a demo in the training room and then given a "checksheet" that directed you through self-paced exercises.

Your coach was to "check you out" to ensure that your questions were answered, your exercises were complete, and that you thoroughly understood how to use the new tool. Please help us evaluate this training so we can improve it the next time we roll out a new process or tool.

Please reply to this e-mail by 11/20 . . . it's quick and easy!

Thanks,

Peg

Your job title:

1. How much do you use the Auto SA/RTV process?

_____ Often (several times a day)

_____ Some (several times a week)

_____ A little (once in a while)

_____ Never

2. How were you trained in the new process? (check all that apply)

_____ Demo by coach

_____ Used the checksheet, procedure, work instructions, and Maserati to practice

_____ Used the procedure and work instruction without checksheet

_____ Coach answered my questions/showed me how to find my own answers

_____ Coach checked me out to see if I was proficient

_____ Learned completely on my own

_____ Didn't get trained/not using the tool

3. If you were trained using a checksheet, how much did it help you learn?

_____ It helped me a great deal

_____ It helped me a bit

_____ It interfered with my learning

_____ Didn't use checksheet

Exhibit 23.1. Survey for Level 1 *(continued)*

---

4. If you used a checksheet, what *did* you like about it?

5. If you used a checksheet, what *didn't* you like about it?

6. If you had a coach, what did the coach *do well?* Optional: What was your coach's name?

7. If you had a coach, what could the coach *do better* next time?

8. Overall, how would you rate this form of training?

   _____ Liked it a lot

   _____ Liked it somewhat

   _____ Didn't like it much

9. Overall, how can we improve training in manufacturing on oracle and business tools?

Level 4 was measured in the following five ways, as predetermined before we began the training project:

1. Reduction in the dollar amount of write-off for untraceable RTVs. (The goal was elimination of this type of write-off.)
2. Decrease in queue and reduce aging of RTVs in the system. (In the old process, buyers who were not proficient in the manual process or who had many RTVs would build up a backlog of RTVs to be completed, some as many as ninety days old. When this happened, Cisco was not collecting the credit from the vendor and the boards were aging, potentially becoming outdated.)
3. Reduction in the dollar value of RTV inventory in the plant at any given time waiting for the process to complete.
4. Immediate increase in productivity in the Cost Accounting Department by eliminating the inspection, verification, and

resolution of problems related to RTVs. (As a result, Cost Accounting did not have to hire an additional person, which would have been done otherwise.)
5. Immediate increase in productivity in the buyer and material handling groups because of the new process and because subject matter experts would no longer be required to answer questions and solve process problems.

The major result that the company wanted to see was the elimination of the write-offs due to nontraceable RTVs. Within one quarter these write-offs were reduced by 100 percent. Another measure was the on-hand inventory due to RTVs. At first the number of returns in the system went up by about 10 percent as people used the new process and increased their queues. But within four weeks, the cycle time for the return of boards was reduced from seven to ten days to three days, and RTV inventory moved quickly out of the stockroom and back to the vendor. As far as productivity, one person in Cost Accounting was able to focus on other projects because she was no longer receiving RTV paper authorizations and buyers were no longer asking for help. Productivity among buyers went up by a minimum of 10 percent (ability to process more returns quicker). All of this was measurable by reports developed to track the returns in the system. The trainers in each department increased their productivity by 10 to 30 percent depending on how many RTVs a department had who no longer needed to resolve issues and answer questions about the process.

In Conclusion

All in all, this program was very successful. In conjunction with the implementation of an improved business process, the training facilitated a quicker financial return to the business because of the method used. The following are factors that contributed to our success:

- The training was focused on solving a real business problem; because of this the business partners were fully committed to making it work.
- The training measures were identified by the business partners and agreed to before the training began. The results were to be

collected by the business, and this made measurement of the training fairly straightforward.

- The Training Department did not own the training process. Process designers wrote the reference materials, and experts in each group were able to customize the process details for their students' situations. In this way we were able to train 130 people over a two- to three-week period.

- The 100% Proficiency™ training method ensured consistency across groups and proof of proficiency via the checkouts. The materials continue to be used successfully by the coaches to train new hires and transfers.

- Training continued on the job because the students received reinforcement and feedback from their trainers and managers as a normal course of the business measurement process.

This training project was perceived by the business managers and the participants as the most successful information systems training program they had ever experienced. Cost Accounting was impressed with the success of its implementation and the results. The trainers were relieved when few people asked them for help after the system went live, and our Training Department was perceived as a real business partner. As a result, there is now a requirement in Manufacturing that all new processes be introduced using the 100% Proficiency™ training method and that the business owners, information systems developers, and Training Department measure and communicate the results at all four levels of evaluation.

Index

ONALD L. KIRKPATRICK is Professor Emeritus, University of Wisconsin, and a widely respected teacher, author, and consultant. He has over thirty years of experience as professor of management at the University of Wisconsin and has held professional training and human resource positions with International Minerals and Chemical Corporation and Bendix Corporation. He is the author of eight management inventories and five books: *How to Manage Change Effectively, How to Improve Performance Through Appraisal and Coaching, How to Train and Develop Supervisors, How to Plan and Conduct Productive Business Meetings,* and *No-Nonsense Communication.* The first two titles received the Best Book of the Year award from the Society for Human Resource Management. Kirkpatrick is past president of the American Society for Training and Development and is best known for developing the internationally accepted four-level approach for evaluating training programs. In 1997 he was inducted into *TRAINING* magazine's Hall of Fame. He received his B.B.A., M.B.A., and Ph.D. degrees from the University of Wisconsin, Madison. He lives in Elm Grove, Wisconsin, and is a senior elder at Elmbrook Church and an active member of Gideons International.

Berrett-Koehler Publishers

ERRETT-KOEHLER is an independent publisher of books, periodicals, and other publications at the leading edge of new thinking and innovative practice on work, business, management, leadership, stewardship, career development, human resources, entrepreneurship, and global sustainability.

Since the company's founding in 1992, we have been committed to supporting the movement toward a more enlightened world of work by publishing books, periodicals, and other publications that help us to integrate our values with our work and work lives, and to create more humane and effective organizations.

We have chosen to focus on the areas of work, business, and organizations, because these are central elements in many people's lives today. Furthermore, the work world is going through tumultuous changes, from the decline of job security to the rise of new structures for organizing people and work. We believe that change is needed at all levels—individual, organizational, community, and global—and our publications address each of these levels.

We seek to create new lenses for understanding organizations, to legitimize topics that people care deeply about but that current business orthodoxy censors or considers secondary to bottom-line concerns, and to uncover new meaning, means, and ends for our work and work lives.

See next page for other books from Berrett-Koehler Publishers

Other leading-edge business books from Berrett-Koehler Publishers

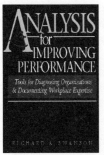

Analysis for Improving Performance
Tools for Diagnosing Organizations and Documenting Workplace Expertise

Richard A. Swanson

*A*NALYSIS FOR *IMPROVING PERFORMANCE* details the front-end work essential to the success of any performance improvement effort. Swanson shows how to do the rigorous preparatory analysis that defines successful performance improvement efforts, and maps the critical steps for insuring that a performance improvement program will meet its objectives.

Paperback, 298 pages, 9/96 • ISBN 1-57675-001-9 CIP
Item no. 50019-245

Hardcover, 7/94 • ISBN 1-881052-48-6 CIP • **Item no. 52486-2456**

Human Resource Development Research Handbook
Linking Research and Practice

Richard A. Swanson and Elwood F. Holton III, Editors

*T*HE *HUMAN RESOURCE DEVELOPMENT RESEARCH HANDBOOK* gives practitioners the tools they need to stay on the leading edge of the profession. Each chapter is written in straightforward language by a leading researcher and offers real-world examples to clearly show how research and theory are not just for academics, but are practical tools to solve everyday problems.

Paperback, 225 pages, 3/97 • ISBN 1-881052-68-0 CIP
Item no. 52680-245 $24.95

Structured On-the-Job Training
Unleashing Employee Expertise in the Workplace

Ronald Jacobs and Michael Jones

*J*ACOBS AND *JONES* describe an approach to on-the-job training that combines the structure of off-site training with the inherent efficiency of training conducted in the actual job setting. *Structured On-the-Job Training* provides step-by-step guidelines for designing and delivering effective training in the actual job setting.

Hardcover, 220 pages, 1/95 • ISBN 1-881052-20-6 CIP
Item no. 52206-245 $29.95

Available at your favorite bookstore, or call (800) 929-2929

Performance Consulting

Moving Beyond Training

Dana Gaines Robinson and James C. Robinson

PERFORMANCE CONSULTING provides a conceptual framework and many how-to's for moving from the role of a traditional trainer to that of a performance consultant. Dozens of useful tools, illustrative exercises, and a case study that threads through the book show how the techniques described are applied in an organizational setting.

Paperback, 320 pages, 1/96 • ISBN 1-881052-84-2 CIP
Item no. 52842-245

Hardcover, 4/95 • ISBN 1-881052-30-3 CIP • **Item no. 52303-176**

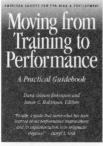

Moving from Training to Performance

A Practical Guidebook

Dana Gaines Robinson and James C. Robinson

MOVING FROM TRAINING TO PERFORMANCE shows how today's performance improvement departments can take a more active role in helping organizations meet their service and financial goals. This book offers practical, action-oriented techniques from some of the most highly respected contributors in the field—Geoff Bellman, Geary Rummler, Paul Elliott, Jim Fuller, Harold Stolovitch, Erica Keeps, and other experts—paired with real-life case studies of organizations such as Johnson & Johnson, Andersen Consulting, Prudential HealthCare System, Steelcase, PNC Bank, and others that have achieved exceptional results by successfully making the transition to performance at each level of alignment.

Paperback, 300 pages, 7/98 • ISBN 1-57675-039-6 CIP
Item no. 50396-245 $29.95

On-The-Level

Performance Communication That Works
New Edition

Patricia McLagan and Peter Krembs

DESIGNED TO HELP managers and employees plan and execute more effective and less fearful communication, *On The Level* provides tips, action steps, and practical tools to help everyone in and around the workplace communicate "on-the-level."

Paperback, 140 pages, 8/95 • ISBN 1-881052-76-1 CIP
Item no. 52761-245 $19.95

Available at your favorite bookstore, or call (800) 929-2929